Table of Contents

Earth and Space Science

Rocks and minerals

The physical properties (as opposed to chemical structures) used to identify minerals are hardness, luster, color, cleavage, streak, form (the external shape), and other special properties. Senses other than sight, such as touch, taste, and smell, may be used to observe physical properties. Hardness is the resistance a mineral has to scratches. The Mohs Hardness Scale is used to rate hardness from 1 to 10. Color can often not be determined definitively as some minerals can be more than one color. Luster is determined by reflected light. Luster can be described as metallic (shiny), sub-metallic (dull), non-metallic (vitreous, like glass), or earthy (like dirt or powder). Streak is the true color of the mineral in powdered form. It can be determined by rubbing the specimen across an unglazed porcelain tile. Fracture or cleavage is how a mineral reacts to stress, such as being struck with a hammer. Other properties that can be used to identify rocks and minerals include magnetism, a salty taste, or a pungent odor in a streak test.

Minerals are naturally occurring, inorganic solids with a definite chemical composition and an orderly internal crystal structure. A polymorph is two minerals with the same chemical composition, but a different crystal structure. Rocks are aggregates of one or more minerals, and may also contain mineraloids (minerals lacking a crystalline structure) and organic remains. The three types of rocks are sedimentary, igneous, and metamorphic. Rocks are classified based on their formation and the minerals they contain. Minerals are classified by their chemical composition. Geology is the study of the planet Earth as it pertains to the composition, structure, and origin of its rocks. Petrology is the study of rocks, including their composition, texture, structure, occurrence, mode of formation, and history. Mineralogy is the study of minerals.

Sedimentary rock

Sedimentary rocks are formed by the process of lithification, which involves compaction, the expulsion of liquids from pores, and the cementation of the pre-existing rock. It is pressure and temperature that are responsible for this process. Sedimentary rocks are often formed in layers in the presence of water, and may contain organic remains, such as fossils. Sedimentary rocks are organized into three groups: detrital, biogenic, and chemical. Texture refers to the size, shape, and grains of sedimentary rock. Texture can be used to determine how a particular sedimentary rock was created. Composition refers to the types of minerals present in the rock. The origin of sedimentary rock refers to the type of water that was involved in its creation. Marine deposits, for example, likely involved ocean environments, while continental deposits likely involved dry land and lakes.

Mineral classification

Minerals are classified by chemical composition and internal crystalline structure. They are organized into classes. Native elements such as gold and silver are not classified in this manner. The eight classes are sulfides, oxides\hydroxides, halides, carbonates, sulfates, phosphates, and silicates. These classes are based on the dominant anion (negatively charged ion) or anionic group. Minerals are classified in this way for three main reasons. First, minerals with the same anion have unmistakable resemblances. Second, minerals with the same anion are often found in the same geologic environment. For example, calcite and dolomite, which belong to the same group, are often found together. Last, this method is similar to the naming convention used to identify inorganic compounds in chemistry. Minerals can be further separated into groups on the basis of internal structure.

Metamorphic rock

Metamorphic rock is that which has been changed by great heat and pressure. This results in a variety of outcomes, including deformation, compaction, destruction of the characteristics of the original rock, bending, folding, and formation of new minerals because of chemical reactions, and changes in the size and shape of the mineral grain. For example, the igneous rock ferromagnesian can be changed into schist and gneiss. The sedimentary rock carbonaceous can be changed into marble. The texture of metamorphic rocks can be classified as foliated and unfoliated. Foliation, or layering, occurs when rock is compressed along one axis during recrystallization. This can be seen in schist and shale. Unfoliated rock does not include this banding. Rocks that are compressed equally from all sides or lack specific minerals will be unfoliated. An example is marble.

Igneous rock

Igneous rock is formed from magma, which is molten material originating from beneath the Earth's surface. Depending upon where magma cools, the resulting igneous rock can be classified as intrusive, plutonic, hypabyssal, extrusive, or volcanic. Magma that solidifies at a depth is intrusive, cools slowly, and has a coarse grain as a result. An example is granite. Magma that solidifies at or near the surface is extrusive, cools quickly, and usually has a fine grain. An example is basalt. Magma that actually flows out of the Earth's surface is called lava. Some extrusive rock cools so quickly that crystals do not have time to form. These rocks have a glassy appearance. An example is obsidian. Hypabyssal rock is igneous rock that is formed at medium depths.

Earth's structure

The Earth is ellipsoid, not perfectly spherical. This means the diameter is different through the poles and at the equator. Through the poles, the Earth is about 12,715 km in diameter. The approximate center of the Earth is at a depth of 6,378 km. The Earth is divided into a crust, mantle, and core. The core consists of a solid inner portion. Moving outward, the molten outer core occupies the space from about a depth of 5,150 km to a depth of 2,890 km. The mantle consists of a lower and upper layer. The lower layer includes the D' (D prime) and D" (D double-prime) layers. The solid portion of the upper mantle and crust together form the lithosphere, or rocky sphere. Below this, but still within the mantle, is the asthenosphere, or weak sphere. These layers are distinguishable because the lithosphere is relatively rigid, while the asthenosphere resembles a thick liquid.

Maps

Traditional maps represent land in two dimensions, while topographic maps represent elevation through the use of contour lines. Contour lines help show changes to elevations above the surface of the Earth and on the ocean floor. They also help show the shape of Earth's surface features. The United States Geological Survey (USGS) produces frequently used quadrangle maps in various scales. A quadrangle topographic map is bounded by two lines of latitude and two lines of longitude. A 7.5-minute map shows an area that spans 7.5 minutes of latitude and 7.5 minutes of longitude. The name of the quadrangle map appears at the top, and usually indicates the name of a prominent feature. Topographic maps that show much less detail are also available. They might show a much larger area, such as a country or state. USGS quad maps also refer to adjacent quad maps. Other information contained on quad maps includes the projection and grid used, scale, contour intervals, and magnetic declination, which is the difference between true north and magnetic north.

Earth's chemical composition

The Earth's core consists of hot iron and forms of nickel. The mantle consists of different materials, including iron, magnesium, and calcium. The crust covers the mantle, consists of a thin layer of much lighter rocks, and is further subdivided into continental and oceanic portions. The continental portion consists mainly of silicates, such as granite. The oceanic portion consists of heavier, volcanic rocks, such as basalt. The upper 10 miles of the lithosphere layer (the crust and part of the mantle) is made up of 95% igneous rock (or its metamorphic equivalent), 4% shale, 0.75% sandstone, and 0.25% limestone. There are over 4,000 known minerals, but only about 20 make up some 95% of all rocks. There are, however, more than 3,000 individual kinds of minerals in the Earth's crust. Silicates are the largest group of minerals.

Mountains

Orogeny refers to the formation of mountains, particularly the processes of folding and faulting caused by plate tectonics. Folding is when layers of sedimentary rock are pressed together by continental plate movements. Sections of rock that are folded upward are called anticlines. Sections of rock that are folded downward are called synclines. Examples of folded mountains are the Alps and the Himalayans. Fault-block mountains are created when tectonic plate movement produces tension that results in displacement. Mountains in the Southwest United States are examples of fault-blocking mountains. Mountains can also be caused by volcanic activity and erosion.

Tectonic Convection

Heat is transferred through the process of convection, which is a cycle. Hot material rises and spreads, cooling as it spreads. The cool material then sinks, where it is heated again. The process of convection can be seen in a pot of boiling water. It is believed this same process is happening deep within the Earth. Greater depths are associated with more pressure and heat. The weight of all the rocks causes the increase in pressure, while the decay of heavy radioactive elements such as uranium produces heat. This creates hot areas of molten material that find their way upward and to the surface in an effort to equalize, which means pressure and temperature are reduced. This causes the processes involved in plate tectonics.

Plate tectonic theory

The theory of plate tectonics states that the lithosphere, the solid portion of the mantle and Earth's crust, consists of major and minor plates. These plates are on top of and move with the viscous upper mantle, which is heated because of the convection cycle that occurs in the interior of the Earth. There are different estimates as to the exact number of major and minor plates. The number of major plates is believed to be between 9 and 15, and it is thought that there may be as many as 40 minor plates. The United States is atop the North American plate. The Pacific Ocean is atop the Pacific plate. The point at which these two plates slide horizontally along the San Andreas fault is an example of a transform plate boundary. The other two types of boundaries are divergent (plates that are spreading apart and forming new crust) and convergent (the process of subduction causes one plate to go under another). The movement of plates is what causes other features of the Earth's crust, such as mountains, volcanoes, and earthquakes.

Volcanic activities and plate tectonics

Volcanoes can occur along any type of tectonic plate boundary. At a divergent boundary, as plates move apart, magma rises to the surface, cools, and forms a ridge. An example of this is the mid-Atlantic ridge. Convergent boundaries, where one plate slides under another, are often areas with a lot of volcanic activity. The subduction process creates magma. When it rises to the surface, volcanoes can be created. Volcanoes can also be created in the middle of a plate over hot spots. Hot spots are locations where narrow plumes of magma rise through the mantle in a fixed place over a long period of time. The Hawaiian Islands and Midway are examples. The plate shifts and the island moves. Magma continues to rise through the mantle, however, which produces another island. Volcanoes can be active, dormant, or extinct. Active volcanoes are those that are erupting or about to erupt. Dormant volcanoes are those that might erupt in the future and still have internal volcanic activity. Extinct volcanoes are those that will not erupt.

Types of volcanoes

The three types of volcanoes are shield, cinder cone, and composite. A shield volcano is created by a long-term, relatively gentle eruption. This type of volcanic mountain is created by each progressive lava flow that occurs over time. A cinder cone volcano is created by explosive eruptions. Lava is spewed out of a vent into the air. As it falls to the ground, the lava cools into cinders and ash, which build up around the volcano in a cone shape. A composite volcano is a combination of the other two types of volcanoes. In this type, there are layers of lava flows and layers of ash and cinder.

Seismic deformation and seismic waves

There are two types of deformations created by an earthquake fault rupture: static and dynamic. Static deformation permanently displaces the ground. Examples are when a road or railroad track becomes distorted by an earthquake. Plate tectonics stresses the fault by creating tension with slow plate movements. An earthquake releases the tension. Plate tectonics also cause a second type of deformation. This type results in dynamic motions that take the form of seismic waves. These sound waves can be compressional waves, also known as primary or P waves, or shear waves, also known as secondary or S waves. P waves travel fastest, with speeds ranging between 1.5 and 8 kilometers per second. Shear waves are slower. P waves shake the ground in the direction they are propagating. S waves shake perpendicularly or transverse to the direction of propagation. Seismographs use a simple pendulum to record earthquake movement in a record called a seismogram. A seismogram can help seismologists estimate the distance, direction, Richter magnitude, and type of faulting of an earthquake.

Earthquakes plate tectonics

Most earthquakes are caused by tectonic plate movement. They occur along fractures called faults or fault zones. Friction in the faults prevents smooth movement. Tension builds up over time, and the release of that tension results in earthquakes. Faults are grouped based on the type of slippage that occurs. The types of faults are dip-slip, strike-slip, and oblique-slip. A dip-slip fault involves vertical movement along the fault plane. In a normal dip-slip fault, the wall that is above the fault plane moves down. In a reverse dip-slip fault, the wall above the fault plane moves up. A strike-slip fault involves horizontal movement along the fault plane. Oblique-slip faults involve both vertical and horizontal movement. The Richter magnitude scale measures how much seismic energy was released by an earthquake.

Erosion

Erosion is the wearing away of rock materials from the Earth's surface. Erosion can be classified as natural geologic erosion and erosion due to human activity. Natural geologic erosion occurs due to weathering and gravity. Factors involved in natural geologic erosion are typically long term forces. Human activity such as development, farming, and deforestation occurs over shorter periods of time. Soil, which supports plant growth, is the topmost layer of organic material. One type of erosion is sheet erosion, which is the gradual and somewhat uniform removal of surface soil. Rills are small rivulets that cut into soil. Gullies are rills that have become enlarged due to extended water run-off. Sandblows are caused by wind blowing away particles. Negative effects of erosion include sedimentation in rivers, which can pollute water and damage ecosystems. Erosion can also result in the removal of topsoil, which destroys crops and prevents plants from growing. This reduces food production and alters ecosystems.

Hydrologic cycle

The hydrologic, or water, cycle refers to water movement on, above, and in the Earth. Water can be in any one of its three states during different phases of the cycle. The three states of water are liquid water, frozen ice, and water vapor. Processes involved in the hydrologic cycle include precipitation, canopy interception, snow melt, runoff, infiltration, subsurface flow, evaporation, sublimation, advection, condensation, and transpiration. Precipitation is when condensed water vapor falls to Earth. Examples include rain, fog drip, and various forms of snow, hail, and sleet. Canopy interception is when precipitation lands on plant foliage instead of falling to the ground and evaporating. Snow melt is runoff produced by melting snow. Infiltration occurs when water flows from the surface into the ground. Subsurface flow refers to water that flows underground. Evaporation is when water in a liquid state changes to a gas. Sublimation is when water in a solid state (such as snow or ice) changes to water vapor without going through a liquid phase. Advection is the movement of water through the atmosphere. Condensation is when water vapor changes to liquid water. Transpiration is when water vapor is released from plants into the air.

Deposition

Deposition, or sedimentation, is the geological process in which previously eroded material is transported or added to a land form or land mass. Erosion and sedimentation are complementary geological processes. Running water causes a substantial amount of deposition of transported materials in both fresh water and coastal areas. Examples include gravity transporting material down the slope of a mountain and depositing it at the base of the slope. Another example is when sandstorms deposit particles in other locations. When glaciers melt and retreat, it can result in the deposition of sediments. Evaporation is also considered to cause deposition since dissolved materials are left behind when water evaporates. Deposition can include the build up of organic materials. For example, chalk is partially made up of the small calcium carbonate skeletons of marine plankton, which helps create more calcium carbonate from chemical processes.

Weathering

There are two basic types of weathering: mechanical and chemical. Weathering is a very prominent process on the Earth's surface. Materials weather at different rates, which are known as differential weathering. Mechanical and chemical weathering is interdependent. For example, chemical weathering can loosen the bonds between molecules and allow mechanical weathering to take place. Mechanical weathering can expose the surfaces of land masses and allow chemical weathering to take place. Impact, abrasion, frost wedging, root wedging, salt wedging, and uploading are types of mechanical weathering. Types of chemical weathering are dissolution, hydration, hydrolysis, oxidation, biological, and carbonation. The primary type of chemical weathering is caused by water dissolving a mineral. The more acidic water is, the more effective it is at weathering. Carbonic and sulfuric acids can enter rain when they are present in the atmosphere. This lowers the pH value of rain, making it more acidic. Normal rain water has a pH value of 5.5. Acid rain has a pH value of 4 or less.

Radioactive dating

Radioactive dating, also known as radiometric dating, is a technique that can be used to determine the age of rocks and even the Earth itself. The process compares the amount of radioactive material in a rock to the amount of material that has "decayed." Decay refers to the fact that the nuclide of an element loses subatomic particles over time. The process includes a parent element that undergoes changes to create a daughter element, also known as the decay product. The daughter element can also be unstable and lose particles, creating another daughter element. This is known as a decay chain. Decay occurs until all the elements are stable. Three types of dating techniques are radiocarbon dating, potassium-argon dating, and uranium-lead dating. These techniques can be used to date a variety of natural and manmade materials, including archaeological artifacts.

Mass extinction

Mass extinction, also known as an extinction event, is a decrease in the number of species over a short period of time. While there are many theories as to the causes of mass extinction, it occurs when a relatively large number of species die off or when fewer species evolve than expected. Extinction events are classified as major and minor. It is generally accepted that there have been five major extinction events in Earth's history. The five most significant mass extinction events are Ordovician-Silurian, Permian-Triassic, Late Devonian, Triassic-Jurassic, and Cretaceous-Tertiary.

Uniformitarianism, catastrophism, and superposition

Uniformitarianism: Also known as gradualism, uniformitarianism is the belief among modern geologists that the forces, processes, and laws that we see today have existed throughout geologic time. It involves the belief that the present is the key to the past, and that relatively slow processes have shaped the geological features of Earth.

Catastrophism: This is the belief that the Earth was shaped by sudden, short-term catastrophic events.

Superposition: In geology, and in the field of stratigraphy in particular, the law of superposition is that underground layers closer to the surface were deposited more recently.

Geologic time scale

One year is 365.25 days long. The International System of Units (SI) suggests the symbol "a" for a standard year or annum. The prefixes "M" for mega and "G" for giga are used to refer to one million and one billion years, respectively. Ma stands for a megannum (10^6 years) and Ga stands for a gigannum (10^9 years). For example, it can be said that the Earth was formed 4.5 billion years ago, or 4.5 Ga. The term "ago" is understood. Use of the abbreviation "mya" for millions of years (ago) is discouraged, but it is still occasionally used. The abbreviation "BP" stands for "before present." The "present" is defined as January 1, 1950, since present changes from year to year. Another abbreviation used is BCE, which stands for "Before the Common Era." Christian and current can also be used in place of common.

Geologists use the geologic time scale when discussing Earth's chronology and the formation of rocks and minerals. Age is calculated in millions of years before the present time. Units of time are often delineated by geologic or paleontologic events. Smaller units of time such as eras are distinguished by the abundance and/or extinction of certain plant and animal life. For example, the extinction of the dinosaurs marks the end of the Mesozoic era and the beginning of the Cenozoic, the present, era. We are in the Holocene epoch. The supereon encompasses the greatest amount of time. It is composed of eons. Eons are divided into eras, eras into periods, and periods into epochs. Layers of rock also correspond to periods of time in geochronology. Current theory holds that the Earth was formed 4.5 billion years ago.

Development of geologic time scale

The first known observations of stratigraphy were made by Aristotle, who lived before the time of Christ. He observed seashells in ancient rock formations and on the beach, and concluded that the fossilized seashells were similar to current seashells. Avicenna, a Persian scholar from the 11th century, also made early advances in the development of stratigraphy with the concept of superposition. Nicolas Steno, a Danish scientist from the 17th century, expounded upon this with the belief that layers of rock are piled on top of each other. In the 18th century, Abraham Werner categorized rocks from four different periods: the Primary, Secondary, Tertiary, and Quaternary periods. This fell out of use when the belief emerged that rock layers containing the same fossils had been deposited at the same time, and were therefore from the same age. British geologists created the names for many of the time divisions in use today. For example, the Devonian period was named after the county of Devon, and the Permian period was named after Perm, Russia.

Relative and absolute time

A numerical, or "absolute," age is a specific number of years, such as 150 million years ago. A "relative" age refers to a time range, such as the Mesozoic era. It is used to determine whether one rock formation is older or younger than another formation. Radioactive dating is a form of absolute dating and stratigraphy is a form of relative dating. Radioactive dating techniques have provided the most information about the absolute age of rocks and other geological features. Together, geochronologists have created a geologic time scale. Biostratigraphy uses plant and animal fossils within rock to determine its relative age.

Stratigraphy

Stratigraphy is a branch of geology that involves the study of rock layers and layering. Sedimentary rocks are the primary focus of stratigraphy. Subfields include lithostratigraphy, which is the study of the vertical layering of rock types, and biostratigraphy, which is the study of fossil evidence in rock layers. Magnetostratigraphy is the study of changes in detrital remnant magnetism (DRM), which is used to measure the polarity of Earth's magnetic field at the time a stratum was deposited. Chronostratigraphy focuses on the relative dating of rock strata based on the time of rock formation. Unconformity refers to missing layers of rock.

Fossils

Fossils provide a wealth of information about the past, particularly about the flora and fauna that once occupied the Earth, but also about the geologic history of the Earth itself and how Earth and its inhabitants came to be. Some fossilized remains in the geohistorical record exemplify ongoing processes in the Earth's environment, such as weathering, glaciation, and volcanism. These have all led to evolutionary changes in plants and animals. Other fossils support the theory that catastrophic events caused drastic changes in the Earth and its living creatures. One example of this type of theory is that a meteor struck the Earth and caused dinosaurs to become extinct. Both types of fossils provide scientists with a way to hypothesize whether these types of events will happen again.

Fossils are preservations of plants, animals, their remains, or their traces that date back to about 10,000 years ago. Fossils and where they are found in rock strata makes up the fossil record. Fossils are formed under a very specific set of conditions. The fossil must not be damaged by predators and scavengers after death, and the fossil must not decompose. Usually, this happens when the organism is quickly covered with sediment. This sediment builds up and molecules in the organism's body are replaced by minerals. Fossils come in an array of sizes, from single-celled organisms to large dinosaurs.

Atmospheric layers

Earth's atmosphere has five main layers. From lowest to highest, these are the troposphere, the stratosphere, the mesosphere, the thermosphere, and the exosphere. Between each pair of layers is a transition layer called a pause. The troposphere includes the tropopause, which is the transitional layer of the stratosphere. Energy from Earth's surface is transferred to the troposphere. Temperature decreases with altitude in this layer. In the stratosphere, the temperature is inverted, meaning that it increases with altitude. The stratosphere includes the ozone layer, which helps block ultraviolet light from the Sun. The stratopause is the transitional layer to the mesosphere. The temperature of the mesosphere decreases with height. It is considered the coldest place on Earth, and has an average temperature of -85 degrees Celsius. Temperature increases with altitude in the thermosphere, which includes the thermopause. Just past the thermosphere is the exobase, the base layer of the exosphere. Beyond the five main layers are the ionosphere, homosphere, heterosphere, and magnetosphere.

Earth's atmosphere

The atmosphere consists of 78% nitrogen, 21% oxygen, and 1% argon. It also includes traces of water vapor, carbon dioxide and other gases, dust particles, and chemicals from Earth. The atmosphere becomes thinner the farther it is from the Earth's surface. It becomes difficult to breathe at about 3 km above sea level. The atmosphere gradually fades into space. The lowest layer of the atmosphere is called the troposphere. Its thickness varies at the poles and the equator, varying from about 7 to 17 km. This is where most weather occurs. The stratosphere is next, and continues to an elevation of about 51 km. The mesosphere extends from the stratosphere to an elevation of about 81 km. It is the coldest layer and is where meteors tend to ablate. The next layer is the thermosphere. It is where the International Space Station orbits. The exosphere is the outermost layer, extends to 10,000 km, and mainly consists of hydrogen and helium.

Tropospheric circulation

Most weather takes place in the troposphere. Air circulates in the atmosphere by convection and in various types of "cells." Air near the equator is warmed by the Sun and rises. Cool air rushes under it, and the higher, warmer air flows toward Earth's poles. At the poles, it cools and descends to the surface. It is now under the hot air, and flows back to the equator. Air currents coupled with ocean currents move heat around the planet, creating winds, weather, and climate. Winds can change direction with the seasons. For example, in Southeast Asia and India, summer monsoons are caused by air being heated by the Sun. This air rises, draws moisture from the ocean, and causes daily rains. In winter, the air cools, sinks, pushes the moist air away, and creates dry weather.

Layers above Earth's surface

The ozone layer, although contained within the stratosphere, is determined by ozone (O_3) concentrations. It absorbs the majority of ultraviolet light from the Sun. The ionosphere is part of both the exosphere and the thermosphere. It is characterized by the fact that it is a plasma, a partially ionized gas in which free electrons and positive ions are attracted to each other, but are too energetic to remain fixed as a molecule. It starts at about 50 km above Earth's surface and goes to 1,000 km. It affects radio wave transmission and auroras. The ionosphere pushes against the inner edge of the Earth's magnetosphere, which is the highly magnetized, non-spherical region around the Earth. The homosphere encompasses the troposphere, stratosphere, and mesosphere. Gases in the homosphere are considered well mixed. In the heterosphere, the distance that particles can move without colliding is large. As a result, gases are stratified according to their molecular weights. Heavier gases such as oxygen and nitrogen occur near the bottom of the heterosphere, while hydrogen, the lightest element, is found at the top.

Hydrosphere

Much of Earth is covered by a layer of water or ice called the hydrosphere. Most of the hydrosphere consists of ocean water. The water cycle and the many processes involved in it take place in the hydrosphere. There are several theories regarding how the Earth's hydrosphere was formed. Earth contains more surface water than other planets in the inner solar system. Outgassing, the slow release of trapped water vapor from the Earth's interior, is one theory used to explain the existence of water on Earth. This does not really account for the quantity of water on Earth, however. Another hypothesis is that the early Earth was subjected to a period of bombardment by comets and water-rich asteroids, which resulted in the release of water into the Earth's environment. If this is true, much of the water on the surface of the Earth today originated from the outer parts of the solar system beyond Neptune.

Formation of Earth's atmosphere

It is generally believed that the Earth's atmosphere evolved into its present state. Some believe Earth's early atmosphere contained hydrogen, helium, methane, ammonia, and some water vapor. These elements also played a role in planet formation. Earth's early atmosphere was developed before the emergence of living organisms as we know them today. Eventually, the hot hydrogen and helium escaped Earth's gravity and drifted off. Others believe the early atmosphere contained a large amount of carbon dioxide. Either way, there was probably little oxygen at the time. One theory is that a second stage of the atmosphere evolved over several hundred million years through a process during which methane, ammonia, and water vapor broke down and reformed into nitrogen, hydrogen, and carbon dioxide. About two billion years ago, higher levels of oxygen were found in the atmosphere, which is indicated by large deposits of iron ore. At the same time, iron ores created in oxygen-poor environments stopped forming. The oxygen in the atmosphere today comes mainly from plants and microorganisms such as algae.

Paleozoic era

The Paleozoic era began about 542 Ma and lasted until 251 Ma. It is further divided into six periods. The Paleozoic era began after the supercontinent Pannotia started to break up and at the end of a global ice age. By the end of the era, the supercontinent Pangaea had formed. The beginning of the Paleozoic era is marked by Cambrian Explosion, a time when there were abundant life forms according to the fossil record. The end of the era is marked by one of the major extinction events, the Permian extinction, during which almost 90 percent of the species living at the time became extinct. Many plant and animal forms appeared on the land and in the sea during this era. It is also when large land plants first appeared in the fossil record. There are many invertebrates found in the fossil record of the Paleozoic era, and fish, amphibians, and reptiles also first appeared in the fossil record during this era. There were also large swamps and forests, some of which were formed into coal deposits that exist today.

Earth's formation

Earth's early development began after a supernova exploded. This led to the formation of the Sun out of hydrogen gas and interstellar dust. These same elements swirled around the newly-formed Sun and formed the planets, including Earth. Scientists theorize that about 4.5 billion years ago, Earth was a chunk of rock surrounded by a cloud of gas. It is believed it lacked water and the type of atmosphere that exists today. Heat from radioactive materials in the rock and pressure in the Earth's interior melted the interior. This caused the heavier materials, such as iron, to sink. Lighter silicate-type rocks rose to the Earth's surface. These rocks formed the Earth's earliest crust. Other chemicals also rose to the Earth's surface, helping to form the water and atmosphere. There is one material that has been dated by scientists and found to be 4.4 billion years old. The material is zircon, which consists of zirconium, silicon, and oxygen. Zircon is a mineral that has a high resistance to weathering.

Cenozoic era

The Cenozoic era began about 65.5 Ma and continues to the present. It is marked by the Cretaceous-Tertiary extinction event (extinction of the dinosaurs as well as many invertebrates and plants). The Cenozoic era is further divided into the Paleogene, Neogene, and Quaternary periods. During the Cenozoic era, Pangaea continued to drift, and the plates eventually moved into their present positions. The Pleistocene Ice Age, also known as Quaternary glaciation or the current ice age began about 2.58 Ma and includes the glaciation occurring today. Mammals continued to evolve and other plants and animals came into existence during this era. The fossil record includes the ancestors of the horse, rhinoceros, and camel. It also includes the first dogs and cats and the first humanlike creatures. The first humans appeared less than 200,000 years ago.

Mesozoic era

The Mesozoic era is known as the Age of the Dinosaurs. It is also the era during which the dinosaurs became extinct. The fossil record also shows the appearance of mammals and birds. Trees that existed included gymnosperms, which have uncovered seeds and are mostly cone bearing, and angiosperms, which have covered seeds and are flowering plants. The angiosperm group is currently the dominant plant group. It was also during this era that the supercontinent Pangaea divided into the continental pieces that exist today. During the Cretaceous period, sea levels rose until one-third of the Earth's present land mass was underwater, and then receded. This period created huge marine deposits and chalk. The extinction of the dinosaurs happened about 65 Ma, and was believed to have been triggered by the impact of an asteroid.

Ocean

The ocean is the salty body of water that encompasses the Earth. It has a mass of 1.4 x 10^{24} grams. Geographically, the ocean is divided into three large oceans: the Pacific Ocean, the Atlantic Ocean, and the Indian Ocean. There are also other divisions, such as gulfs, bays, and various types of seas, including Mediterranean and marginal seas. Ocean distances can be measured by latitude, longitude, degrees, meters, miles, and nautical miles. The ocean accounts for 70.8% of the surface of the Earth, amounting to 361,254,000 km^2. The ocean's depth is greatest at Challenger Deep in the Mariana Trench. The ocean floor here is 10,924 meters below sea level. The depths of the ocean are mapped by echo sounders and satellite altimeter systems. Echo sounders emit a sound pulse from the surface and record the time it takes to return. Satellite altimeters provide better maps of the ocean floor.

Ocean's importance

The ocean covers 71 percent of the Earth's surface and contains 97 percent of the planet's water. The ocean is an important part of the biosphere, the hydrologic cycle, and tropospheric circulation. It also plays a key role in Earth's weather and climate, which influence the daily lives of humans. The main uses of the ocean and coastal areas for humans are food, transport, oil, gas, and recreation. It is estimated that the ocean provides a means of support for almost 50 percent of all species on Earth. Roughly 20 percent of the animal protein in human diets comes from the ocean.

Seawater

Salinity is a measure of the amount of dissolved salts in ocean water. It is defined in terms of conductivity. Salinity is influenced by the geologic formations in the area, with igneous formations leading to lower salinity and sedimentary formations leading to higher salinity. Dryer areas with greater rates of evaporation also have higher salt concentrations. Areas where fresh water mixes with ocean water have lower salt concentrations. Hydrogen and oxygen make up about 96.5% of sea water. The major constituents of the dissolved solids of sea water at an atomic level are chlorine (55.3%), sodium (30.8%), magnesium (3.7%), sulfur (2.6%), calcium (1.2%), and potassium (1.1%). The salinity of ocean water is fairly constant, ranging from 34.60 to 34.80 parts per thousand, which is 200 parts per million. Measuring variation on this small of a scale requires instruments that are accurate to about one part per million.

Ocean floor

The ocean floor includes features similar to those found on land, such as mountains, ridges, plains, and canyons. The oceanic crust is a thin, dense layer that is about 10 km thick. The greatest volume of water is contained in the basins with lesser volumes that occupy the low-lying areas of the continents, which are known as the continental shelves. The continental slope connects the shelf to the ocean floor of the basin. The continental rise is a slightly sloping area between the slope and the basin. A seamount is an undersea volcanic peak that rises to a height of at least 1,000 meters. A guyot is a seamount with a flat top. A mid-ocean ridge is a continuous undersea mountain chain.

Sills are low parts of ridges separating ocean basins or other seas. Trenches are long, narrow troughs. Many isolated peaks and seamounts are scattered throughout the ocean basins, and interrupt ocean currents.

Gyres and the Coriolis effect

Gyres are surface ocean currents that form large circular patterns. In the Northern Hemisphere, they flow clockwise. In the Southern Hemisphere, they flow counterclockwise. These directions are caused by the Coriolis effect. The Coriolis effect occurs due to the fact that the Earth is a rotating object. In the Northern Hemisphere, currents appear to be curving to the right. In the Southern Hemisphere, currents appear to be curving to the left. This is because the Earth is rotating. Gyres tend to flow in the opposite direction near the Earth's poles. In the portion of the Pacific Ocean north of the equator, the major currents are North Pacific, California, North Equatorial, and Kuroshio. In the South Pacific, they are South Equatorial, East Australia, South Pacific, and Peru. In the North Atlantic, they are the North Atlantic Drift, Canary, North Equatorial, and Gulf Stream. In the South Atlantic, they are South Equatorial, Brazil, South Atlantic, and Benguela.

Ocean currents

Surface currents are caused by winds. Subsurface currents, which occur deep beneath the ocean's surface, are caused by land masses and the Earth's rotation. The density of ocean water can also affect currents. Sea water with a higher salinity is denser than sea water with a lower salinity. Water from denser areas flows to areas with water that is less dense. Currents are classified by temperature. Colder polar sea water flows south towards warmer water, forming cold currents. Warm water currents swirl around the basins and equator. In turn, heat lost and gained by the ocean creates winds. Ocean currents play a significant role in transferring this heat toward the poles, which aids in the development of many types of weather phenomena.

Upwelling and Ekman transport

Upwelling occurs where wind blows parallel to a coast. This causes the ocean surface to move away from the coast. Deep-sea water, which is usually cold and rich in nutrients, rises to takes its place. Ekman transport refers to the impact of the Coriolis effect when wind moves water. Wind blowing in one direction tries to move the surface layer of water in a straight line, but the rotation of the Earth causes water to move in a curved direction. The wind continues to blow the surface of the water and the surface water turns slightly. Below the surface, the water turns even more, eventually creating a spiral. This creates water movement at a right angle to the wind direction. The importance of upwelling is that it brings the nutrient-rich dead and rotting sea creatures closer to the ocean's surface. Here, they are consumed by phytoplankton, which is in turn eaten by zooplankton. Fish eat the zooplankton, and larger creatures and humans eat the fish. Downwelling is the opposite of upwelling.

Deep sea currents

Deep sea currents are often likened to a conveyor belt because they circumnavigate the entire ocean, albeit weakly, and slowly mix deeper and shallower water. In the winter, deep circulation carries cold water from high latitudes to lower latitudes throughout the world. This takes place in areas where most water is at a depth of between 4 and 5 km. This water mass can be as cold as or colder than 4°C. Surface ocean temperatures average about 17°C, but can vary from -2°C to 36°C. The vast cold mass of sea water is also dense and has a high saline content, which forces it to sink at high latitudes. It spreads out, stratifies, and fills the ocean basins. Deep mixing occurs and then the water upwells. The manner in which deep sea currents move can be described as abyssal circulation.

Ocean waves

Most waves in the ocean are formed by winds. The stronger the winds are, the larger the waves will be. The highest point of a wave is the crest. The lowest point of a wave is the trough. The wavelength is measured from crest to crest. The wave height is measured from the trailing trough to the peak of the crest. The wave frequency refers to the number of wave crests passing a designated point each second. A wave period is the time it takes for a wave crest to reach the point of the wave crest of the previous wave. The energy in the wave runs into the shallow sea floor. This causes the wave to become steeper and then fall over, or break.

Other types of waves

Waves that reach the shore are not all the same size. They can be larger or smaller than average. About once an hour, there is usually a wave that is twice the size of others. There are even larger, but rare, rogue waves, which often travel alone and in a direction different than other waves. Swells are waves that have traveled a great distance. These types of waves are usually large waves with flatter crests. They are very regular in shape and size. The sea level slowly rises and falls over the period of a day. These types of waves on the sea surface are known as tides. Tides have wavelengths of thousands of kilometers. They differ from other wave types in that they are created by slow and very small changes in gravity due to the motion of the Sun and the Moon relative to Earth.

Tsunamis

Seismic sea waves or tsunamis (sometimes mistakenly called tidal waves) are formed by seismic activity. A tsunami is a series of waves with long wavelengths and long periods. Far out at sea, the heights of these waves are typically less than one meter. The wavelength may be 100 km and the wave period may range from five minutes to one hour. However, as seismic sea waves approach the shoreline, the bottom of the wave is slowed down by the shallower sea floor. The top is not slowed as much, and wave height increases to as much as 20 meters. These waves can hit the shore at speeds of up to 30 miles per hour. Tsunamis are caused by earthquakes, submarine landslides, and volcanic eruptions.

Beaufort wind scale

The Beaufort wind scale assigns a numerical value to wind conditions and the appearance of the sea. Zero represents a calm, mirror-like sea with no measurable wind. Twelve is the maximum on the Beaufort scale, and represents hurricane force winds with speeds of 35.2 meters per second (m/s). Visibility is greatly reduced, the sea air is filled with foam, and the sea is completely white with driving spray. The scale is as follows: 1 is light wind with a speed of 1.2 m/s; 2 is a light breeze of 2.8 m/s; 3 is a gentle breeze of 4.9 m/s; 4 is a moderate breeze of 7.7 m/s; and 5 is a fresh breeze of 10.5 m/s. At 5, there are moderate waves, many white caps, and some spray. Six is a strong breeze of 13.1 m/s; 7 is a near gale with wind speeds of 15.8 m/s; 8 is gale force winds of 18.8 m/s; 9 is strong gales of 22.1 m/s; 10 is considered a storm with wind speeds of 25.9 m/s; and 11 is a violent storm.

Shoreline

The area where land meets the sea is called the shoreline. This marks the average position of the ocean. Longshore currents create longshore drift or transport (also called beach drift). This is when ocean waves move toward a beach at an angle, which moves water along the coast. Sediment is eroded from some areas and deposited in others. In this way, it is moved along the beach. Rip currents are strong, fast currents that occur when part of longshore current moves away from the beach. Hard, man-made structures built perpendicular to the beach tend to trap sand on the up-current side. Erosion occurs on the down-current side. Features formed by the sediment deposited by waves include spits, bay-mouth bars, tombolos, barrier islands, and buildups. Sand is composed of weather-resistant, granular materials like quartz and orthoclase. In some locations, it is composed of rock and basalt.

Tides

The gravitational pull of the Sun and Moon causes the oceans to rise and fall each day, creating high and low tides. Most areas have two high tides and two low tides per day. Because the Moon is closer to the Earth than the Sun, its gravitational pull is much greater. The water on the side of the Earth that is closest to the Moon and the water on the opposite side experience high tide. The two low tides occur on the other sides. This changes as the Moon revolves around the Earth. Tidal range is the measurement of the height difference between low and high tide. Tidal range also changes with the location of the Sun and Moon throughout the year, creating spring and neap tides. When all these bodies are aligned, the combined gravitational pull is greater and the tidal range is also greater. This is what creates the spring tide. The neap tide is when the tidal range is at its lowest, which occurs when the Sun and Moon are not at right angles.

Black smokers

Black smokers are a relatively recently discovered feature of the ocean floor. They were first identified in 1977. A black smoker is a type of hydrothermal vent formed when superheated water from below Earth's crust emerges from the ocean floor. This hot water is also rich in sulfides and other minerals from the Earth's crust. When the hot water comes in contact with the cold ocean water, it creates a black chimney-like structure around the vent. Water temperatures around black smokers have been recorded at 400°C. However, water pressure is too great on the sea floor to allow for boiling. The water is also very acidic (twice that of vinegar). It is estimated that the yearly volume of water passing through black smokers is 1.4×10^{14} kg.

Carbon cycle

The carbon and nutrient cycles of the ocean are processes that are due in part to the deep currents, mixing, and upwelling that occur in the ocean. Carbon dioxide (CO_2) from the atmosphere is dissolved into the ocean at higher latitudes and distributed to the denser deep water. Where upwelling occurs, CO_2 is brought back to the surface and emitted into the tropical air. Phytoplankton are typically single-celled organisms that are nourished by the Sun. They are photosynthetic autotrophs, meaning they convert water, carbon dioxide, and solar energy into food. They drift with the currents, produce oxygen as a byproduct, and serve as a food source. Zooplankton feed on phytoplankton. Zooplankton are heterotrophic organisms, meaning they do not synthesize their own food. Zooplankton can be single-celled creatures or much larger organisms, such as jellyfish, mollusks, and crustaceans.

El Niño-Southern Oscillation (ENSO)

The El Niño-Southern Oscillation (ENSO) is a climate pattern of the Pacific Ocean area that lasts 6 to 18 months and causes weather that is different from the expected seasonal patterns and variations. There are two sets of events associated with ENSO: El Niño and La Niña. The usual weather patterns for the Pacific Ocean involve the movement of sea water by winds from the eastern part of the tropical Pacific to the western part of the Pacific Ocean. This pattern causes cold deep water upwells in the eastern Pacific. This creates wet weather and is considered a low-pressure system. Conversely, the eastern Pacific is a dry, high-pressure system. El Niño weakens upwelling because equalization in air pressure leads to less wind, which leads to more water staying in the eastern Pacific. La Niña increases upwelling because winds grow stronger because of higher air pressures across the Pacific. Both El Niño and La Niña cause extreme weather events such as droughts, heavy rain, and flooding.

Rift valley

Rift valleys occur both on land and in the ocean. They are a result of plate tectonics, and occur when plates are spreading apart. In the ocean, this is part of the crust development cycle in which new crust is created at mid-ocean ridges and old crust is lost at the trenches. The Mid-Atlantic Ridge is an example of this. It occurs at divergent Eurasian and North American plates and in the South Atlantic, African, and South American plates. The East Pacific Rise is also a mid-oceanic ridge. The most extensive rift valley is located along the crest of the mid-ocean ridge system. It is a result of sea floor spreading.

Beaches

Weathering erodes the parent material of beaches, rock and soil, into sand, which is typically quartz. Other parts of the soil such as clay and silt are deposited in areas of the continental shelf. The larger sand particles get deposited in the form of a beach. This includes a near shore, which is underwater, a fore shore, the area typically considered the beach, and a back shore. The offshore starts about 5 meters from the shoreline and extends to about 20 meters. The beach also includes wet and dry parts and a fore dune and rear dune. Waves typically move sand from the sea to the beach, and gravity and wave action move it back again. Wind gradually pushes sand particles uphill in a jumping motion called saltation. Sand stays deposited in the form of dunes and the dunes appear as if they roll backward. Storms can both erode a beach and provide additional deposition.

North Atlantic Oscillation (NAO)

The North Atlantic Oscillation is a climatic occurrence that affects winter weather in the Northern Hemisphere, particularly in the east coast regions of the United States, Europe, and North Africa. Atmospheric pressure over the North Atlantic caused by the Icelandic Low and the high pressure Azores leads to the North Atlantic Oscillation. There is both a "positive" and "negative" phase of the NAO. The positive phase is when strong winds caused by a large difference in air pressure send wet winter storms from eastern North America to northern Europe. Weaker winds associated with a smaller difference in air pressure cause eastern North America and northern Europe to have fewer winter storms. Instead, the weather is rainy in southern Europe and North Africa.

Weather, climate, and meteorology

Meteorology is the study of the atmosphere, particularly as it pertains to forecasting the weather and understanding its processes. Weather is the condition of the atmosphere at any given moment. Most weather occurs in the troposphere. Weather includes changing events such as clouds, storms, and temperature, as well as more extreme events such as tornadoes, hurricanes, and blizzards. Climate refers to the average weather for a particular area over time, typically at least 30 years. Latitude is an indicator of climate. Changes in climate occur over long time periods.

Weather phenomena

Common atmospheric conditions that are frequently measured are temperature, precipitation, wind, and humidity. These weather conditions are often measured at permanently fixed weather stations so weather data can be collected and compared over time and by region. Measurements may also be taken by ships, buoys, and underwater instruments. Measurements may also be taken under special circumstances. The measurements taken include temperature, barometric pressure, humidity, wind speed, wind direction, and precipitation. Usually, the following instruments are used: A thermometer is used for measuring temperature; a barometer is used for measuring barometric/air pressure; a hygrometer is used for measuring humidity; an anemometer is used for measuring wind speed; a weather vane is used for measuring wind direction; and a rain gauge is used for measuring precipitation.

Latitudinal variation of solar radiation

Latitude is a measurement of the distance from the equator. The distance from the equator indicates how much solar radiation a particular area receives. The equator receives more sunlight, while polar areas receive less. The Earth tilts slightly on its rotational axis. This tilt determines the seasons and affects weather. There are eight biomes or ecosystems with particular climates that are associated with latitude. Those in the high latitudes, which get the least sunlight, are tundra and taiga. Those in the mid latitudes are grassland, temperate forest, and chaparral. Those in latitudes closest to the equator are the warmest. The biomes are desert and tropical rain forest. The eighth biome is the ocean, which is unique because it consists of water and spans the entire globe. Insolation refers to incoming solar radiation. Diurnal variations refer to the daily changes in insolation. The greatest insolation occurs at noon.

Tilt of the Earth

The tilt of the Earth on its axis is 23.5°. This tilt causes the seasons and affects the temperature because it affects the amount of Sun the area receives. When the Northern or Southern Hemispheres are tilted toward the Sun, the hemisphere tilted toward the sun experiences summer and the other hemisphere experiences winter. This reverses as the Earth revolves around the Sun. Fall and spring occur between the two extremes. The equator gets the same amount of sunlight every day of the year, about 12 hours, and doesn't experience seasons. Both poles have days during the winter when they are tilted away from the Sun and receive no daylight. The opposite effect occurs during the summer. There are 24 hours of daylight and no night. The summer solstice, the day with the most amount of sunlight, occurs on June 21st in the Northern Hemisphere and on December 21st in the Southern Hemisphere. The winter solstice, the day with the least amount of sunlight, occurs on December 21st in the Northern Hemisphere and on June 21st in the Southern Hemisphere.

Breezes

Sea breezes and land breezes help influence an area's prevailing winds, particularly in areas where the wind flow is light. Sea breezes, also called onshore breezes, are the result of the different capacities for absorbing heat of the ocean and the land. The sea can be warmed to a greater depth than the land. It warms up more slowly than the land's surface. Land heats air above it as its temperature increases. This heated; warmer is less dense and rises as a result. The cooler air above the sea and higher sea level pressure create a wind flow in the direction of the land. Coastal areas often receive these cooler breezes. Land cools slower at night than the ocean, and coastal breezes weaken at this time. When the land becomes so cool that it is cooler than the sea surface, the pressure over the ocean is lower than the land. This creates a land breeze. This can cause rain and thunderstorms over the ocean.

Wind

Winds are the result of air moving by convection. Masses of warm air rise, and cold air sweeps into their place. The warm air also moves, cools, and sinks. The term "prevailing wind" refers to the wind that usually blows in an area in a single direction. Dominant winds are the winds with the highest speeds. Belts or bands that run latitudinal and blow in a specific direction are associated with convection cells. Hadley cells are formed directly north and south of the equator. The Farrell cells occur at about 30° to 60°. The jet stream runs between the Farrell cells and the polar cells. At the higher and lower latitudes, the direction is easterly. At mid latitudes, the direction is westerly. From the North Pole to the south, the surface winds are Polar High Easterlies, Subpolar Low Westerlies, Subtropical High or Horse Latitudes, North-East Trade winds, Equatorial Low or Doldrums, South-East Trades, Subtropical High or Horse Latitudes, Subpolar Low Easterlies, and Polar High.

Thunderstorms

A thunderstorm is one of the many weather phenomena that can be created during the ongoing process of heat moving through Earth's atmosphere. Thunderstorms form when there is moisture to form rain clouds, unstable air, and lift. Unstable air is usually caused by warm air rising quickly through cold air. Lift can be caused by fronts, sea breezes, and elevated terrain, such as mountains. Single cell thunderstorms have one main draft. Multicell clusters have clusters of storms. Multicell lines have severe thunderstorms along a squall line. Supercell thunderstorms are large and severe, and have the capacity to produce destructive tornadoes. Thunder is a sonic shock wave caused by the rapid expansion of air around lightning. Lightning is the discharge of electricity during a thunderstorm. Lightning can also occur during volcanic eruptions or dust storms.

Atmospheric variations

Terrain affects several local atmospheric conditions, including temperature, wind speed, and wind direction. When there are land forms, heating of the ground can be greater than the heating of the surrounding air than it would be at the same altitude above sea level. This creates a thermal low in the region and amplifies any existing thermal lows. It also changes the wind circulation. Terrain such as hills and valleys increase friction between the air and the land, which disturbs the air flow. This physical block deflects the wind, and the resulting air flow is called a barrier jet. Just as the heating of the land and air affect sea and land breezes along the coast, rugged terrain affects the wind circulation between mountains and valleys.

Cyclones

Cyclones generally refer to large air masses rotating in the same direction as the Earth. They are formed in low pressure areas. Cyclones vary in size. Some are mesoscale systems, which vary in size from about 5 km to hundreds of kilometers. Some are synoptic scale systems, which are about 1,000 km in size. The size of subtropical cyclones is somewhere in between. Cold-core polar and extratropical cyclones are synoptic scale systems. Warm-core tropical, polar low and mesocyclones are mesoscale systems. Extratropical cyclones, sometimes called mid-latitude cyclones or wave cyclones, occur in the middle latitudes. They have neither tropical nor polar characteristics. Extratropical cyclones are everyday phenomena which, along with anticyclones, drive the weather over much of the Earth. They can produce cloudiness, mild showers, heavy gales, and thunderstorms. Anticyclones occur when there is a descending pocket of air of higher than average pressure. Anticyclones are usually associated with clearing skies and drier, cooler air.

Tornados

During a tornado, wind speeds can be upward of 300 miles per hour. Tornados are rotating funnel-like clouds. They have a very high energy density, which means they are very destructive to a small area. They are also short-lived. About 75% of the world's tornadoes occur in the United States, mostly in an area of the Great Plains known as Tornado Alley. If there are two or more columns of air, it is referred to as a multiple vortex tornado. A satellite tornado is a weak tornado that forms near a larger one within the same mesocyclone. A waterspout is a tornado over water. The severity of tornadoes is measured using the Enhanced Fujita Scale. An EF-0 rating is associated with a 3-second wind gust between 65 and 85 miles per hour, while an EF-5 is associated with wind speeds of greater than 200 mph.

Humidity

Humidity refers to water vapor contained in the air. The amount of moisture contained in air depends upon its temperature. The higher the air temperature, the more moisture it can hold. These higher levels of moisture are associated with higher humidity. Absolute humidity refers to the total amount of moisture air is capable of holding at a certain temperature. Relative humidity is the ratio of water vapor in the air compared to the amount the air is capable of holding at its current temperature. As temperature decreases, absolute humidity stays the same and relative humidity increases. A hygrometer is a device used to measure humidity. The dew point is the temperature at which water vapor condenses into water at a particular humidity.

Hurricanes

A hurricane is one of the three weather phenomena that can occur as a result of a tropical cyclone. A tropical cyclone is a warm-core, low-pressure condition that circles in the same direction as the Earth. A tropical depression has sustained winds of up to 30 miles per hour (mph), with rotational winds around a center. A tropical storm appears more circular and has more rotation than a tropical depression. Its winds range from 39 to 73 mph. A hurricane appears well-organized and sometimes has a recognizable eye with strong rotation. Its wind speed is more than 73 mph. Hurricanes are classified using the Saffir-Simpson Scale, which ranges from category 1 to category 5. A category 5 hurricane has wind speeds greater than 155 mph. Hurricanes are named alphabetically through the season starting with "A." The letters "Q," "U," and "Z" are not used. There are six lists of names that are used from year to year. The names of devastating hurricanes are retired from the list.

Precipitation

After clouds reach the dew point, precipitation occurs. Precipitation can take the form of a liquid or a solid. It is known by many names, including rain, snow, ice, dew, and frost. Liquid forms of precipitation include rain and drizzle. Rain or drizzle that freezes on contact is known as freezing rain or freezing drizzle. Solid or frozen forms of precipitation include snow, ice needles or diamond dust, sleet or ice pellets, hail, and graupel or snow pellets. Virga is a form of precipitation that evaporates before reaching the ground. It usually looks like sheets or shafts falling from a cloud. The amount of rainfall is measured with a rain gauge. Intensity can be measured according to how fast precipitation is falling or by how severely it limits visibility. Precipitation plays a major role in the water cycle since it is responsible for depositing much of the Earth's fresh water.

Heat waves

A heat wave is a stretch of hotter than normal weather. Some heat waves may involve high humidity and last longer than a week. Heat waves can form if a warm high-pressure weather system stalls in an area. The jet stream is a flow that moves air through the middle latitudes. When this shifts, it can bring a pattern of unusually warm weather into a region, creating a heat wave. Heat can be trapped by cities. If there is no rain or clouds to help cool the weather, the heat wave can linger. In humans, heat waves can lead to heat stroke, heat exhaustion, cramps, dehydration, and even death. Plants can dry up and crops can fail. There is also a greater threat of fires during a heat wave in dry areas.

Cloud types

Most clouds can be classified according to the altitude of their base above Earth's surface. High clouds occur at altitudes between 5,000 and 13,000 meters. Middle clouds occur at altitudes between 2,000 and 7,000 meters. Low clouds occur from the Earth's surface to altitudes of 2,000 meters. Types of high clouds include cirrus (Ci), thin wispy mare's tails that consist of ice; cirrocumulus (Cc), small, pillow-like puffs that often appear in rows; and cirrostratus (Cs), thin, sheetlike clouds that often cover the entire sky. Types of middle clouds include altocumulus (Ac), gray-white clouds that consist of liquid water; and altostratus (As), grayish or blue-gray clouds that span the sky. Types of low clouds include stratus (St), gray and fog-like clouds consisting of water droplets that take up the whole sky; stratocumulus (Sc), low-lying, lumpy gray clouds; and nimbostratus (Ns), dark gray clouds with uneven bases that indicate rain or snow. Two types of clouds, cumulus (Cu) and cumulonimbus (Cb), are capable of great vertical growth. They can start at a wide range of altitudes, from the Earth's surface to altitudes of 13,000 meters.

Cloud formation

Clouds form when air cools and warm air is forced to give up some of its water vapor because it can no longer hold it. This vapor condenses and forms tiny droplets of water or ice crystals called clouds. Particles, or aerosols, are needed for water vapor to form water droplets. These are called condensation nuclei. Clouds are created by surface heating, mountains and terrain, rising air masses, and weather fronts. Clouds precipitate, returning the water they contain to Earth. Clouds can also create atmospheric optics. They can scatter light, creating colorful phenomena such as rainbows, colorful sunsets, and the green flash phenomenon.

Air masses and weather fronts

Air masses are large volumes of air in the troposphere of the Earth. They are categorized by their temperature and by the amount of water vapor they contain. Arctic and Antarctic air masses are cold, polar air masses are cool, and tropical and equatorial air masses are hot. Other types of air masses include maritime and monsoon, both of which are moist and unstable. There are also continental and superior air masses, which are dry. A weather front separates two masses of air of different densities. It is the principal cause of meteorological phenomena. Air masses are quickly and easily affected by the land they are above. They can have certain characteristics, and then develop new ones when they get blown over a different area.

Nonstandard cloud types

Contrails, or condensation trails, are thin white streaks caused by jets. These are created from water vapor condensing and freezing the jet's exhaust particles. Contrails can be further classified as short-lived, persistent non-spreading, and persistent. Lenticular or lee wave, clouds are created by an air current over an obstacle, such as a mountain. They appear to be stationary, but are actually forming, dissipating, and reforming in the same place. Kelvin-Helmholtz clouds are formed by winds with different speeds or directions. They look like ocean waves. Mammatus clouds hang down from the base of a cloud, usually a cumulonimbus cloud. They often occur during the warmer months.

Pressure systems

The concept of atmospheric pressure involves the idea that air exerts a force. An imaginary column of air 1 square inch in size rising through the atmosphere would exert a force of 14.7 pounds per square inch (psi). Both temperature and altitude affect atmospheric pressure. Low and high pressure systems tend to want to equalize. Air tends to move from areas of high pressure to areas of low pressure. When air moves into a low pressure system, the air that was there gets pushed up, creating lower temperatures and pressures. Water vapor condenses and forms clouds and possibly rain and snow. A barometer is used to measure air pressure.

Bergeron system

The Bergeron classification system uses three sets of letters to identify the following characteristics of air masses: moisture content, thermal characteristics from where they originated, and the stability of the atmosphere. The first, moisture content, uses the following letters: "c" represents the dry continental air masses and "m" stands for the moist maritime air masses. The second set of abbreviations are as follows: "T" indicates the air mass is tropical in origin; "P" indicates the air mass is polar in origin; "A" indicates the air mass is Antarctic in origin; "M" stands for monsoon; "E" indicates the air mass is equatorial in origin; and "S" is used to represent superior air, which is dry air formed by a downward motion. The last set of symbols provides an indicator of the stability of the mass. "K" indicates the mass is colder than the ground below it, while "w" indicates the mass is warmer than the ground. For example, cP is a continental polar air mass, while cPk is a polar air mass blowing over the Gulf Stream, which is warmer than the mass.

Frontal systems

A cold front is a mass of cold air, usually fast moving and dense, that moves into a warm air front, producing clouds. This often produces a temperature drop and rain, hail (frozen rain), thunder, and lightning. A warm front is pushed up by a fast moving cold front. It is often associated with high wispy clouds, such as cirrus and cirrostratus clouds. A stationary front forms when a warm and cold front meet, but neither is strong enough to move the other. Winds blowing parallel to the fronts keep the front stationary. The front may remain in the same place for days until the wind direction changes and both fronts become a single warm or cold front. In other cases, the entire front dissipates. An occluded front is when a cold front pushes into a warm front. The warm air rises and the two masses of cool air join. These types of fronts often occur in areas of low atmospheric pressure.

Weather fronts and maps

A weather front is the area between two differing masses of air that affects weather. Frontal movements are influenced by the jet stream and other high winds. Movements are determined by the type of front. Cold fronts move up to twice as fast as warm ones. It is in the turbulent frontal area that commonplace and dramatic weather events take place. This area also creates temperature changes. Weather phenomena include rain, thunderstorms, high winds, tornadoes, cloudiness, clear skies, and hurricanes. Different fronts can be plotted on weather maps using a set of designated symbols. Surface weather maps can also include symbols representing clouds, rain, temperature, air pressure, and fair weather.

Cold fronts are represented on weather maps as a blue line. Solid blue triangles are used to indicate the direction of movement. Warm fronts are represented with a red line. Solid red semi-circles are used to indicate the direction of the front. The cold and warm front symbols are merged and alternated to point in opposite directions to indicate a stationary front. An occluded front is represented by a purple line with alternating solid purple triangles and semi-circles. A surface trough is represented by an orange dashed line. A squall or shear line is represented by a red line. Two dots and a dash are alternated to form the line. A dry line is represented by an orange line with semi-circles in outline form. A tropical wave is represented by a straight orange line. An "L" is used to indicate an area of low atmospheric pressure and an "H" is used to indicate an area of high atmospheric pressure.

Weather phenomena

Shearline: This evolves from a stationary front that has gotten smaller. Wind direction shifts over a short distance.

Dry line or dew point line: This separates two warm air masses of differing moisture content. At lower altitudes, the moist air mass wedges under the drier air. At higher altitudes, the dry air wedges under the moist air. This is a frequent occurrence in the Midwest and Canada, where the dry air of the Southwest and the moister air of the Gulf of Mexico meet. This can lead to extreme weather events, including tornadoes and thunderstorms.

Squall line: Severe thunderstorms can form at the front of or ahead of a cold front. In some cases, severe thunderstorms can also outrun cold fronts. A squall line can produce extreme weather in the form of heavy rain, hail, lightning, strong winds, tornadoes, and waterspouts.

Tropical waves or easterly waves: These are atmospheric troughs or areas of low air pressure that travel westward in the tropics, causing clouds and thunderstorms.

Astronomy

Astronomy is the scientific study of celestial objects and their positions, movements, and structures. Celestial does not refer to the Earth in particular, but does include its motions as it moves through space. Other objects include the Sun, the Moon, planets, satellites, asteroids, meteors, comets, stars, galaxies, the universe, and other space phenomena. The term astronomy has its roots in the Greek words "astro" and "nomos," which means "laws of the stars."

Weather forecasting

Short and long-term weather forecasting is important because the day-to-day weather greatly affects humans and human activity. Severe weather and natural events can cause devastating harm to humans, property, and sources of livelihood, such as crops. The persistence method of forecasting can be used to create both short and long-term forecasts in areas that change very little or change slowly. It assumes that the weather tomorrow will be similar to the weather today. Barometric pressure is measured because a change in air pressure can indicate the arrival of a cold front that could lead to precipitation. Long-term forecasts based on climate data are useful to help people prepare for seasonal changes and severe events such as hurricanes.

Universe structure

What can be seen of the universe is believed to be at least 93 billion light years across. To put this into perspective, the Milky Way galaxy is about 100,000 light years across. Our view of matter in the universe is that it forms into clumps. Matter is organized into stars, galaxies, clusters of galaxies, superclusters, and the Great Wall of galaxies. Galaxies consist of stars, some with planetary systems. Some estimates state that the universe is about 13 billion years old. It is not considered dense, and is believed to consist of 73 percent dark energy, 23 percent cold dark matter, and 4 percent regular matter. Cosmology is the study of the universe. Interstellar medium (ISM) is the gas and dust in the interstellar space between a galaxy's stars.

Universe origin

The universe can be said to consist of everything and nothing. The universe is the source of everything we know about space, matter, energy, and time. There are likely still phenomena that have yet to be discovered. The universe can also be thought of as nothing, since a vast portion of the known universe is empty space. It is believed that the universe is expanding. The Big Bang theory, which is widely accepted among astronomers, was developed to explain the origin of the universe. There are other theories regarding the origin of the universe, such as the Steady-State theory and the Creationist theory. The Big Bang theory states that all the matter in the universe was once in one place. This matter underwent a huge explosion that spread the matter into space. Galaxies formed from this material and the universe is still expanding.

Stars

Black hole: A black hole is a space where the gravitational field is so powerful that everything, including light, is pulled into it. Once objects enter the surface, the event horizon, they cannot escape.

Quasar: Quasar stands for quasi-stellar radio source, which is an energetic galaxy with an active galactic nucleus. Quasars were first identified by their emissions of large amounts of electromagnetic energy, such as radio waves and visible light. These emissions differed from those associated with other galaxies.

Blazar: A blazar is a very violent phenomenon in galaxies with supermassive black holes.

Dark matter: Although its existence has not yet been proven, dark matter may account for a large proportion of the universe's mass. It is undetectable because it does not emit any radiation, but is believed to exist because of gravitational forces exerted on visible objects.

Galaxies

Galaxies consist of stars, stellar remnants, and dark matter. Dwarf galaxies contain as few as 10 million stars, while giant galaxies contain as many as 1 trillion stars. Galaxies are gravitationally bound, meaning the stars, star systems, other gases, and dust orbits the galaxy's center. The Earth exists in the Milky Way galaxy and the nearest galaxy to ours is the Andromeda galaxy. Galaxies can be classified by their visual shape into elliptical, spiral, irregular, and starburst galaxies. It is estimated that there are more than 100 billion galaxies in the universe ranging from 1,000 to 100,000 parsecs in diameter. Galaxies can be megaparsecs apart. Intergalactic space consists of a gas with an average density of less than one atom per cubic meter. Galaxies are organized into clusters which form superclusters. Dark matter may account for up to 90% of the mass of galaxies. Dark matter is still not well understood.

Time measurements

A sidereal day is four minutes shorter than a solar day. A solar day is the time it takes the Earth to complete one revolution and face the Sun again. From noon to noon is 24 hours. A sidereal day is measured against a distant "fixed" star. As the Earth completes one rotation, it has also completed part of its revolution around the Sun, so it completes a sidereal rotation in reference to the fixed star before it completes a solar rotation. The Sun travels along the ecliptic in 365.25 days. This can be tracked day after day before dawn. After one year, the stars appear back in their original positions. As a result, different constellations are viewable at different times of the year. Sidereal years are slightly longer than tropical years. The difference is caused by the precession of the equinoxes. A calendar based on the sidereal year will be out of sync with the seasons at a rate of about one day every 71 years.

Large units of distance

An astronomical unit, also known as AU, is a widely used measurement in astronomy. One AU is equal to the distance from the Earth to the Sun, which is 150 million km, or 93 million miles. These distances can also be expressed as 149.60×10^9 m or 92.956×10^6 mi. A light year (ly) is the distance that light travels in a vacuum in one year. A light year is equal to about 10 trillion km, or 64,341 AU, and is used to measure large astronomical units. Also used for measuring large distances is the parsec (pc), which is the preferred unit since it is better suited for recording observational data. A parsec is the parallax of one arcsecond, and is about 31 trillion km (about 19 trillion miles), or about 3.26 light years. It is used to calculate distances by triangulation. The AU distance from the Earth to the Sun is used to form the side of a right triangle.

Star life cycle

There are different life cycle possibilities for stars after they initially form and enter into the main sequence stage. Small, relatively cold red dwarfs with relatively low masses burn hydrogen slowly, and will remain in the main sequence for hundreds of billions of years. Massive, hot supergiants will leave the main sequence after just a few million years. The Sun is a mid-sized star that may be in the main sequence for 10 billion years. After the main sequence, the star expands to become a red giant. Depending upon the initial mass of the star, it can become a black dwarf (from a medium-sized star), and then a small, cooling white dwarf. Massive stars become red supergiants (and sometimes blue supergiants), explode in a supernova, and then become neutron stars. The largest stars can become black holes.

Star birth

A nebula is a cloud of dust and gas that is composed primarily of hydrogen (97%) and helium (3%). Gravity causes parts of the nebula to clump together. This accretion continues adding atoms to the center of an unstable protostar. Equilibrium between gravity pulling atoms and gas pressure pushing heat and light away from the center is achieved. A star dies when it is no longer able to maintain equilibrium. A protostar may never become a star if it does not reach a critical core temperature. It may become a brown dwarf or a gas giant instead. If nuclear fusion of hydrogen into helium begins, a star is born. The "main sequence" of a star's life involves nuclear fusion reactions. During this time, the star contracts over billions of years to compensate for the heat and light energy lost. In the star's core, temperature, density, and pressure increase as the star contracts and the cycle continues.

Hertzsprung-Russell diagram

A Hertzsprung-Russell diagram (H-R diagram or HRD) is a plot or scattergraph depicting stars' temperatures and comparing them with stars' luminosities or magnitudes. This can help determine the age and evolutionary state of a star. A Hertzsprung-Russell diagram is also known as a color-magnitude diagram (CMD). It helps represent the life cycles of stars. In these plots, temperatures are plotted from highest to lowest, which aids in the comparison of H-R diagrams and observations. Hertzsprung-Russell diagrams can have many variations. Most of the stars in these diagrams lie along the line called main sequence, which contains stars that are fusing hydrogen. Other groupings include white dwarfs, subgiants, giants, and supergiants.

Spectral classification

Stars use the Morgan-Keenan classification system, which is based on spectral traits that indicate the ionization of the chromosphere. The following letter designations are used to indicate temperature, from hottest to coolest: O, B, A, F, G, K, and M. The phrase "Oh, be a fine girl/guy, kiss me" can be used as a memory aid. Different types of stars also have different corresponding colors. O stars are blue; A stars are white; G stars are yellow; and M stars are red. The numbers 0 to 9 are used to indicate tenths between two star classes. Zero indicates 0/10 and 9 indicates 9/10. Luminosity output is an indicator of size, and is expressed with the Roman numerals I, II, III, IV, and V. Supergiants are included in class I, giants are included in class III, and main sequence stars are included in class V. Using the Sun as an example, the spectral type G2V could be expressed as "a yellow two-tenths towards an orange main sequence star."

Sun

The Sun is at the center of the solar system. It is composed of 70% hydrogen (H) and 28% helium (He). The remaining 2% is made up of metals. The Sun is one of 100 billion stars in the Milky Way galaxy. Its diameter is 1,390,000 km, its mass is 1.989 x 10^{30} kg, its surface temperature is 5,800 K, and its core temperature is 15,600,000 K. The Sun represents more than 99.8% of the total mass of the solar system. At the core, the temperature is 15.6 million K, the pressure is 250 billion atmospheres, and the density is more than 150 times that of water. The surface is called the photosphere. The chromosphere lies above this, and the corona, which extends millions of kilometers into space, is next. Sunspots are relatively cool regions on the surface with a temperature of 3,800 K. Temperatures in the corona are over 1,000,000 K. Its magnetosphere, or heliosphere, extends far beyond Pluto.

Solar system formation

A planetary system consists of the various non-stellar objects orbiting a star, such as planets, dwarf planets, moons, asteroids, meteoroids, comets, and cosmic dust. The Sun, together with its planetary system, which includes Earth, is known as the solar system. The theory of how the solar system was created is that it started with the collapse of a cloud of interstellar gas and dust, which formed the solar nebula. This collapse is believed to have occurred because the cloud was disturbed. As it collapsed, it heated up and compressed at the center, forming a flatter protoplanetary disk with a protostar at the center. Planets formed as a result of accretion from the disk. Gas cooled and condensed into tiny particles of rock, metal, and ice. These particles collided and formed into larger particles, and then into object the size of small asteroids. Eventually, some became large enough to have significant gravity.

Solar system components

The solar system is a planetary system of objects that exist in an ecliptic plane. Objects orbit around and are bound by gravity to a star called the Sun. Objects that orbit around the Sun include: planets, dwarf planets, moons, asteroids, meteoroids, cosmic dust, and comets. The definition of planets has changed. At one time, there were nine planets in the solar system. There are now eight. Planetary objects in the solar system include four inner, terrestrial planets: Mercury, Venus, Earth, and Mars. They are relatively small, dense, rocky, lack rings, and have few or no moons. The four outer, or Jovian, planets are Jupiter, Saturn, Uranus, and Neptune, which are large and have low densities, rings, and moons. They are also known as gas giants. Between the inner and outer planets is the asteroid belt. Beyond Neptune is the Kuiper belt. Within these belts are five dwarf planets: Ceres, Pluto, Haumea, Makemake, and Eris.

Sun's energy

The Sun's energy is produced by nuclear fusion reactions. Each second, about 700,000,000 tons of hydrogen are converted (or fused) to about 695,000,000 tons of helium and 5,000,000 tons of energy in the form of gamma rays. In nuclear fusion, four hydrogen nuclei are fused into one helium nucleus, resulting in the release of energy. In the Sun, the energy proceeds towards the surface and is absorbed and re-emitted at lower and lower temperatures. Energy is mostly in the form of visible light when it reaches the surface. It is estimated that the Sun has used up about half of the hydrogen at its core since its birth. It is expected to radiate in this fashion for another 5 billion years. Eventually, it will deplete its hydrogen fuel, grow brighter, expand to about 260 times its diameter,

and become a red giant. The outer layers will ablate and become a dense white dwarf the size of the Earth.

Inner terrestrial planets

Mercury: Mercury is the closest to the Sun and is also the smallest planet. It orbits the Sun every 88 days, has no satellites or atmosphere, has a Moon-like surface with craters, appears bright, and is dense and rocky with a large iron core.

Venus: Venus is the second planet from the Sun. It orbits the Sun every 225 days, is very bright, and is similar to Earth in size, gravity, and bulk composition. It has a dense atmosphere composed of carbon dioxide and some sulfur. It is covered with reflective clouds made of sulfuric acid and exhibits signs of volcanism. Lightning and thunder have been recorded on Venus's surface.

Earth: Earth is the third planet from the Sun. It orbits the Sun every 365 days. Approximately 71% of its surface is salt-water oceans. The Earth is rocky, has an atmosphere composed mainly of oxygen and nitrogen, has one moon, and supports millions of species. It contains the only known life in the solar system.

Mars: Mars it the fourth planet from the Sun. It appears reddish due to iron oxide on the surface, has a thin atmosphere, has a rotational period similar to Earth's, and has seasonal cycles. Surface features of Mars include volcanoes, valleys, deserts, and polar ice caps. Mars has impact craters and the tallest mountain, largest canyon, and perhaps the largest impact crater yet discovered.

Solar system size

The Earth is about 12,765 km (7,934 miles) in diameter. The Moon is about 3,476 km (2,160 mi) in diameter. The distance between the Earth and the Moon is about 384,401 km (238,910 mi). The diameter of the Sun is approximately 1,390,000 km (866,000 mi). The distance from the Earth to the Sun is 149,598,000 km, also known as 1 Astronomical Unit (AU). The star that is nearest to the solar system is Proxima Centauri. It is about 270,000 AU away. Some distant galaxies are so far away that their light takes several billion years to reach the Earth. In other words, people on Earth see them as they looked billions of years ago.

Oort Cloud, asteroid belt, and Kuiper Belt

The asteroid belt is between Mars and Jupiter. The many objects contained within are composed of rock and metal similar to those found on the terrestrial planets. The Kuiper Belt is beyond Neptune's orbit, but the influence of the gas giants may cause objects from the Kuiper Belt to cross Neptune's orbit. Objects in the Kuiper Belt are still being discovered. They are thought to be composed of the frozen forms of water, ammonia, and methane, and may be the source of short-period comets. It is estimated that there are 35,000 Kuiper Belt objects greater than 100 km in diameter and perhaps 100 million objects about 20 km in diameter. There is also a hypothetical Oort Cloud that may exist far beyond the Kuiper Belt and act as a source for long-period comets.

Outer planets

Jupiter: Jupiter is the fifth planet from the Sun and the largest planet in the solar system. It consists mainly of hydrogen, and 25% of its mass is made up of helium. It has a fast rotation and has clouds in the tropopause composed of ammonia crystals that are arranged into bands sub-divided into

lighter-hued zones and darker belts causing storms and turbulence. Jupiter has wind speeds of 100 m/s, a planetary ring, 63 moons, and a Great Red Spot, which is an anticyclonic storm.

Saturn: Saturn is the sixth planet from the Sun and the second largest planet in the solar system. It is composed of hydrogen, some helium, and trace elements. Saturn has a small core of rock and ice, a thick layer of metallic hydrogen, a gaseous outer layer, wind speeds of up to 1,800 km/h, a system of rings, and 61 moons.

Uranus: Uranus is the seventh planet from the Sun. Its atmosphere is composed mainly of hydrogen and helium, and also contains water, ammonia, methane, and traces of hydrocarbons. With a minimum temperature of 49 K, Uranus has the coldest atmosphere. Uranus has a ring system, a magnetosphere, and 13 moons.

Neptune: Neptune is the eighth planet from the Sun and is the planet with the third largest mass. It has 12 moons, an atmosphere similar to Uranus, a Great Dark Spot, and the strongest sustained winds of any planet (wind speeds can be as high as 2,100 km/h). Neptune is cold (about 55 K) and has a fragmented ring system.

Meteors, meteoroids, and meteorites

A meteoroid is the name for a rock from space before it enters the Earth's atmosphere. Most meteoroids burn up in the atmosphere before reaching altitudes of 80 km. A meteor is the streak of light from a meteoroid in the Earth's atmosphere, and is also known as a shooting star. Meteor showers are associated with comets, happen when the Earth passes through the debris of a comet, and are associated with a higher than normal number of meteors. Meteorites are rocks that reach the Earth's surface from space. Fireballs are very bright meteors with trails that can last as long as 30 minutes. A bolide is a fireball that burns up when it enters Earth's atmosphere. There are many types of meteorites, and they are known to be composed of various materials. Iron meteorites consist of iron and nickel with a criss-cross, or Widmanstatten, internal metallic crystalline structure. Stony iron meteorites are composed of iron, nickel, and silicate materials. Stony meteorites consist mainly of silicate and also contain iron and nickel.

Comets

A comet consists of frozen gases and rocky and metallic materials. Comets are usually small and typically have long tails. A comet's tail is made of ionized gases. It points away from the Sun and follows the comet as it approaches the Sun. The tail precedes the head as the comet moves away from the Sun. It is believed that as many as 100 billion comets exist. About 12 new ones are discovered each year. Their orbits are elliptical, not round. Some scientists theorize that short-period comets originate from the Kuiper Belt and long-period comets originate from the Oort Cloud, which is thought to be 100,000 AU away. Comets orbit the Sun in time periods varying from a few years to hundreds of thousands of years. A well-known comet, Halley's Comet, has an orbit of 76 years. It is 80 percent water, and consists of frozen water, carbon dioxide (dry ice), ammonia, and methane.

Earth-Moon-Sun system

The Earth-Moon-Sun system is responsible for eclipses. From Earth, the Sun and the Moon appear to be about the same size. An eclipse of the Sun occurs during a new Moon, when the side of the Moon facing the Earth is not illuminated. The Moon passes in front of the Sun and blocks its view

from Earth. Eclipses do not occur every month because the orbit of the Moon is at about a 5° angle to the plane of Earth's orbit. An eclipse of the Moon happens during the full Moon phase. The Moon passes through the shadow of the Earth and blocks sunlight from reaching it, which temporarily causes darkness. During a lunar eclipse, there are two parts to the shadow. The umbra is the dark, inner region. The sun is completely blocked in this area. The penumbra is a partially lighted area around the umbra. Earth's shadow is four times longer than the Moon's shadow.

Natural satellites

There are about 335 moons, or satellites, that orbit the planets and objects in the solar system. Many of these satellites have been recently discovered, a few are theoretical, some are asteroid moons (moons orbiting asteroids), some are moonlets (small moons), and some are moons of dwarf planets and objects that have not been definitively categorized, such as trans-Neptunian objects. Mercury and Venus do not have any moons. There are several moons larger than the dwarf planet Pluto and two larger than Mercury. Some consider the Earth and Moon a pair of double planets rather than a planet and a satellite. Some satellites may have started out as asteroids. They were eventually captured by a planet's gravity and became moons.

Remote sensing

Remote sensing refers to the gathering of data about an object or phenomenon without physical or intimate contact with the object being studied. The data can be viewed or recorded and stored in many forms (visually with a camera, audibly, or in the form of data). Gathering weather data from a ship, satellite, or buoy might be thought of as remote sensing. The monitoring of a fetus through the use of ultrasound technology provides a remote image. Listening to the heartbeat of a fetus is another example of remote sensing. Methods for remote sensing can be grouped as radiometric, geodetic, or acoustic. Examples of radiometric remote sensing include radar, laser altimeters, light detection and ranging (LIDAR) used to determine the concentration of chemicals in the air, and radiometers used to detect various frequencies of radiation. Geodetic remote sensing involves measuring the small fluctuations in Earth's gravitational field. Examples of acoustic remote sensing include underwater sonar and seismographs.

Phases of the Moon

It takes about one month for the Moon to go through all its phases. Waxing refers to the two weeks during which the Moon goes from a new moon to a full moon. About two weeks is spent waning, going from a full moon to a new moon. The lit part of the Moon always faces the Sun. The phases of waxing are: new moon, during which the Moon is not illuminated and rises and sets with the Sun; crescent moon, during which a tiny sliver is lit; first quarter, during which half the Moon is lit and the phase of the Moon is due south on the meridian; gibbous, during which more than half of the Moon is lit and has a shape similar to a football; right side, during which the Moon is lit; and full moon, during which the Moon is fully illuminated, rises at sunset, and sets at sunrise. After a full moon, the Moon is waning. The phases of waning are: gibbous, during which the left side is lit and the Moon rises after sunset and sets after sunrise; third quarter, during which the Moon is half lit and rises at midnight and sets at noon; crescent, during which a tiny sliver is lit; and new moon, during which the Moon is not illuminated and rises and sets with the Sun.

Tropic of Cancer, Tropic of Capricorn; Antarctic and Arctic Circles

Tropic of Cancer: This is located at 23.5 degrees north. The Sun is directly overhead at noon on June 21st in the Tropic of Cancer, which marks the beginning of summer in the Northern Hemisphere.

Tropic of Capricorn: This is located at 23.5 degrees south. The Sun is directly overhead at noon on December 21st in the Tropic of Capricorn, which marks the beginning of winter in the Northern Hemisphere.

Arctic Circle: This is located at 66.5 degrees north, and marks the start of when the Sun is not visible above the horizon. This occurs on December 21st, the same day the Sun is directly over the Tropic of Capricorn.

Antarctic Circle: This is located at 66.5 degrees south, and marks the start of when the Sun is not visible above the horizon. This occurs on June 21st, which marks the beginning of winter in the Southern Hemisphere and is when the Sun is directly over the Tropic of Cancer.

Latitude, longitude, and equator

For the purposes of tracking time and location, the Earth is divided into sections with imaginary lines. Lines that run vertically around the globe through the poles are lines of longitude, sometimes called meridians. The Prime Meridian is the longitudinal reference point of 0. Longitude is measured in 15-degree increments toward the east or west. Degrees are further divided into 60 minutes, and each minute is divided into 60 seconds. Lines of latitude run horizontally around the Earth parallel to the equator, which is the 0 reference point and the widest point of the Earth. Latitude is the distance north or south from the equator, and is also measured in degrees, minutes, and seconds.

Geosynchronous and geostationary orbits

A geosynchronous orbit around the Earth has an orbital period matching the Earth's sidereal rotation period. Sidereal rotation is based on the position of a fixed star, not the Sun, so a sidereal day is slightly shorter than a 24-hour solar day. A satellite in a geosynchronous orbit appears in the same place in the sky at the same time each day. Technically, any object with an orbit time period equal to the Earth's rotational period is geosynchronous. A geostationary orbit is a geosynchronous orbit that is circular and at zero inclination, which means the object is located directly above the equator. Geostationary orbits are useful for communications satellites because they are fixed in the same spot relative to the Earth. A semisynchronous orbit has an orbital period of half a sidereal day.

Equinox, solstice, perihelion, and aphelion

Equinox: This occurs twice each year when the Sun crosses the plane of the Earth's celestial equator. During an equinox, Earth is not tilted away from or towards the Sun. The length of day and night are roughly equal. The two equinoxes are the March equinox and the September equinox.

Solstice: The summer solstice, the day with the most amount of sunlight, occurs on June 21st in the Northern Hemisphere and on December 21st in the Southern Hemisphere. The winter solstice, the day with the least amount of sunlight, occurs on December 21st in the Northern Hemisphere and on June 21st in the Southern Hemisphere.

Perihelion: This is the point in an object's orbit when it is closest to the Sun.

Aphelion: This is the point in an object's orbit when it is farthest from the Sun.

Piloted space missions

The Soviet space program successfully completed the first space flight by orbiting Yuri Gagarin in 1961 on Vostok 1. His orbit lasted 1 hour, 48 minutes. Later in 1961, the U.S. completed its first piloted space flight by launching Alan Shepard into space in the Mercury-Redstone 3. This space mission was suborbital. The first woman in space was Valentina Tereshkova, who orbited the Earth 48 times aboard Vostok 6 in 1963. The first space flight with more than one person and also the first that didn't involve space suits took place on the Voskhod in 1964. The first person on the Moon was American Neil Armstrong. In 1969, he traveled to the Moon on Apollo 11, which was the 11th manned space flight completed in the Apollo program, which was conducted from 1968 to 1972. In 2003, Yang Liwei became the first person from China to go into space. He traveled onboard the Shenzhou 5. The Space Shuttle Orbiter has included piloted space shuttles from 1981 until the present. The program was suspended after two space shuttle disasters: Challenger in 1986 and Columbia in 2003.

Notable satellites

The first satellite to orbit the Earth was the Soviet Union's Sputnik 1 in 1957. Its two radio transmitters emitted beeps that were received by radios around the world. Analysis of the radio signals was used to gather information about the electron density of the ionosphere. Soviet success escalated the American space program. In 1958, the U.S. put Explorer 1 into orbit. The Osumi was the first Japanese satellite, which was put into orbit in 1970. The Vanguard 1 is the satellite that has orbited the Earth the longest. It was put into orbit in 1958 and was still in orbit in June, 2009. The Mir Space Station orbited Earth for 11 years, and was assembled in space starting in 1986. It was almost continuously occupied until 1999. The International Space Station began being assembled in orbit in 1998. At 43,000 cubic feet, it is the largest manned object sent into space. It circles the Earth every 90 minutes.

Limitations of space exploration

There are many limitations of space exploration. The main limitation is knowledge. Space exploration is currently time-consuming, dangerous, and costly. Manned and unmanned missions, even within the solar system, take years of planning and years to complete. The associated financial costs are great. Interstellar travel and intergalactic is not yet realistically feasible. Technological advances are needed before these types of missions can be carried out. By some estimates, it would take more than 70 years to travel to Proxima Centauri (the nearest star) using the fastest rocket technology available. It would take much longer using less advanced technologies. Space travel is dangerous for many reasons. Rocket fuel is highly explosive. Non-Earth environments are uninhabitable for humans. Finally, astronauts are exposed to larger than usual amounts of radiation.

Unpiloted space missions

The first artificial object to reach another space object was Luna 2. It crashed on the Moon in 1959. The first automatic landing was by Luna 9. It landed on the Moon in 1966. Mariner 2's flyby of Venus in 1962 was the first successful interplanetary flyby. Venera 7 landing on and transmitting data from Venus was the first interplanetary surface landing, which took place in 1970. The first soft landing on Mars was in 1971. Unpiloted spacecraft have also made successful soft landings on the asteroids Eros and Itokawa, as well as Titan, a moon of Saturn. The first flyby of Jupiter was in 1973 by Pioneer 10. Pioneer 10 was also the first craft of its kind to leave the solar system. The first flyby of Mercury was in 1974 by Mariner. The first flyby of Saturn was in 1979 by Pioneer 11. The first flyby of Uranus was in 1986 by Voyager 2, which also flew by Neptune in 1989.

Granite and basalt

Both granite and basalt are plentiful igneous rocks, but granite is intrusive and basalt is extrusive. Intrusive rocks come from magma within the Earth's crust and cool slowly. Extrusive rocks are formed from lava on the Earth's surface and cool more quickly than intrusive rocks. Granite is an igneous rock with a medium to coarse texture that is formed from magma. It can be a variety of colors. It is intrusive, massive, hard, and coarse grained. It forms a major part of continental crust. It can be composed of potassium feldspar, plagioclase feldspar, and quartz, as well as various amounts of muscovite, biotite, and hornblende-type amphiboles. Basalt is extrusive and usually colored gray to black. It has a fine grain due to quicker cooling. Basalt is porphyritic, meaning it contains larger crystals in a fine matrix. Basalt is usually composed of amphibole and pyroxene, and sometimes of plagioclase, feldspathoids, and olivine.

Moon facts

The Moon is the fifth largest satellite in the solar system. It orbits the Earth about every 27.3 days. The changes of the Earth, Sun, and Moon in relation to each other cause the phases of the Moon, which repeat every 29.5 days. The Moon's gravitational pull (along with the Sun's) is responsible for the tides on Earth. Its diameter is about 3,474 km and its gravity is about 17% of Earth's. The lunar maria (plural of mare) on the Moon's surface is dark thin layers composed of dark basalt. They were formed by ancient volcanoes. There are many impact craters on the Moon. There were numerous impact craters on Earth at one time, but they have been transformed by erosion over time. Very few are still visible

Greenhouse effect

The greenhouse effect refers to a naturally occurring and necessary process. Greenhouse gasses, which are ozone, carbon dioxide, water vapor, and methane, trap infrared radiation that is reflected toward the atmosphere. This is actually beneficial in that warm air is trapped. Without the greenhouse effect, it is estimated that the temperature on Earth would be 30 degrees less on average. The problem occurs because human activity generates more greenhouse gases than necessary. The practices that increase the amount of greenhouse gases are the burning of natural gas and oil, farming practices that result in the release of methane and nitrous oxide, factory operations that produce gases, and deforestation practices that decrease the amount of oxygen available to offset greenhouse gases. Population growth also increases the volume of gases released. Excess greenhouse gases cause more infrared radiation to become trapped, which increases the temperature at the Earth's surface.

Ecosystems

Human impacts on ecosystems take many forms and have many causes. They include widespread disruptions and specific niche disturbances. Humans practice many forms of environmental manipulation that affect plants and animals in many biomes and ecosystems. Many human practices involve the consumption of natural resources for food and energy production, the changing of the environment to produce food and energy, and the intrusion on ecosystems to provide shelter. These general behaviors include a multitude of specific behaviors, including the use and overuse of pesticides, the encroachment upon habitat, over hunting and over fishing, the introduction of plant and animal species into non-native ecosystems, not recycling, and the introduction of hazardous wastes and chemical byproducts into the environment. These behaviors have led to a number of consequences, such as acid rain, ozone depletion, deforestation, urbanization, accelerated species loss, genetic abnormalities, endocrine disruption in populations, and harm to individual animals.

Human affairs and the environment

Since the industrial revolution, science and technology has had a profound impact on human affairs. There has been a rapid increase in the number of discoveries in many fields. Many major and minor discoveries have led to a great improvement in the quality of life of many people. This includes longer life spans because of better nutrition, access to medical care, and a decrease in workplace health hazards. Not all of these problems have been solved, and many still exist in one form or another. For example, even though there are means to recycle, not every business does so because of economic factors. These advances, while improving the lives of many humans, have also taken their toll on the environment. A possible solution may arise when the carrying capacity for humans on Earth is reached. The population will decline, and solutions will have to be found. Otherwise, an immediate halt or decrease in the human behaviors that are causing environmental damage will need to happen.

Global warming

Rising temperatures may lead to an increase in sea levels as polar ice melts, lower amounts of available fresh water as coastal areas flood, species extinction because of changes in habitat, increases in certain diseases, and a decreased standard of living for humans. Less fresh water and losses of habitat for humans and other species can also lead to decreased agricultural production and food supply shortages. Increased desertification leads to habitat loss for humans and certain other species. Decreases in animal populations from losses of habitat and increased hunting by other species can lead to extinction. Increases in severe weather, such as huge sustained snowstorms, may also occur at unlikely latitudes. Even though global warming results in weather that is drier and warmer overall, it still gets cold enough to snow. There may be more moisture in the atmosphere due to evaporation. Global warming may cause the permanent loss of glaciers and permafrost. There might also be increases in air pollution and acid rain.

Waste disposal methods

Landfills: Methane (CH_4) is a greenhouse gas emitted from landfills. Some is used to generate electricity and some gets into the atmosphere. CO_2 is also emitted, and landfill gas can contain nitrogen, oxygen, water vapor, sulfur, mercury, and radioactive contaminants such as tritium. Landfill leachate contains acids from car batteries, solvents, heavy metals, pesticides, motor oil, paint, household cleaning supplies, plastics, and many other potentially harmful substances. Some of these are dangerous when they get into the ecosystem. Lead, mercury, and others are toxic.

Incinerators: These contribute to air pollution in that they can release nitric and sulfuric oxides, which cause acid rain.

Sewage: When dumped in raw form into oceans, sewage can introduce fecal contaminants and pathogenic organisms, which can harm ocean life and cause disease in humans.

Price of consumerism

The economics of capitalism and even of communism with an increased tendency to a market economy are such that economic growth and quality of living are associated with a wasteful cycle of production. Goods are produced as cheaply as possible with little or no regard for the ecological effects. The ultimate goal is profitability. The production process is wasteful, and often introduces hazardous byproducts into the environment. Furthermore, after the product (which is not necessary for survival) has been consumed, it may be dumped into a landfill instead of recycled. When consumer products get dumped in landfills, they can leach contamination into groundwater. Landfills can also leach gases. These are or have been dumping grounds for illegal substances, business and government waste, construction industry waste, and medical waste. These items also get dumped at illegal dump sites in urban and remote areas.

Ethical and moral issues

Ethical and moral concerns related to genetic engineering arise in the scientific community and in smaller communities within society. Religious and moral beliefs can conflict with the economic interests of businesses, and with research methods used by the scientific community. For example, the United States government allows genes to be patented. A company has patented the gene for breast and ovarian cancer and will only make it available to researchers for a fee. This leads to a decrease in research, a decrease in medical solutions, and possibly an increase in the occurrence of breast and ovarian cancers. The possibility of lateral or incidental discoveries as a result of research is also limited. For example, a researcher working on a genetic solution to treat breast cancer might accidentally discover a cure for prostate cancer. This, however, would not occur if the researcher could not use the patented gene in the first place.

Types of energy production

Coal-fired power plants: These generate electricity, and are the largest source of greenhouse gases, including sulfur oxides responsible for acid rain, carbon dioxide, mercury, and nitrogen oxides.

Nuclear power plants: Spent nuclear waste (fuel rods) is incredibly toxic to humans, causing burns, sickness, and hair loss at low levels. Higher levels result in death. Storage facilities tend to be placed on Native American lands and in communities of color. Dirty bombs can be made with uranium. The process of uranium mining (as well as the processes used to mine other precious metals) pollutes, introducing chemicals into the surrounding area and drastically changing its natural balance and beauty. Tailings can contaminate ground, surface, and well water. Some nuclear waste can remain harmful for billions of years. Strontium-90 is one radioactive pollutant. Other radioactive isotopes are also released. A huge amount of water is necessary for cooling.

Gasoline: The burning of gas and other fossil fuels releases carbon dioxide (a greenhouse gas) into the atmosphere.

Mathematics Practice Test

Practice Questions

1. Determine the number of diagonals of a dodecagon.
   a. 12
   b. 24
   c. 54
   d. 108

2. A circular bracelet contains 5 charms, A, B, C, D, and E, attached at specific points around the bracelet, with the clasp located between charms A and B. The bracelet is unclasped and stretched out into a straight line. On the resulting linear bracelet, charm C is between charms A and B, charm D is between charms A and C, and charm E is between charms C and D. Which of these statements is (are) necessarily true?

   I. The distance between charms B and E is greater than the distance between charms A and D.
   II. Charm E is between charms B and D.
   III. The distance between charms D and E is less than the distance of bracelet between charms A and C.

   a. I, II, and III
   b. II and III
   c. II only
   d. None of these is necessarily true.

3. In a town of 35,638 people, about a quarter of the population is under the age of 35. Of those, just over a third attend local K-12 schools. If the number of students in each grade is about the same, how many fourth graders likely reside in the town?
   a. Fewer than 100
   b. Between 200 and 300
   c. Between 300 and 400
   d. More than 400

4. Identical rugs are offered for sale at two local shops and one online retailer, designated Stores A, B, and C, respectively. The rug's regular sales price is $296 at Store A, $220 at Store B, and $198.00 at Store C. Stores A and B collect 8% in sales tax on any after-discount price, while Store C collects no tax but charges a $35 shipping fee. A buyer has a 30% off coupon for Store A and a $10 off coupon for Store B. Which of these lists the stores in order of lowest to highest final sales price after all discounts, taxes, and fees are applied?
   a. Store A, Store B, Store C
   b. Store B, Store C, Store A
   c. Store C, Store A, Store C
   d. Store C, Store B, Store A

5. Two companies offer monthly cell phone plans, both of which include free text messaging. Company A charges a $25 monthly fee plus five cents per minute of phone conversation, while Company B charges a $50 monthly fee and offers unlimited calling. Both companies charge the same amount when the total duration of monthly calls is

a. 500 hours.
b. 8 hours and 33 minutes.
c. 8 hours and 20 minutes.
d. 5 hours.

6. A dress is marked down by 20% and placed on a clearance rack, on which is posted a sign reading, "Take an extra 25% off already reduced merchandise." What fraction of the original price is the final sales price of the dress?

a. $\frac{9}{20}$
b. $\frac{11}{20}$
c. $\frac{2}{5}$
d. $\frac{3}{5}$

7. On a floor plan drawn at a scale of 1:100, the area of a rectangular room is 30 cm^2. What is the actual area of the room?

a. 30,000 cm^2
b. 3,000 cm^2
c. 3,000 m^2
d. 30 m^2

8. The ratio of employee wages and benefits to all other operational costs of a business is 2:3. If a business's operating expenses are $130,000 per month, how much money does the company spend on employee wages and benefits?

a. $43,333.33
b. $86,666.67
c. $52,000.00
d. $78,000.00

9. The path of ball thrown into the air is modeled by the first quadrant graph of the equation $h = -16t^2 + 64t + 5$, where h is the height of the ball in feet and t is time in seconds after the ball is thrown. What is the average rate of change in the ball's height with respect to time over the interval $[1, 3]$?

a. 0 feet/second
b. 48 feet/second
c. 53 feet/second
d. 96 feet/second

10. Zeke drove from his house to a furniture store in Atlanta and then back home along the same route. It took Zeke three hours to drive to the store. By driving an average of 20 mph faster on his return trip, Zeke was able to save an hour of diving time. What was Zeke's average driving speed on his round trip?

a. 24 mph
b. 48 mph
c. 50 mph
d. 60 mph

11. The graph below shows Aaron's distance from home at times throughout his morning run. Which of the following statements is (are) true?

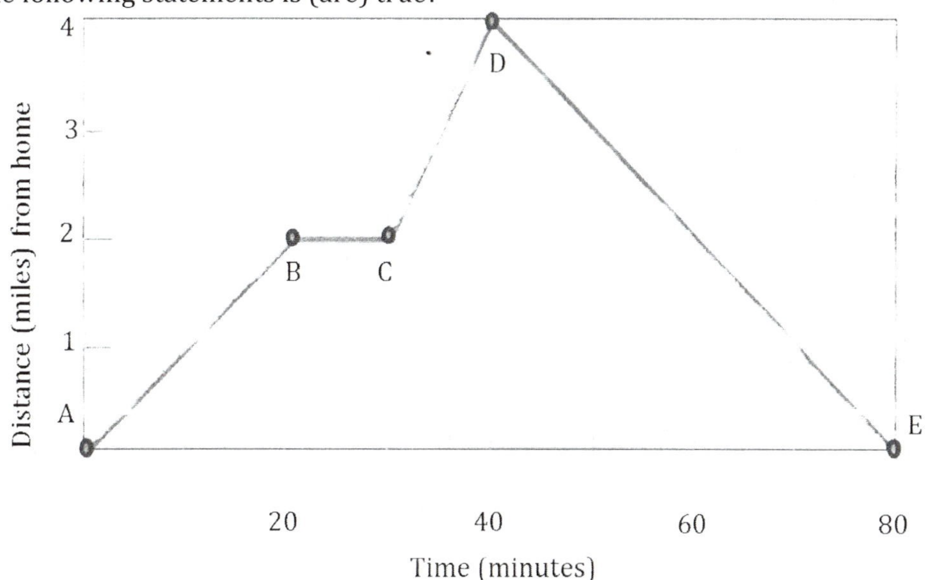

I. Aaron's average running speed was 6 mph.
II. Aaron's running speed from point A to point B was the same as his running speed from point D to E.
III. Aaron ran a total distance of four miles.

a. I only
b. II only
c. I and II
d. I, II, and III

12. Use the operation table to determine $(a * b) * (c * d)$.

$*$	a	b	c	d
a	d	a	b	c
b	a	b	c	d
c	b	c	d	a
d	c	d	a	b

a. a
b. b
c. c
d. d

13. Complete the analogy.

$$x^3 \text{ is to } \sqrt[3]{y} \text{ as ...}$$

a. $x + a$ is to $x - y$.
b. e^x is to $ln\, y, y > 0$.
c. $\frac{1}{x}$ is to $y, x, y \neq 0$.
d. $sin\, x$ is to $cos\, y$.

14. Which of these statements is (are) true for deductive reasoning?
I. A general conclusion is drawn from specific instances.
II. If the premises are true and proper reasoning is applied, the conclusion must be true.
a. Statement I is true
b. Statement II is true
c. Both statements are true
d. Neither statement is true

15. Given that premises "all a are b," "all b are d," and "no b are c" are true and that premise "all b are e" is false, determine the validity and soundness of the following arguments:
Argument I: All a are b. No b are c. Therefore, no a are c.
Argument II: All a are b. All d are b. Therefore, all d are a.
Argument III: All a are b. All b are e. Therefore, all a are e.

a.

	Invalid	**Valid**	**Sound**
Argument I		X	X
Argument II	X		
Argument III		X	

b.

	Invalid	**Valid**	**Sound**
Argument I	X		
Argument II		X	X
Argument III	X		

c.

	Invalid	**Valid**	**Sound**
Argument I		X	X
Argument II		X	X
Argument III	X		

d.

	Invalid	**Valid**	**Sound**
Argument I		X	X
Argument II	X		
Argument III	X		

16. If $p \rightarrow q$ is true, which of these is also necessarily true?

a. $q \rightarrow p$
b. $\sim p \rightarrow \sim q$
c. $\sim q \rightarrow \sim p$
d. None of these

17. Given statements p and q, which of the following is the truth table for the statement $q \leftrightarrow \sim(p \wedge q)$?

a.

p	q	$q \leftrightarrow \sim(p \wedge q)$
T	T	F
T	F	T
F	T	T
F	F	T

b.

p	q	$q \leftrightarrow \sim(p \wedge q)$
T	T	T
T	F	T
F	T	T
F	F	F

c.

p	q	$q \leftrightarrow \sim(p \wedge q)$
T	T	F
T	F	F
F	T	F
F	F	T

d.

p	q	$q \leftrightarrow \sim(p \wedge q)$
T	T	F
T	F	F
F	T	T
F	F	F

18. Which of the following is the truth table for logic circuit shown below?

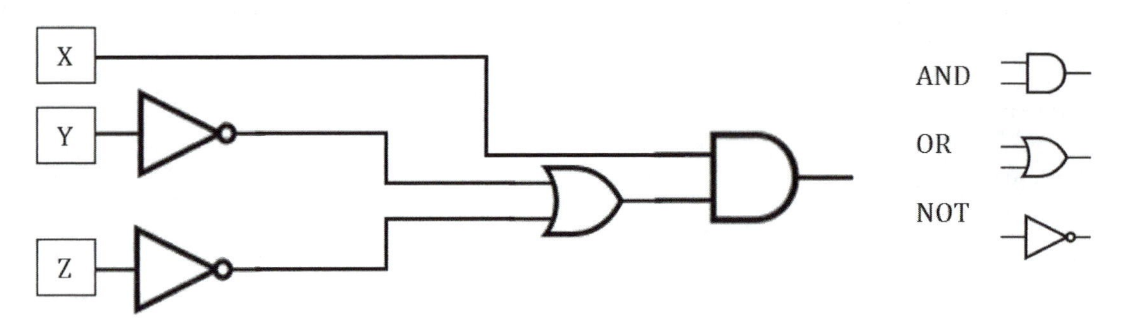

a.

X	Y	Z	Output
0	0	0	1
0	0	1	0
0	1	0	0
0	1	1	0
1	0	0	0
1	0	1	0
1	1	0	0
1	1	1	1

b.

X	Y	Z	Output
0	0	0	0
0	0	1	1
0	1	0	1
0	1	1	1
1	0	0	1
1	0	1	1
1	1	0	1
1	1	1	1

c.

X	Y	Z	Output
0	0	0	0
0	0	1	0
0	1	0	0
0	1	1	1
1	0	0	1
1	0	1	1
1	1	0	1
1	1	1	0

d.

X	Y	Z	Output
0	0	0	0
0	0	1	0
0	1	0	0
0	1	1	0
1	0	0	1
1	0	1	1
1	1	0	1
1	1	1	0

19. Which of these is a major contribution of the Babylonian civilization to the historical development of mathematics?

a. The division of an hour into 60 minutes, and a minute into 60 seconds, and a circle into 360 degrees
b. The development of algebra as a discipline separate from geometry
c. The use of deductive reasoning in geometric proofs
d. The introduction of Boolean logic and algebra

20. Which mathematician is responsible for what is often called the most remarkable and beautiful mathematical formula, $e^{i\pi} + 1 = 0$?

a. Pythagoras
b. Euclid
c. Euler
d. Fermat

21. Which of these demonstrates the relationship between the sets of prime numbers, real numbers, natural numbers, complex numbers, rational numbers, and integers?
$\mathbb{P}$ - Prime; $\mathbb{R}$ - Real; $\mathbb{N}$ - Natural; $\mathbb{C}$ - Complex; $\mathbb{Q}$ - Rational; $\mathbb{Z}$ - Integer

a. $\mathbb{P} \subseteq \mathbb{Q} \subseteq \mathbb{R} \subseteq \mathbb{Z} \subseteq \mathbb{C} \subseteq \mathbb{N}$
b. $\mathbb{P} \subseteq \mathbb{N} \subseteq \mathbb{Z} \subseteq \mathbb{Q} \subseteq \mathbb{R} \subseteq \mathbb{C}$
c. $\mathbb{C} \subseteq \mathbb{R} \subseteq \mathbb{Q} \subseteq \mathbb{Z} \subseteq \mathbb{N} \subseteq \mathbb{P}$
d. None of these

22. To which of the following sets of numbers does -4 **NOT** belong?

a. The set of whole numbers
b. The set of rational numbers
c. The set of integers
d. The set of real numbers

23. Which of these forms a group?

a. The set of prime numbers under addition
b. The set of negative integers under multiplication
c. The set of negative integers under addition
d. The set of non-zero rational numbers under multiplication

24. Simplify $\frac{2+3i}{4-2i}$.

a. $\frac{1}{10} + \frac{4}{5}i$
b. $\frac{1}{10}$
c. $\frac{7}{6} + \frac{2}{3}i$
d. $\frac{1}{10} + \frac{3}{10}i$

25. Simplify $|(2 - 3i)^2 - (1 - 4i)|$.

a. $\sqrt{61}$
b. $-6 - 8i$
c. $6 + 8i$
d. 10

26. Which of these sets forms a group under multiplication?

a. $\{-i, 0, i\}$
b. $\{-1, 1, i, -i\}$
c. $\{i, 1\}$
d. $\{ i, -i, 1\}$

27. The set $\{a, b, c, d\}$ forms a group under operation #. Which of these statements is (are) true about the group?

#	a	b	c	d
a	c	d	b	a
b	d	c	a	b
c	b	a	d	c
d	a	b	c	d

I. The identity element of the group is d.
II. The inverse of c is c.
III. The operation # is commutative.

a. I
b. III
c. I, III
d. I, II, III

28. If the square of twice the sum of x and three is equal to the product of twenty-four and x, which of these is a possible value of x?

a. $6 + 3\sqrt{2}$
b. $\frac{3}{2}$
c. $-3i$
d. -3

29. Given that x is a prime number and that the greatest common factor of x and y is greater than 1, compare the two quantities.

Quantity A	Quantity B
y	the least common multiple of x and y

a. Quantity A is greater.
b. Quantity B is greater.
c. The two quantities are the same.
d. The relationship cannot be determined from the given information.

30. If a, b, and c are even integers and $3a^2 + 9b^3 = c$, which of these is the largest number which must be factor of c?

a. 2
b. 3
c. 6
d. 12

31. Which of these relationships represents y as a function of x?

a. $x = y^2$

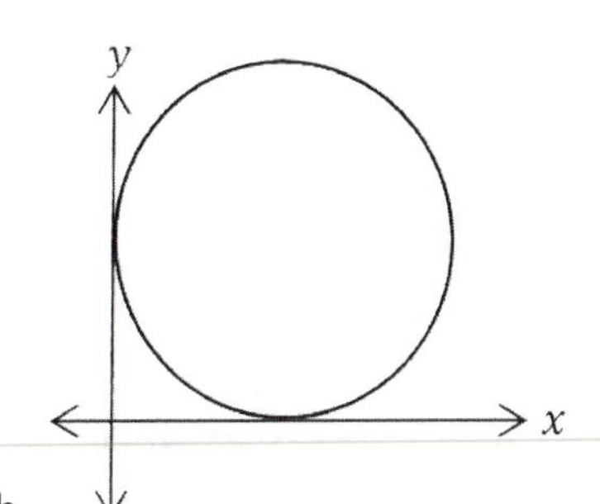

b.

c. $y = [\![x]\!]s$

x y

0 1
1 2
2 3
4

d.

32. Express the area of the given triangle as a function of x.

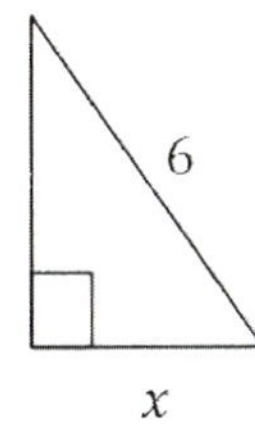

a. $A(x) = 3x$

b. $A(x) = \frac{x\sqrt{36-x^2}}{2}$

c. $A(x) = \frac{x^2}{2}$

d. $A(x) = 18 - \frac{x^2}{2}$

33. Find $[g \circ f\,]x$ when $f(x) = 2x + 4$ and $g(x) = x^2 - 3x + 2$.

a. $4x^2 + 10x + 6$

b. $2x^2 - 6x + 8$

c$4x^2 + 13x + 18$.

d. $2x^2 - 3x + 6$

34. Given the partial table of values for $f(x)$ and $g(x)$, find $f(g(-4))$. (Assume that $f(x)$ and $g(x)$ are the simplest polynomials that fit the data.)

x	f(x)	g(x)
-2	8	1
-1	2	3
0	0	5
1	2	7
2	8	9

a. 69
b. 31
c. 18
d. -3

35. If $f(x)$ and $g(x)$ are inverse functions, which of these is the value of x when $f(g(x)) = 4$?
a. -4
b. $\frac{1}{4}$
c. 2
d. 4

36. Determine which pair of equations are **NOT** inverses.
a. $y = x + 6; y = x - 6$
b. $y = 2x + 3; y = 2x - 3$
c. $y = \frac{2x+3}{x-1}; y = \frac{x+3}{x-2}$
d. $y = \frac{x-1}{2}; \; y = 2x + 1$

37. Which of these statements is (are) true for function $g(x)$?

$$g(x) = \begin{cases} 2x - 1 & x \geq 2 \\ -x + 3 & x < 2 \end{cases}$$

I. $g(3) = 0$
II. The graph of $g(x)$ is discontinuous at $x = 2$.
III. The range of $g(x)$ is all real numbers.

a. II
b. III
c. I, II
d. II, III

38. Which of the following piecewise functions can describe the graph below?

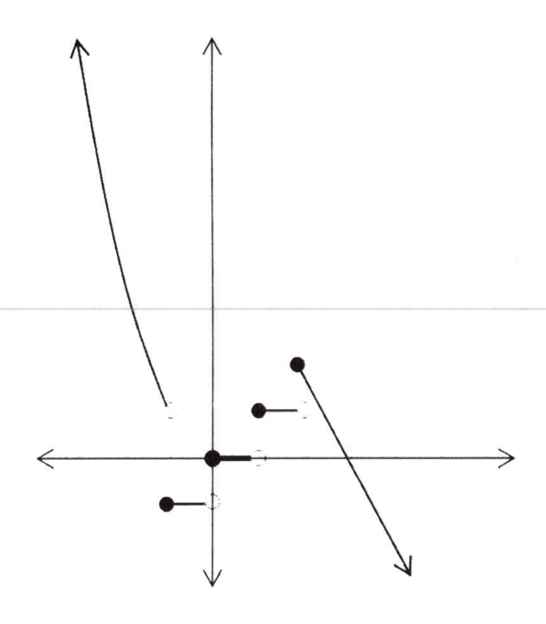

a. $f(x) = \begin{cases} x^2 & x < -1 \\ [\![x]\!] & -1 \leq x < 2 \\ -2x + 6 & x \geq 2 \end{cases}$

b. $f(x) = \begin{cases} x^2 & x \leq -1 \\ [\![x]\!] & -1 \leq x \leq 2 \\ -2x + 6 & x > 2 \end{cases}$

c. $f(x) = \begin{cases} (x+1)^2 & x < -1 \\ [\![x]\!] + 1 & -1 \leq x < 2 \\ -2x + 6 & x \geq 2 \end{cases}$

d. $f(x) = \begin{cases} (x+1)^2 & x < -1 \\ [\![x - 1]\!] & -1 \leq x < 2 \\ -2x + 6 & x \geq 2 \end{cases}$

39. Which of the following could be the graph of $y = a(x+b)(x+c)^2$ if $a > 0$?

a.

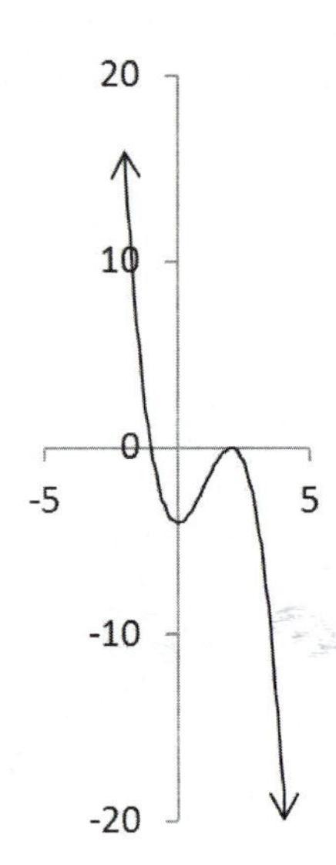

c.

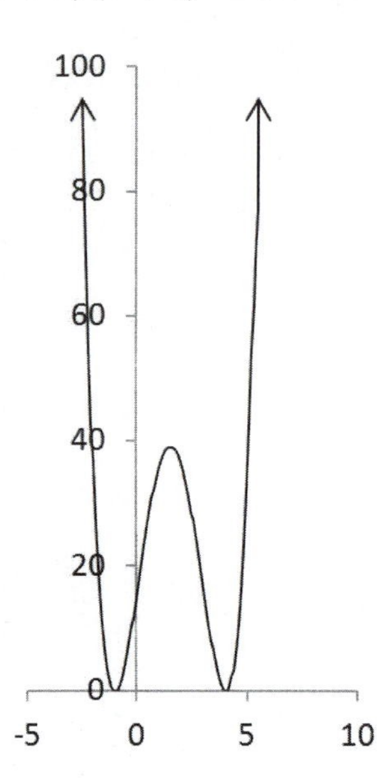

b.

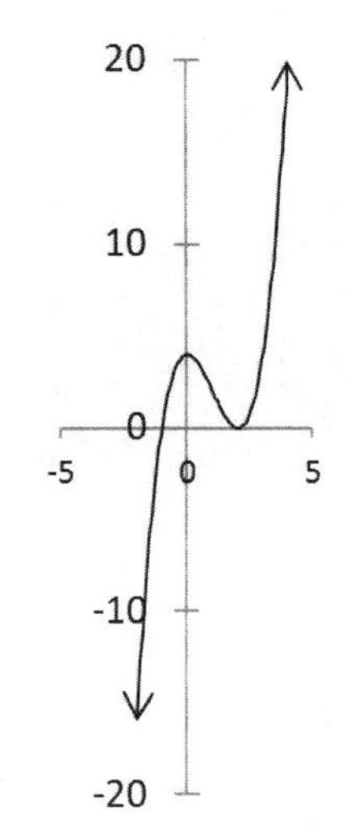

d.

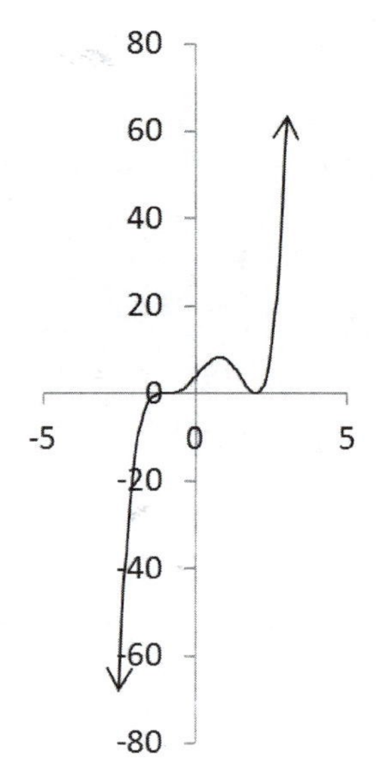

40. A school is selling tickets to its production of *Annie Get Your Gun*. Student tickets cost $3 each, and non-student tickets are $5 each. In order to offset the costs of the production, the school must earn at least $300 in ticket sales. Which graph shows the number of tickets the school must sell to offset production costs?

a.

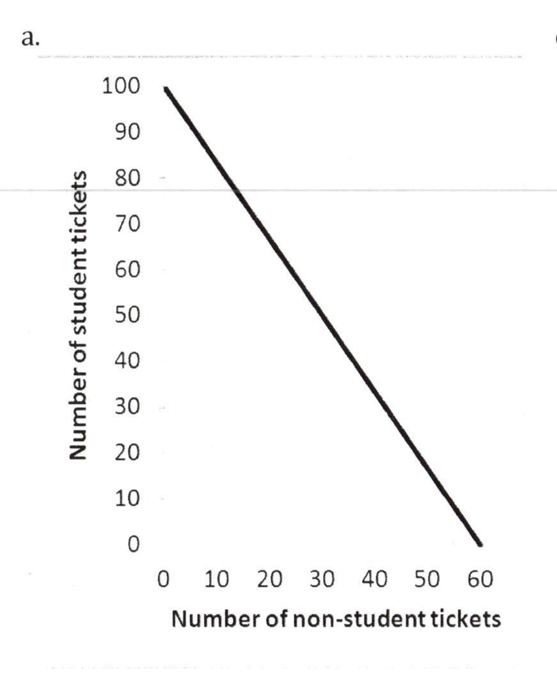

b.

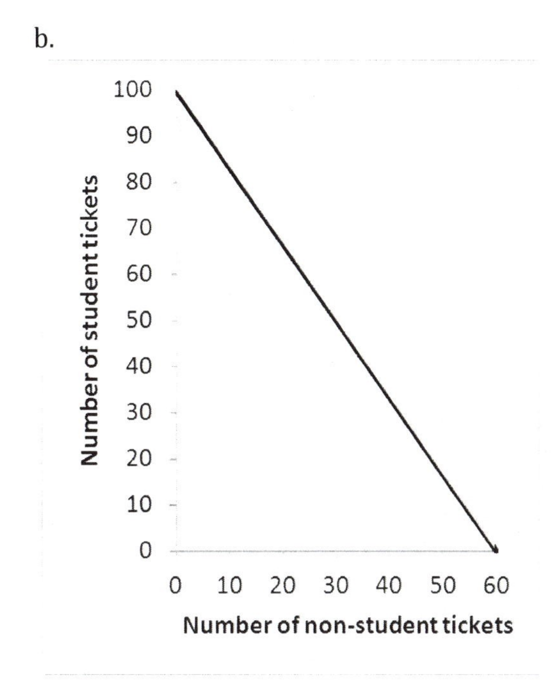

c.

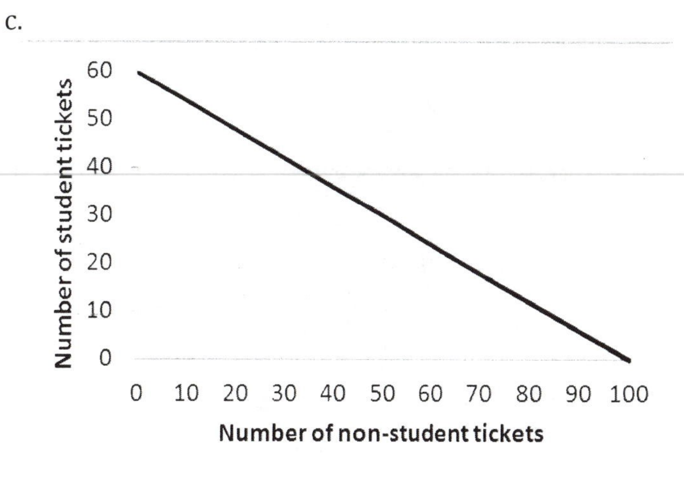

d.

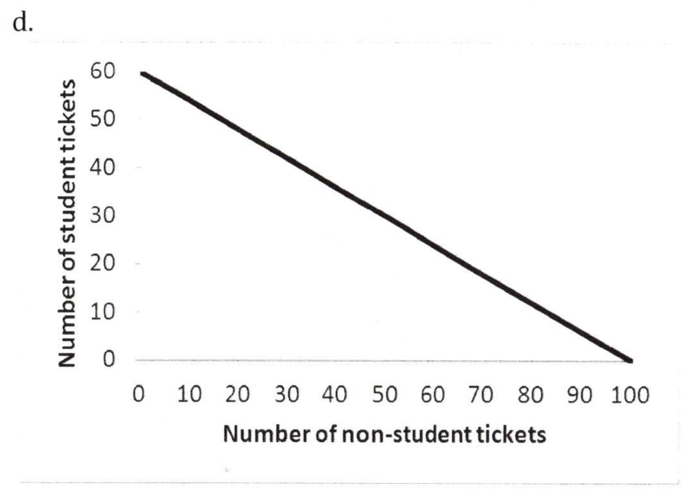

41. Which of these is the equation graphed below?

a. $y = -2x^2 - 4x + 1$
b. $y = -x^2 - 2x + 5$
c. $y = -x^2 - 2x + 2$
d. $y = -\frac{1}{2}x^2 - x + \frac{5}{2}$

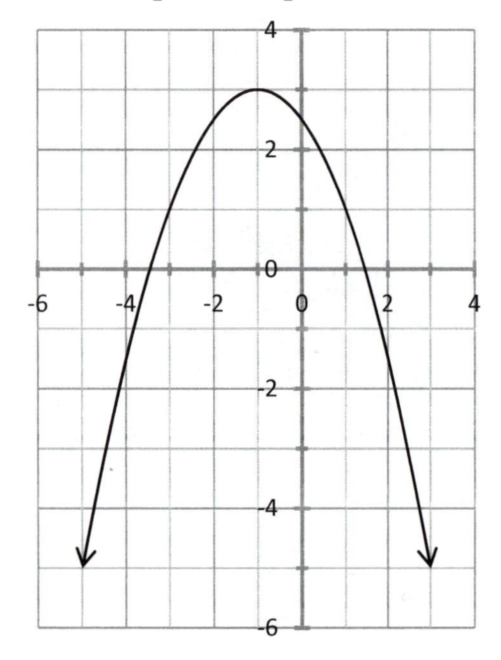

42. Solve $7x^2 + 6x = -2$.

a. $x = \frac{-3\pm\sqrt{23}}{7}$
b. $x = \pm i\sqrt{5}$
c. $x = \pm\frac{2i\sqrt{2}}{7}$
d. $x = \frac{-3\pm i\sqrt{5}}{7}$

43. Solve the system of equations.

$$3x + 4y = 2$$
$$2x + 6y = -2$$

a. $\left(0,\frac{1}{2}\right)$
b. $\left(\frac{2}{5},\frac{1}{5}\right)$
c. $(2,-1)$
d. $\left(-1,\frac{5}{4}\right)$

44. Which system of linear inequalities has no solution?

a. $x - y < 3$
   $x - y \geq -3$

b. $y \leq 6 - 2x$
   $\frac{1}{3}y + \frac{2}{3}x \geq 2$

c. $6x + 2y \leq 12$
   $3x \geq 8 - y$

d. $x + 4y \leq -8$
   $y + 4x > -8$

45. The cost of admission to a theme park is shown below.

Under age 10	Ages 10-55	Over age 65
$15	$25	$20

Yesterday, the theme park sold 810 tickets and earned $14,500. There were twice as many children under 10 at the park as there were other visitors. If x, y, and z represent the number of $15, $25, and $20 tickets sold, respectively, which of the following matrix equations can be used to find the number of each type of ticket sold?

a. $\begin{bmatrix} 1 & 1 & 1 \\ 15 & 25 & 20 \\ 1 & -2 & -2 \end{bmatrix} \begin{bmatrix} x \\ y \\ z \end{bmatrix} = \begin{bmatrix} 810 \\ 14500 \\ 0 \end{bmatrix}$

b. $\begin{bmatrix} 1 & 1 & 1 \\ 15 & 25 & 20 \\ 1 & -2 & -2 \end{bmatrix} \begin{bmatrix} 810 \\ 14500 \\ 0 \end{bmatrix} = \begin{bmatrix} x \\ y \\ z \end{bmatrix}$

c. $\begin{bmatrix} 1 & 15 & 1 \\ 1 & 25 & -2 \\ 1 & 20 & -2 \end{bmatrix} \begin{bmatrix} x \\ y \\ z \end{bmatrix} = \begin{bmatrix} 810 \\ 14500 \\ 0 \end{bmatrix}$

d. $\begin{bmatrix} 1 & 15 & 1 \\ 1 & 25 & -2 \\ 1 & 20 & -2 \end{bmatrix} \begin{bmatrix} 810 \\ 14500 \\ 0 \end{bmatrix} = \begin{bmatrix} x \\ y \\ z \end{bmatrix}$

46. Solve the system of equations.

$$2x - 4y + z = 10$$
$$-3x + 2y - 4z = -7$$
$$x + y - 3z = -1$$

a. $(-1, -3, 0)$
b. $(1, -2, 0)$
c. $(-\frac{3}{4}, -\frac{21}{8}, -1)$
d. No solution

47. Solve $x^4 + 64 = 20x^2$.

a. $x = \{2, 4\}$
b. $x = \{-2, 2, -4, 4\}$
c. $x = \{2i, 4i\}$
d. $x = \{-2i, 2i, -4i, 4i\}$

48. Solve $3x^3y^2 - 45x^2y = 15x^3y - 9x^2y^2$ for x and y.
a. $x = \{0, -3\},\ y = \{0, 5\}$
b. $x = \{0\},\ y = \{0\}$
c. $x = \{0, -3\},\ y = \{0\}$
d. $x = \{0\},\ y = \{0, 5\}$

49. Which of these statements is true for functions $f(x)$, $g(x)$, and $h(x)$?

$$f(x) = 2x - 2$$
$$g(x) = 2x^2 - 2$$
$$h(x) = 2x^3 - 2$$

a. The degree of each polynomial function is 2.
b. The leading coefficient of each function is -2.
c. Each function has exactly one real zero at $x = 1$.
d. None of these is true for functions $f(x)$, $g(x)$, and $h(x)$.

50. Which of these can be modeled by a quadratic function?
a. The path of a sound wave
b. The path of a bullet
c. The distance an object travels over time when the rate is constant
d. Radioactive decay

51. Which of these is equivalent to $\log_y 256$ if $2\log_4 y + \log_4 16 = 3$?
a. 16
b. 8
c. 4
d. 2

52. Simplify $\frac{(x^2y)(2xy^{-2})^3}{16x^5y^2} + \frac{3}{xy}$

a. $\frac{3x+24y^6}{8xy^7}$

b. $\frac{x+6y^6}{2xy^7}$

c. $\frac{x+24y^5}{8xy^6}$

d. $\frac{x+6y^5}{2xy^6}$

53. Given: $f(x) = 10^x$. If $f(x) = 5$, which of these approximates x?
a. 100,000
b. 0.00001
c. 0.7
d. 1.6

54. Which of these could be the equation of the function graphed below?

a. $f(x) = x^2$
b. $f(x) = \sqrt{x}$
c. $f(x) = 2^x$
d. $f(x) = log_2 x$

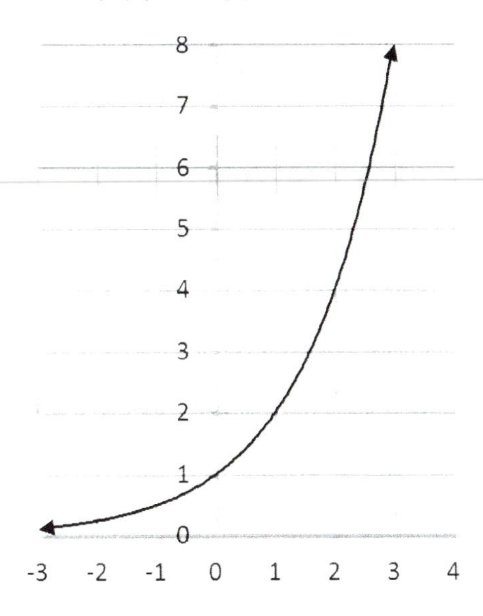

55. Which of these statements is **NOT** necessarily true when $f(x) = \log_b x$ and $b > 1$?

a. The x-intercept of the graph of $f(x)$ is 1.
b. The graph of $f(x)$ passes through $(b, 1)$
c. $f(x) < 0$ when $x < 1$
d. If $g(x) = b^x$, the graph of $f(x)$ is symmetric to the graph of $g(x)$ with respect to $y = x$.

56. A colony of *Escherichia coli* is inoculated from a Petri dish into a test tube containing 50 mL of nutrient broth. The test tube is placed in a 37°C incubator/shaker; after one hour, the number of bacteria in the test tube is determined to be 8×10^6. Given that the doubling time of *E. coli* is 20 minutes with agitation at 37°C, approximately how many bacteria should the test tube contain after eight hours of growth?

a. 2.56×10^8
b. 2.05×10^9
c. 1.7×10^{10}
d. 1.7×10^{13}

57. The strength of an aqueous acid solution is measured by pH. $\text{pH} = -\log[\text{H}^+]$, where $[\text{H}^+]$ is the molar concentration of hydronium ions in the solution. A solution is acidic if its pH is less than 7. The lower the pH, the stronger the acid; for example, gastric acid, which has a pH of about 1, is a much stronger acid than urine, which has a pH of about 6. How many times stronger is an acid with a pH of 3 than an acid with pH of 5?

a. 2
b. 20
c. 100
d. 1000

58. Simplify $\sqrt{\frac{-28x^6}{27y^5}}$.

a. $\frac{2x^3 i\sqrt{21y}}{9y^3}$

b. $\frac{2x^3 i\sqrt{21y}}{27y^4}$

c. $\frac{-2x^3\sqrt{21y}}{9y^3}$

d. $\frac{12x^3 yi\sqrt{7}}{27y^2}$

59. Which of these does **NOT** have a solution set of $\{x: -1 \leq x \leq 1\}$?

a. $-4 \leq 2 + 3(x-1) \leq 2$

b. $-2x^2 + 2 \geq x^2 - 1$

c. $\frac{11-|3x|}{7} \geq 2$

d. $3|2x| + 4 \leq 10$

60. Solve $2 - \sqrt{x} = \sqrt{x - 20}$.

a. $x = 6$

b. $x = 36$

c. $x = 144$

d. No solution

61. Solve $\frac{x-2}{x-1} = \frac{x-1}{x+1} + \frac{2}{x-1}$.

a. $x = 2$

b. $x = -5$

c. $x = 1$

d. No solution

62. Which of these equations is represented by the graph below?

a. $y = \frac{3}{x^2-x-2}$

b. $y = \frac{3x+3}{x^2-x-2}$

c. $y = \frac{1}{x+1} + \frac{1}{x-2}$

d. None of these

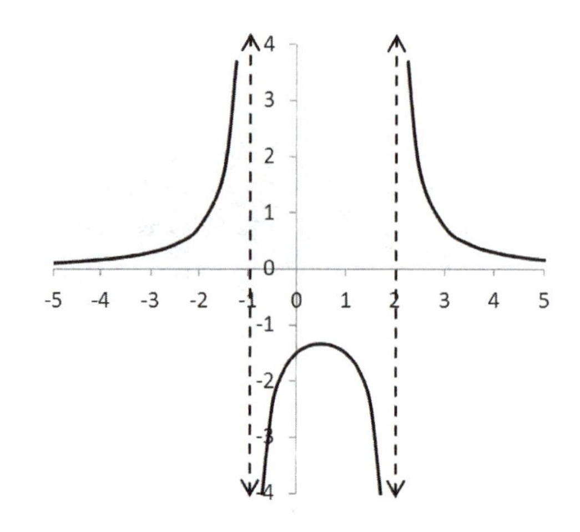

63. Which of the graphs shown represents $f(x) = -2|-x+4| - 1$?

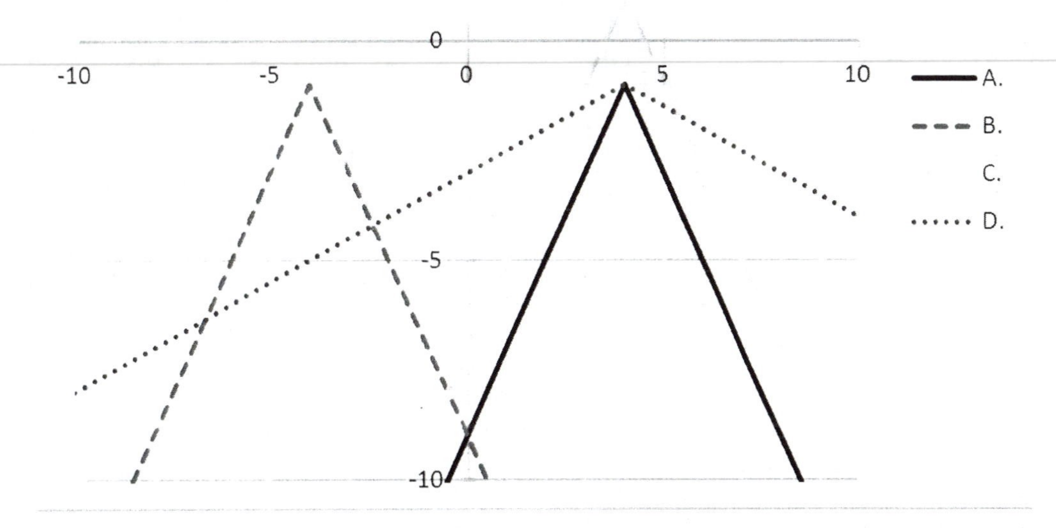

64. Which of these functions includes 1 as an element of the domain and 2 as an element of the range?

a. $y = \frac{1}{x-1} + 1$
b. $y = -\sqrt{x+2} - 1$
c. $y = |x+2| - 3$
d. $y = \begin{cases} x & x < 1 \\ -x-3 & x \geq 1 \end{cases}$

65. Which of the following statements is (are) true when $f(x) = \frac{x^2-x-6}{x^3+2x^2-x-2}$?

I. The graph $f(x)$ has vertical asymptotes at $x = -2$, $x = -1$, and $x = 1$.
II. The x- and y-intercepts of the graph of $f(x)$ are both 3.

a. I
b. II
c. I and II
d. Neither statement is true.

66. In the 1600s, Galileo Galilei studied the motion of pendulums and discovered that the period of a pendulum, the time it takes to complete one full swing, is a function of the square root of the length of its string: $2\pi\sqrt{\frac{L}{g}}$, where L is the length of the string and g is the acceleration due to gravity.

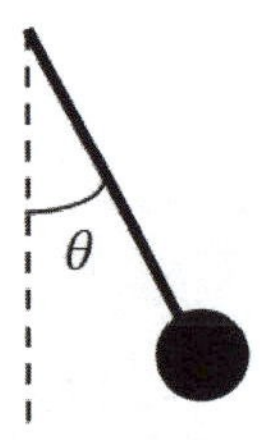

Consider two pendulums released from the same pivot point and at the same angle, $\theta = 30°$. Pendulum 1 has a mass of 100 g, while Pendulum 2 has a mass of 200 g. If Pendulum 1 has a period four times the period of Pendulum 2, what is true of the lengths of the pendulums' strings?

a. The length of Pendulum 1's string is four times the length of Pendulum 2's string.
b. The length of Pendulum 1's string is eight times the length of Pendulum 2's string.
c. The length of Pendulum 1's string is sixteen times the length of Pendulum 2's string.
d. The length of Pendulum 1's string is less than the length of Pendulum 2's string.

67. At today's visit to her doctor, Josephine was prescribed a liquid medication with instructions to take 25 cc's every four hours. She filled the prescription on her way to work, but when it came time to take the medicine, she realized that the pharmacist did not include a measuring cup. Josephine estimated that the plastic spoon in her desk drawer was about the same size as a teaspoon and decided to use it to measure the approximate dosage. She recalled that one cubic centimeter (cc) is equal to one milliliter (mL) but was not sure how many milliliters were in a teaspoon. So, she noted that a two-liter bottle of soda contains about the same amount as a half-gallon container of milk and applied her knowledge of the customary system of measurement to determine how many teaspoons of medicine to take. Which of these calculations might she have used to approximate her dosage?

a. $25 \cdot \frac{1}{1000} \cdot \frac{2}{0.5} \cdot 16 \cdot 48$
b. $25 \cdot \frac{1}{100} \cdot \frac{0.5}{2} \cdot 16 \cdot 4 \cdot 12$
c. $\frac{1000}{25} \cdot \frac{0.5}{2} \cdot 16 \cdot 4 \cdot 12$
d. $\frac{25}{1000} \cdot \frac{1}{4} \cdot 16 \cdot 48$

68. If 1" on a map represents 60 ft, how many yards apart are two points if the distance between the points on the map is 10"?

a. 1800
b. 600
c. 200
d. 2

69. Roxana walks x meters west and $x + 20$ meters south to get to her friend's house. On a neighborhood map which has a scale of 1cm:10 m, the distance between Roxana's house and her friend's house is 10 cm. How far did Roxana walk to her friend's house?

a. 60 m
b. 80 m
c. 100 m
d. 140 m

70. For ΔABC, what is AB?

a. 3
b. 10
c. 12
d. 15

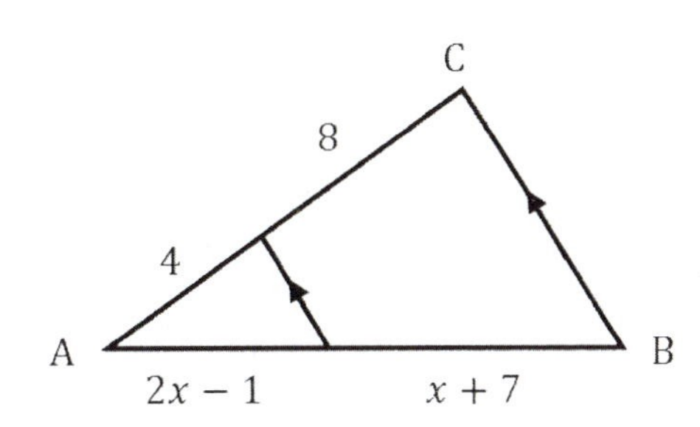

71. To test the accuracy and precision of two scales, a student repeatedly measured the mass of a 10 g standard and recorded these results.

	Trial 1	Trial 2	Trial 3	Trial 4
Scale 1	9.99 g	9.98 g	10.02g	10.01g
Scale 2	10.206 g	10.209 g	10.210 g	10.208 g

Which of these conclusions about the scales is true?

a. Scale 1 has an average percent error of 0.15%, and Scale 2 has an average percent error of 2.08%. Scale 1 is more accurate and precise than Scale 2.
b. Scale 1 has an average percent error of 0.15%, and Scale 2 has an average percent error of 2.08%. Scale 1 is more accurate than Scale 2; however, Scale 2 is more precise.
c. Scale 1 has an average percent error of 0%, and Scale 2 has an average percent error of 2.08%. Scale 1 is more accurate and precise than Scale 2.
d. Scale 1 has an average percent error of 0%, and Scale 2 has an average percent error of 2.08%. Scale 1 is more accurate than Scale 2; however, Scale 2 is more precise.

72. A developer decides to build a fence around a neighborhood park, which is positioned on a rectangular lot. Rather than fencing along the lot line, he fences x feet from each of the lot's boundaries. By fencing a rectangular space 141 yd^2 smaller than the lot, the developer saves $432 in fencing materials, which cost $12 per linear foot. How much does he spend?

a. $160
b. $456
c. $3,168
d. The answer cannot be determined from the given information.

73. Natasha designs a square pyramidal tent for her children. Each of the sides of the square base measures x ft, and the tent's height is h feet. If Natasha were to increase by 1 ft the length of each side of the base, how much more interior space would the tent have?

a. $\frac{h(x^2+2x+1)}{3}$ ft^3
b. $\frac{h(2x+1)}{3}$ ft^3
c. $\frac{x^2h+3}{3}$ ft^3
d. 1 ft^3

74. A rainbow pattern is designed from semi-circles as shown below.

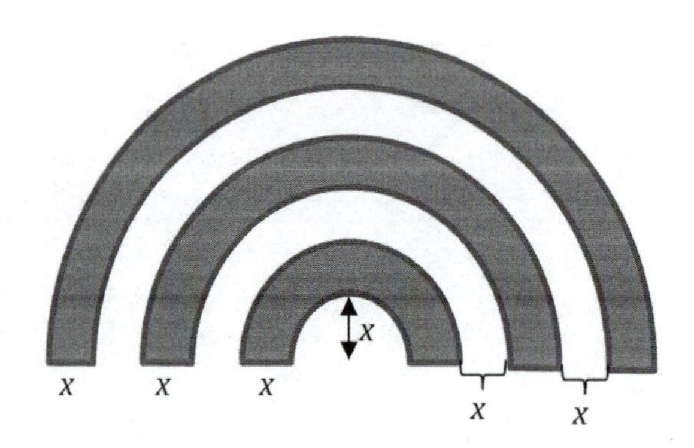

Which of the following gives the area A of the shaded region as a function of x?

a. $A = \frac{21x^2\pi}{2}$
b. $A = 21x^2\pi$
c. $A = 42x^2\pi$
d. $A = 82x^2\pi$

75. Categorize the following statements as axioms of Euclidean, hyperbolic, or elliptical geometry.

I. In a plane, for any line l and point A not on l, no lines which pass through A intersect l.

II. In a plane, for any line l and point A not on l, exactly one line which passes through A does not intersect l.

III. In a plane, for any line l and point A not on l, all lines which pass through A intersect l.

a.

Statement I	Elliptical geometry
Statement II	Euclidean geometry
Statement III	Hyperbolic geometry

b.

Statement I	Hyperbolic geometry
Statement II	Euclidean geometry
Statement III	Elliptical geometry

c.

Statement I	Hyperbolic geometry
Statement II	Elliptical geometry
Statement III	Euclidean geometry

d.

Statement I	Elliptical geometry
Statement II	Hyperbolic geometry
Statement III	Euclidean geometry

76. As shown below, four congruent isosceles trapezoids are positioned such that they form an arch. Find x for the indicated angle.

5x+12.5

a. $x = 11$
b. $x = 20$
c. $x = 24.5$
d. The value of x cannot be determined from the information given.

77. A circle is inscribed inside quadrilateral $ABCD$. $\overline{CD}$ is bisected by the point at which it is tangent to the circle. If $AB = 14, BC = 10, DC = 8$, then

a. $AD = 11$
b. $AD = 2\sqrt{34}$
c. $AD = 12$
d. $AD = 17.5$

78. Which of the following equations gives the area A of the triangle below as a function of a and b?

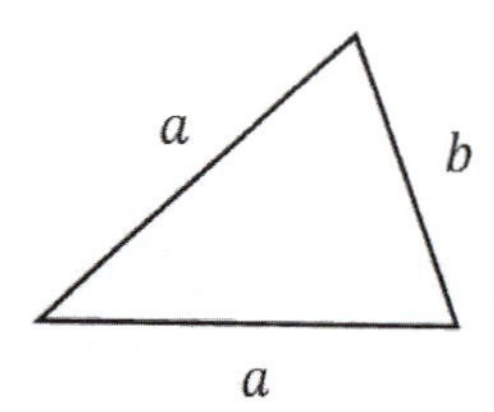

a. $\frac{2a^2-b^2}{4}$
b. $\frac{ab-a^2}{2}$
c. $\frac{b\sqrt{a^2-b^2}}{2}$
d. $\frac{b\sqrt{4a^2-b^2}}{4}$

79. Given the figure and the following information, find DE to the nearest tenth.
$\overline{AD}$ is an altitude of ΔABC
$\overline{DE}$ is an altitude of triangle ΔADC
$BD \cong DC$
$BC = 24; AD = 5$

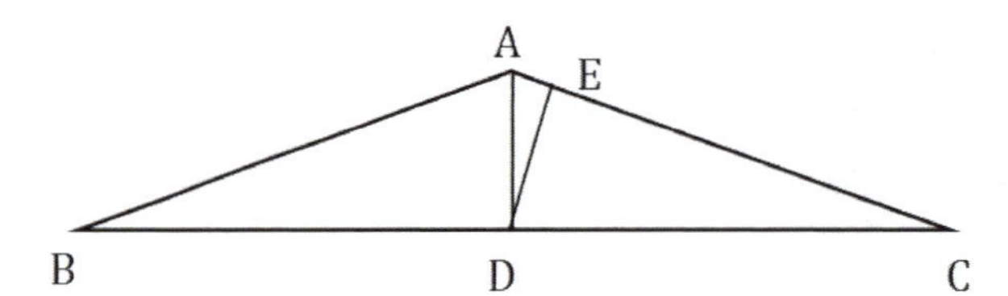

a. 4.2
b. 4.6
c. 4.9
d. 5.4

80. A cube inscribed in a sphere has a volume of 64 cubic units. What is the volume of the sphere in cubic units?

a. $4\pi\sqrt{3}$
b. $8\pi\sqrt{3}$
c. $32\pi\sqrt{3}$
d. $256\pi\sqrt{3}$

Questions 81 and 82 are based on the following proof:

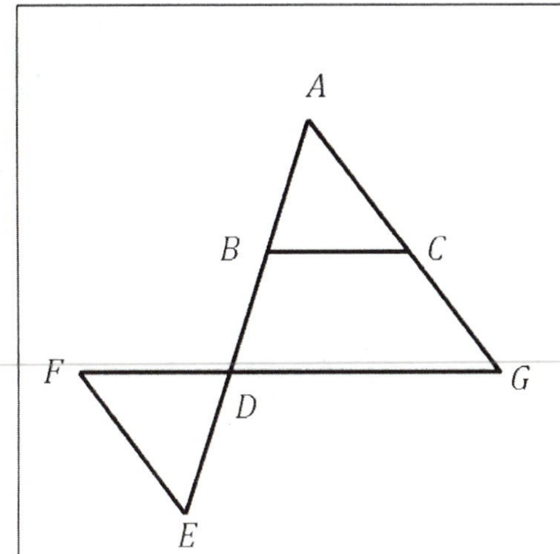

Statement	Reason
1. $\overline{BC} \parallel \overline{FG}$	Given
2.	
3. $\overline{FD} \cong \overline{BC}$	Given
4. $\overline{AB} \cong \overline{DE}$	Given
5. $\Delta ABC \cong \Delta EDF$	___81.___
6. ___82.___	
7. $\overline{FE} \parallel \overline{AG}$	

Given: $\overline{BC} \parallel \overline{FG}$; $\overline{FD} \cong \overline{BC}$; $\overline{AB} \cong \overline{DE}$
Prove: $\overline{FE} \parallel \overline{AG}$

81. Which of the following justifies step 5 in the proof?
    a. AAS
    b. SSS
    c. ASA
    d. SAS

82. Step 6 in the proof should contain which of the following statements?
    a. $\angle BAC \cong \angle DEF$
    b. $\angle ABC \cong \angle EDF$
    c. $\angle ACB \cong \angle EFD$
    d. $\angle GDA \cong \angle EDF$

83. Which of these is **NOT** a net of a cube?

a.
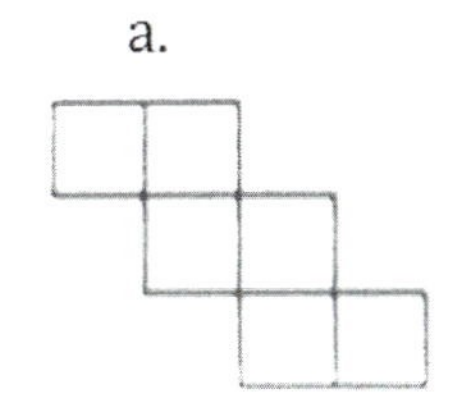

b.
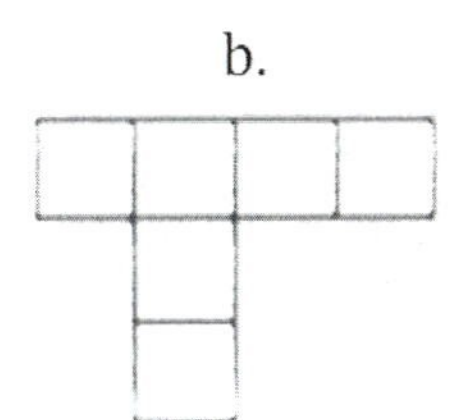

c.
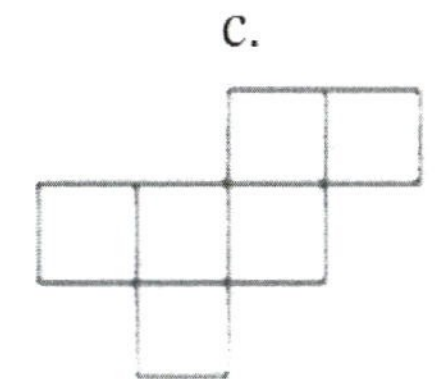

d.
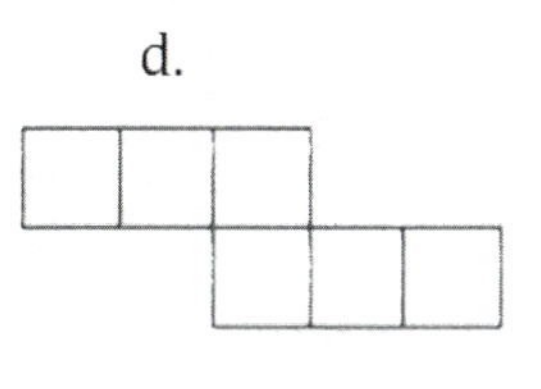

84. Identify the cross-section polygon formed by a plane containing the given points on the cube.

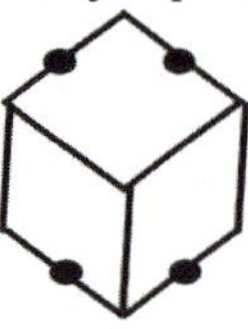

a. Rectangle
b. Trapezoid
c. Pentagon
d. Hexagon

85. Which of these represents the equation of a sphere which is centered in the xyz-space at the point (1, 0, -2) and which has a volume of 36π cubic units?

a. $x^2 + y^2 + z^2 - 2x + 4z = 4$
b. $x^2 + y^2 + z^2 + 2x - 4z = 4$
c. $x^2 + y^2 + z^2 - 2x + 4z = -2$
d. $x^2 + y^2 + z^2 + 2x - 4z = 2$

86. A triangle has vertices $(0,0,0)$, $(0,0,4)$, and $(0,3,0)$ in the xyz-space. In cubic units, what is the difference in the volume of the solid formed by rotating the triangle about the z-axis and the solid formed by rotating the triangle about the y-axis?

a. 0
b. 4π
c. 5π
d. 25

87. If the midpoint of a line segment graphed on the xy-coordinate plane is $(3, -1)$ and the slope of the line segment is -2, which of these is a possible endpoint of the line segment?

a. $(-1,1)$
b. $(0, -5)$
c. $(7,1)$
d. $(5, -5)$

88. The vertices of a polygon are $(2,3)$, $(8,1)$, $(6, -5)$, and $(0, -3)$. Which of the following describes the polygon most specifically?

a. Parallelogram
b. Rhombus
c. Rectangle
d. Square

89. What is the radius of the circle defined by the equation $x^2 + y^2 - 10x + 8y + 29 = 0$?

a. $2\sqrt{3}$
b. $2\sqrt{5}$
c. $\sqrt{29}$
d. 12

90. Which of these describes the graph of the equation $2x^2 - 3y^2 - 12x + 6y - 15 = 0$?

a. Circular
b. Elliptical
c. Parabolic
d. Hyperbolic

91. The graph of $f(x)$ is a parabola with a focus of (a, b) and a directrix of $y = -b$, and $g(x)$ represents a transformation of $f(x)$. If the vertex of the graph of $g(x)$ is $(a, 0)$, which of these is a possible equation for $g(x)$ for nonzero integers a and b?

a. $g(x) = f(x) + b$
b. $g(x) = -f(x)$
c. $g(x) = f(x + a)$
d. $g(x) = f(x - a) + b$

92. A triangle with vertices $A(-4,2), B(-1,3)$, and $C(-5,7)$ is reflected across $y = x + 2$ to give $\Delta A'B'C'$, which is subsequently reflected across the y-axis to give $\Delta A''B''C''$. Which of these statements is true?

a. A 90° rotation of ΔABC about $(-2,0)$ gives ΔA″B″C″.
b. A reflection of ΔABC about the x-axis gives ΔA″B″C″.
c. A 270° rotation of ΔABC about (0,2) gives ΔA″B″C″.
d. A translation of ΔABC two units down gives ΔA″B″C″.

93. For which of these does a rotation of 120° about the center of the polygon map the polygon onto itself?

a. Square
b. Regular hexagon
c. Regular octagon
d. Regular decagon

94. Line segment $\overline{PQ}$ has endpoints (a, b) and (c, b). If $\overline{P'Q'}$ is the translation of $\overline{PQ}$ along a diagonal line such that P' is located at point (c, d), what is the area of quadrilateral $PP'Q'Q$?

a. $|a - c| \cdot |b - d|$
b. $|a - b| \cdot |c - d|$
c. $|a - d| \cdot |b - c|$
d. $(a - c)^2$

95. For the right triangle below, which of the following is a true statement of equality?

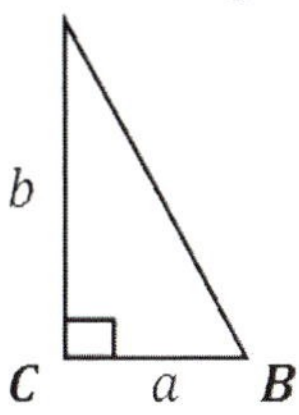

a. $tan\ B = \frac{a}{b}$

b. $cos\ B = \frac{a\sqrt{a^2+b^2}}{a^2+b^2}$

c. $sec\ B = \frac{\sqrt{a^2+b^2}}{b}$

d. $csc\ B = \frac{a^2+b^2}{b}$

96. A man looks out of a window of a tall building at a 45° angle of depression and sees his car in the parking lot. When he turns his gaze downward to a 60° angle of depression, he sees his wife's car. If his car is parked 60 feet from his wife's car, about how far from the building did his wife park her car?

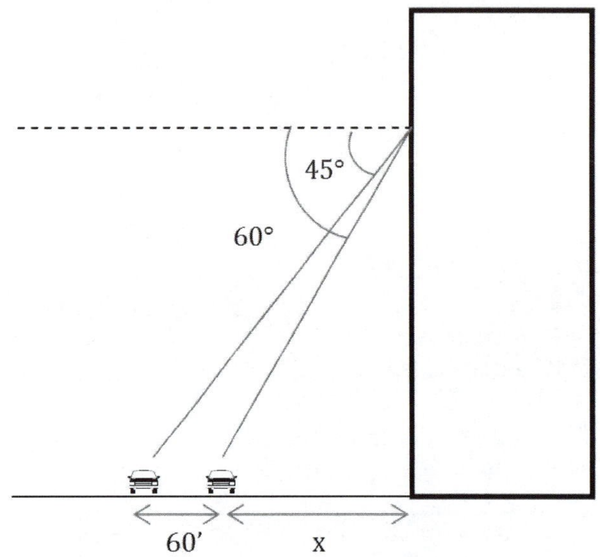

a. 163 feet
b. 122 feet
c. 82 feet
d. 60 feet

97. What is the exact value of $\tan(-\frac{2\pi}{3})$?

a. $\sqrt{3}$
b. $-\sqrt{3}$
c. $\frac{\sqrt{3}}{3}$
d. 1

98. If $\sin\theta = \frac{1}{2}$ when $\frac{\pi}{2} < \theta < \pi$, what is the value of θ?

a. $\frac{\pi}{6}$
b. $\frac{\pi}{3}$
c. $\frac{2\pi}{3}$
d. $\frac{5\pi}{6}$

99. Which of the following expressions is equal to $\cos\theta\cot\theta$?

a. $sin\ \theta$
b. $sec\ \theta\ tan\ \theta$
c. $csc\ \theta - sin\ \theta$
d. $sec\ \theta - sin\ \theta$

100. Solve $\sec^2\theta = 2\tan\theta$ for $0 < \theta \leq 2\pi$.

a. $\theta = \frac{\pi}{6}$ or $\frac{7\pi}{6}$
b. $\theta = \frac{\pi}{4}$ or $\frac{5\pi}{4}$
c. $\theta = \frac{3\pi}{4}$ or $\frac{7\pi}{4}$
d. There is no solution to the equation.

101. A car is driving along the highway at a constant speed when it runs over a pebble, which becomes lodged in one of the tire's treads. If this graph represent the height h of the pebble above the road in inches as a function of time t in seconds, which of these statements is true?

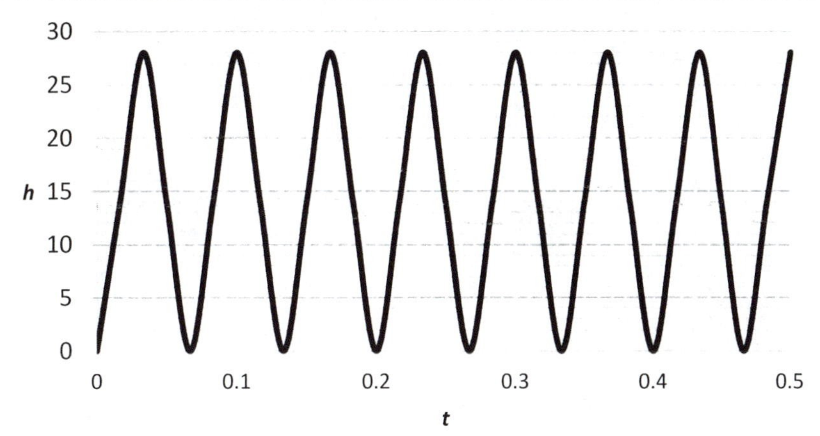

a. The outer radius of the tire is 14 inches, and the tire rotates 900 times per minute.
b. The outer radius of the tire is 28 inches, and the tire rotates 900 times per minute.
c. The outer radius of the tire is 14 inches, and the tire rotates 120 times per minute.
d. The outer radius of the tire is 28 inches, and the tire rotates 120 times per minute.

Below are graphed functions $f(x) = a_1 \sin(b_1 x)$ and $g(x) = a_2 \cos(b_2 x)$; a_1 and a_2 are integers, and b_1 and b_2 are positive rational numbers. Use this information to answer questions 102-103:

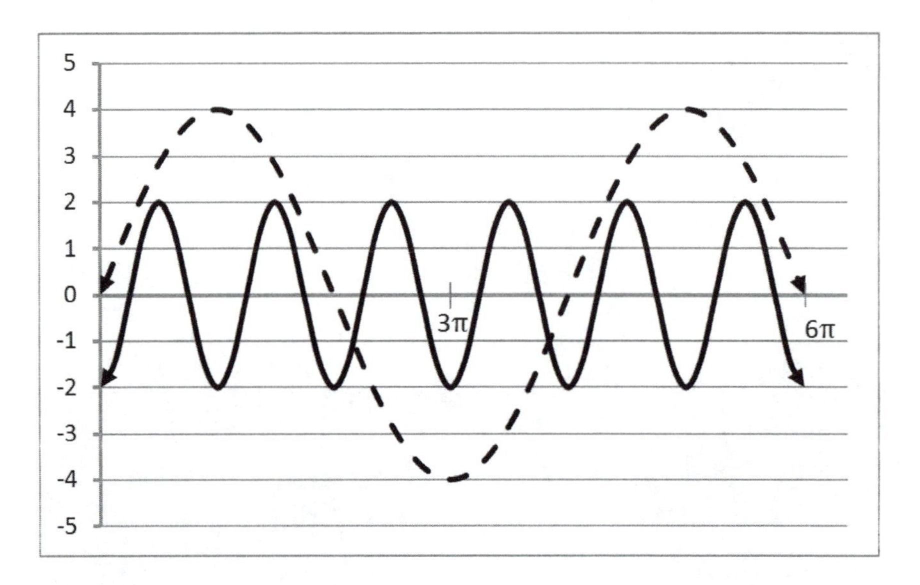

102. Which of the following statements is true?
  a. The graph of $f(x)$ is represented by a solid line.
  b. The amplitude of the graph of $g(x)$ is 4.
  c. $0 < b_1 < 1$.
  d. $b_2 = \pi$.

103. Which of the following statements is true?
  a. $0 < a_2 < a_1$
  b. $a_2 < 0 < a_1$
  c. $0 < a_1 < a_2$
  d. $a_2 < a_1 < 0$

104. A weight suspended on a spring is at its equilibrium point five inches above the top of a table. When the weight is pulled down two inches, it bounces above the equilibrium point and returns to the point from which it was released in one second. Which of these can be used to model the weight's height h above the table as a function of time t in seconds?
  a. $h = -2\cos(2\pi t) + 5$
  b. $h = 5\sin(t) - 2$
  c. $h = -2\sin(2\pi t) + 5$
  d. $h = -2\cos(0.5\pi t) + 3$

105. Evaluate $\lim_{x \to -3} \frac{x^3+3x^2-x-3}{x^2-9}$.
  a. 0
  b. $\frac{1}{3}$
  c. $-\frac{4}{3}$
  d. ∞

106. Evaluate $\lim_{x\to\infty} \frac{x^2+2x-3}{2x^2+1}$.

a. 0
b. $\frac{1}{2}$
c. -3
d. ∞

107. Evaluate $\lim_{x\to 3^+} \frac{|x-3|}{3-x}$.

a. 0
b. −1
c. 1
d. ∞

108. If $f(x) = \frac{1}{4}x^2 - 3$, find the slope of the line tangent to graph of $f(x)$ at $x = 2$.

a. -2
b. 0
c. 1
d. 4

109. If $f(x) = 2x^3 - 3x^2 + 4$, what is $\lim_{h\to 0} \frac{f(2+h)-f(2)}{h}$?

a. -4
b. 4
c. 8
d. 12

110. Find the derivative of $f(x) = e^{3x^2-1}$.

a. $6xe^{6x}$
b. e^{3x^2-1}
c. $(3x^2-1)e^{3x^2-2}$
d. $6xe^{3x^2-1}$

111. Find the derivative of $f(x) = \ln(2x+1)$.

a. $\frac{1}{2x+1}$
b. $2e^{2x+1}$
c. $\frac{2}{2x+1}$
d. $\frac{1}{2}$

112. For functions $f(x)$, $g(x)$, and $h(x)$, determine the limit of the function as x approaches 2 and the continuity of the function at $x = 2$.

a.

$\lim_{x\to 2+} f(x) = 4$ $\lim_{x\to 2-} f(x) = 2$ $f(2) = 2$	$lim_{x\to 2} f(x)$ DNE	The function $f(x)$ is discontinuous at 2.
$\lim_{x\to 2+} g(x) = 2$ $\lim_{x\to 2-} g(x) = 2$ $g(2) = 4$	$\lim_{x\to 2} g(x) = 2$	The function $g(x)$ is discontinuous at 2.
$\lim_{x\to 2+} h(x) = 2$ $\lim_{x\to 2-} h(x) = 2$ $h(2) = 2$	$\lim_{x\to 2} h(x) = 2$	The function $h(x)$ is continuous at 2.

b.

$\lim_{x\to 2+} f(x) = 4$ $\lim_{x\to 2-} f(x) = 2$ $f(2) = 2$	$lim_{x\to 2} f(x)\ DNE$	The function $f(x)$ is continuous at 2.
$\lim_{x\to 2+} g(x) = 2$ $\lim_{x\to 2-} g(x) = 2$ $g(2) = 4$	$lim_{x\to 2} g(x)$ DNE	The function $g(x)$ is continuous at 2.
$\lim_{x\to 2+} h(x) = 2$ $\lim_{x\to 2-} h(x) = 2$ $h(2) = 2$	$\lim_{x\to 2} h(x) = 2$	The function $h(x)$ is continuous at 2.

c.

$\lim_{x\to 2+} f(x) = 4$ $\lim_{x\to 2-} f(x) = 2$ $f(2) = 2$	$\lim_{x\to 2} f(x) = 2$	The function $f(x)$ is continuous at 2.
$\lim_{x\to 2+} g(x) = 2$ $\lim_{x\to 2-} g(x) = 2$ $g(2) = 4$	$\lim_{x\to 2} g(x) = 2$	The function $g(x)$ is discontinuous at 2.
$\lim_{x\to 2+} h(x) = 2$ $\lim_{x\to 2-} h(x) = 2$ $h(2) = 2$	$\lim_{x\to 2} h(x) = 2$	The function $h(x)$ is continuous at 2.

d.

$\lim_{x\to 2+} f(x) = 4$ $\lim_{x\to 2-} f(x) = 2$ $f(2) = 2$	$\lim_{x\to 2} f(x) = 2$	The function $f(x)$ is discontinuous at 2.
$\lim_{x\to 2+} g(x) = 2$ $\lim_{x\to 2-} g(x) = 2$ $g(2) = 4$	$\lim_{x\to 2} g(x) = 2$	The function $g(x)$ is discontinuous at 2.
$\lim_{x\to 2+} h(x) = 2$ $\lim_{x\to 2-} h(x) = 2$ $h(2) = 2$	$\lim_{x\to 2} h(x) = 2$	The function $h(x)$ is continuous at 2.

113. Find $f''(x)$ if $f(x) = 2x^4 - 4x^3 + 2x^2 - x + 1$.
a. $24x^2 - 24x + 4$
b. $8x^3 - 12x^2 + 4x - 1$
c. $32x^2 - 36x^2 + 8$
d. $\frac{2}{5}x^5 - x^4 + \frac{2}{3}x^3 - \frac{1}{2}x^2 + x + c$

114. If $f(x) = 4x^3 - x^2 - 4x + 2$, which of the following statements is(are) true of its graph?
I. The point $\left(-\frac{1}{2}, 3\frac{1}{4}\right)$ is a relative maximum.
II. The graph of f is concave upward on the interval $(-\infty, \frac{1}{2})$.
a. I
b. II
c. I and II
d. Neither I nor II

115. Suppose the path of a baseball hit straight up from three feet above the ground is modeled by the first quadrant graph of the function $h = -16t^2 + 50t + 3$, where t is the flight time of the ball in seconds and h is the height of the ball in feet. What is the velocity of the ball two seconds after it is hit?
a. 39 ft/s upward
b. 19.5 ft/s upward
c. 19.5 ft/s downward
d. 14 ft/s downward

116. A manufacturer wishes to produce a cylindrical can which can hold up to 0.5 L of liquid. To the nearest tenth, what is the radius of the can which requires the least amount of material to make?
a. 2.8 cm
b. 4.3 cm
c. 5.0 cm
d. 9.2 cm

117. Approximate the area A under the curve by using a Riemann sum with $\Delta x = 1$.

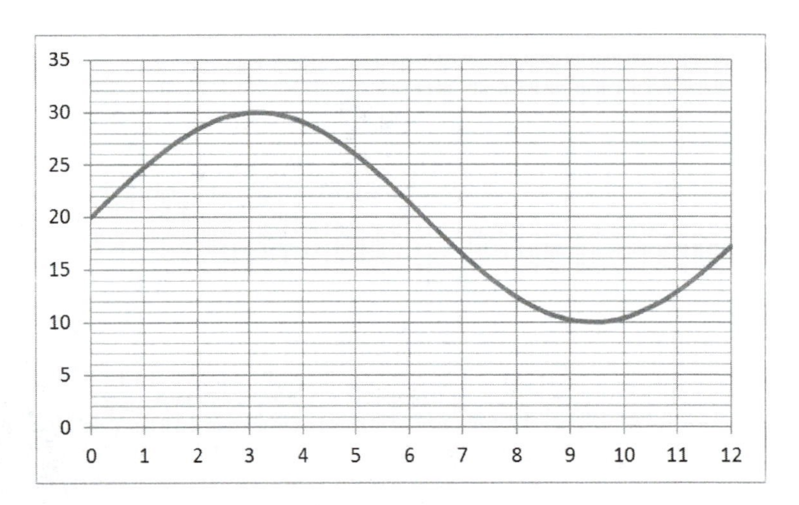

a. $209 < A < 211$
b. $230 < A < 235$
c. $238 < A < 241$
d. $246 < A < 250$

118. To the nearest hundredth, what is the area in square units under the curve of $f(x) = \frac{1}{x}$ on [1,2]?
a. 0.50
b. 0.69
c. 1.30
d. 1.50

119. Calculate $\int 3x^2 + 2x - 1\ dx$.
a. $x^3 + x^2 - x + c$
b. $6x^2 + 2$
c. $\frac{3}{2}x^3 + 2x^2 - x + c$
d. $6x^2 + 2 + c$

120. Calculate $\int 3x^2 e^{x^3}\ dx$
a. $x^3 e^{x^3} + c$
b. $e^{x^3} + c$
c. $x^3 e^{\frac{x^4}{4}} + c$
d. $ln\, x^3 + c$

121. Find the area A of the finite region between the graphs of $y = -x + 2$ and $y = x^2 - 4$.
a. 18
b. $\frac{125}{6}$
c. $\frac{45}{2}$
d. 25

122. The velocity of a car which starts at position 0 at time 0 is given by the equation $v(t) = 12t - t^2$ for $0 \leq t \leq 12$. Find the position of the car when its acceleration is 0.

a. 18
b. 36
c. 144
d. 288

123. Which of these graphs is **NOT** representative of the data set shown below?

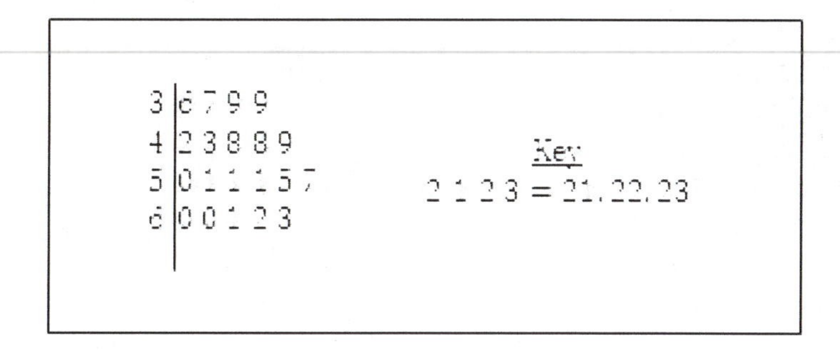

a.

30 35 40 45 50 55 60 65 70

b.

Frequency

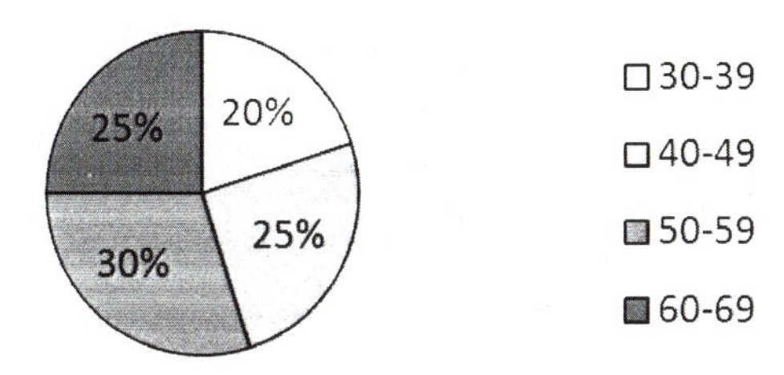

c.

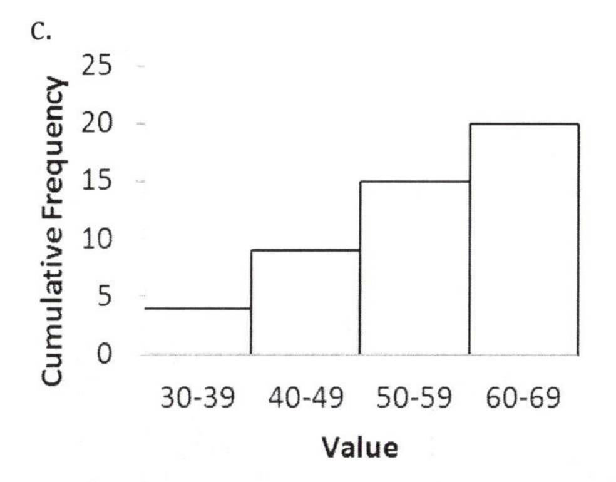

d. All of these graphs represent the data set.

124. Which of these would best illustrate change over time?
a. Pie chart
b. Line graph
c. Box-and-whisker plot
d. Venn diagram

125. Which of these is the least biased sampling technique?
a. To assess his effectiveness in the classroom, a teacher distributes a teacher evaluation to all of his students. Responses are anonymous and voluntary.
b. To determine the average intelligence quotient (IQ) of students in her school of 2,000 students, a principal uses a random number generator to select 300 students by student identification number and has them participate in a standardized IQ test.
c. To determine which video game is most popular among his fellow eleventh graders at school, a student surveys all of the students in his English class.
d. Sixty percent of students at the school have a parent who is a member of the Parent-Teacher Association (PTA). To determine parent opinions regarding school improvement programs, the Parent-Teacher Association (PTA) requires submission of a survey response with membership dues.

126. Which of these tables properly displays the measures of central tendency which can be used for nominal, interval, and ordinal data?
a.

	Mean	Median	Mode
Nominal			x
Interval	x	x	x
Ordinal		x	x

b.

	Mean	Median	Mode
Nominal			x
Interval	x	x	x
Ordinal	x	x	x

c.

	Mean	Median	Mode
Nominal	x	x	x
Interval	x	x	x
Ordinal	x	x	x

d.

	Mean	Median	Mode
Nominal			x
Interval	x	x	
Ordinal	x	x	x

Use the following data to answer questions 127-129:

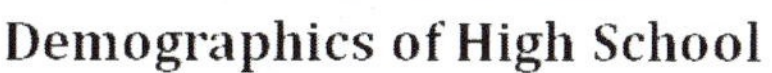

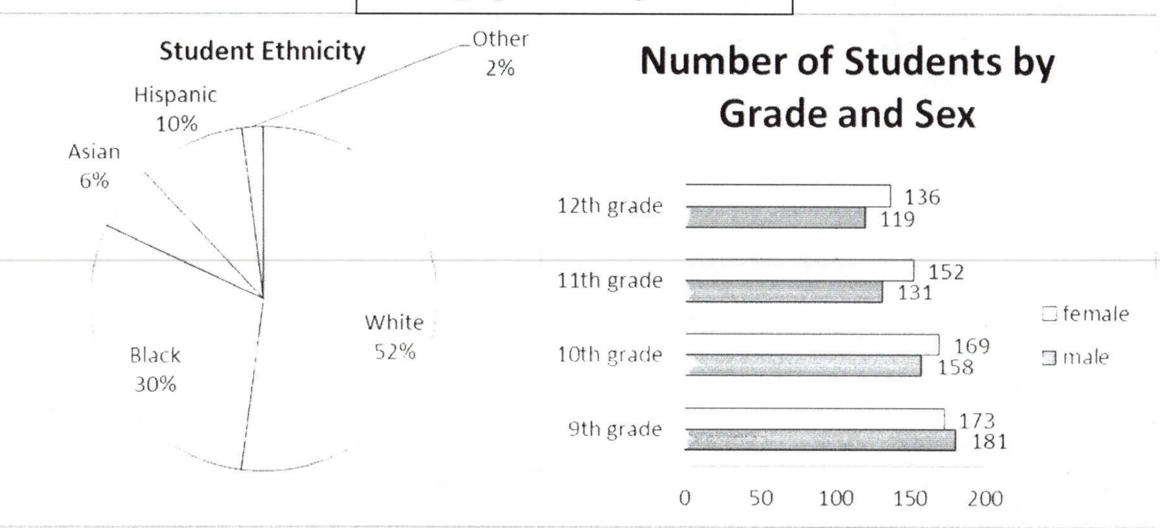

127. Which of these is the greatest quantity?
   a. The average number of male students in the 11th and 12th grades
   b. The number of Hispanic students at the school
   c. The difference in the number of male and female students at the school
   d. The difference in the number of 9th and 12th grader students at the school

128. Compare the two quantities.

Quantity A	Quantity B
The percentage of white students at the school, rounded to the nearest whole number	The percentage of female students at the school, rounded to the nearest whole number

   a. Quantity A is greater.
   b. Quantity B is greater.
   c. The two quantities are the same.
   d. The relationship cannot be determined from the given information.

129. An eleventh grader is chosen at random to represent the school at a conference. What is the approximate probability that the student is male?
   a. 0.03
   b. 0.11
   c. 0.22
   d. 0.46

The box-and-whisker plot displays student test scores by class period. Use the data to answer questions 130 through 132:

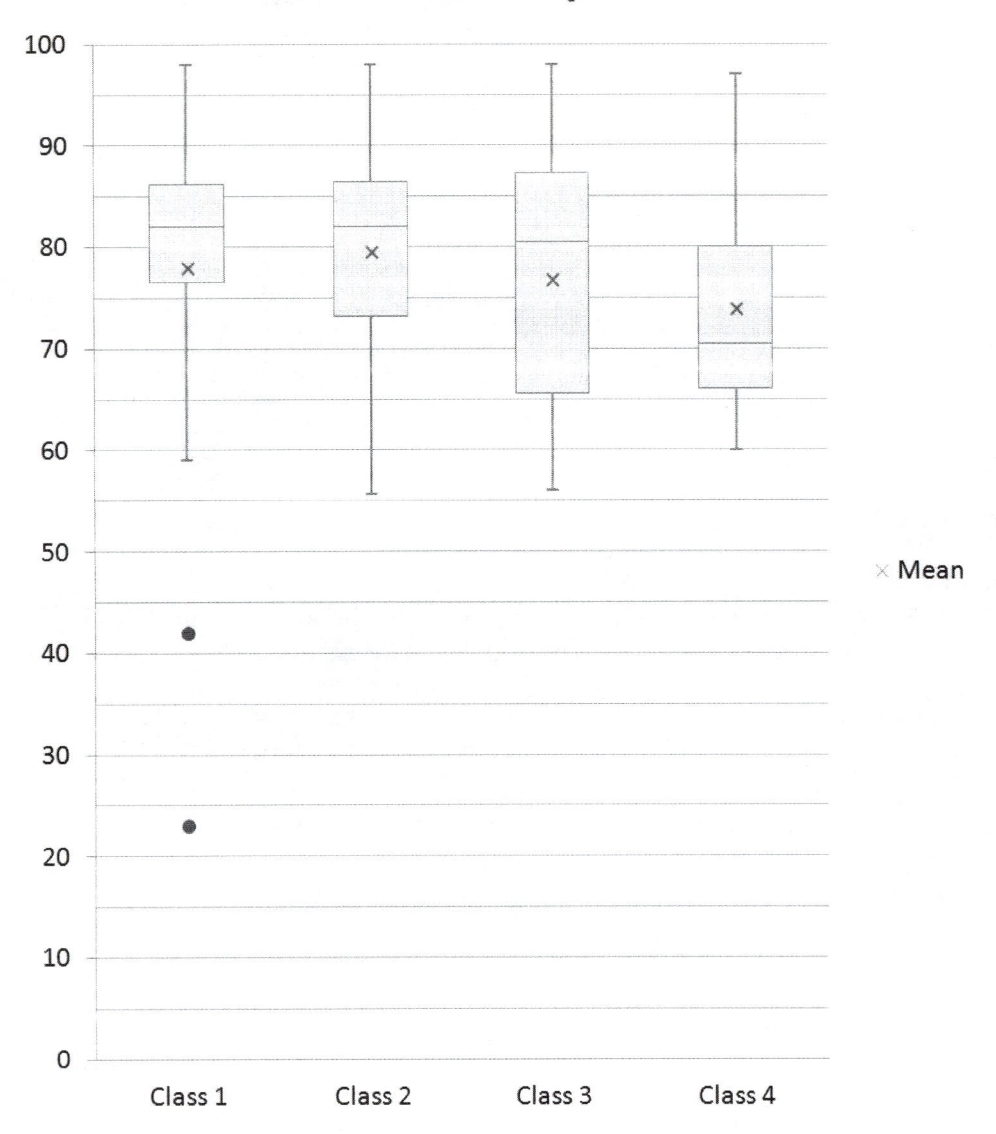

130. Which class has the greatest range of test scores?
   a. Class 1
   b. Class 2
   c. Class 3
   d. Class 4

131. What is the probability that a student chosen at random from class 2 made above a 73 on this test?
   a. 0.25
   b. 0.5
   c. 0.6
   d. 0.75

132. Which of the following statements is true of the data?

a. The mean better reflects student performance in class 1 than the median.
b. The mean test score for class 1 and 2 is the same.
c. The median test score for class 1 and 2 is the same.
d. The median test score is above the mean for class 4.

133. In order to analyze the real estate market for two different zip codes within the city, a realtor examines the most recent 100 home sales in each zip code. She considered a house which sold within the first month of its listing to have a market time of one month; likewise, she considered a house to have a market time of two months if it sold after having been on the market for one month but by the end of the second month. Using this definition of market time, she determined the frequency of sales by number of months on the market. The results are displayed below.

Which of the following is a true statement for these data?

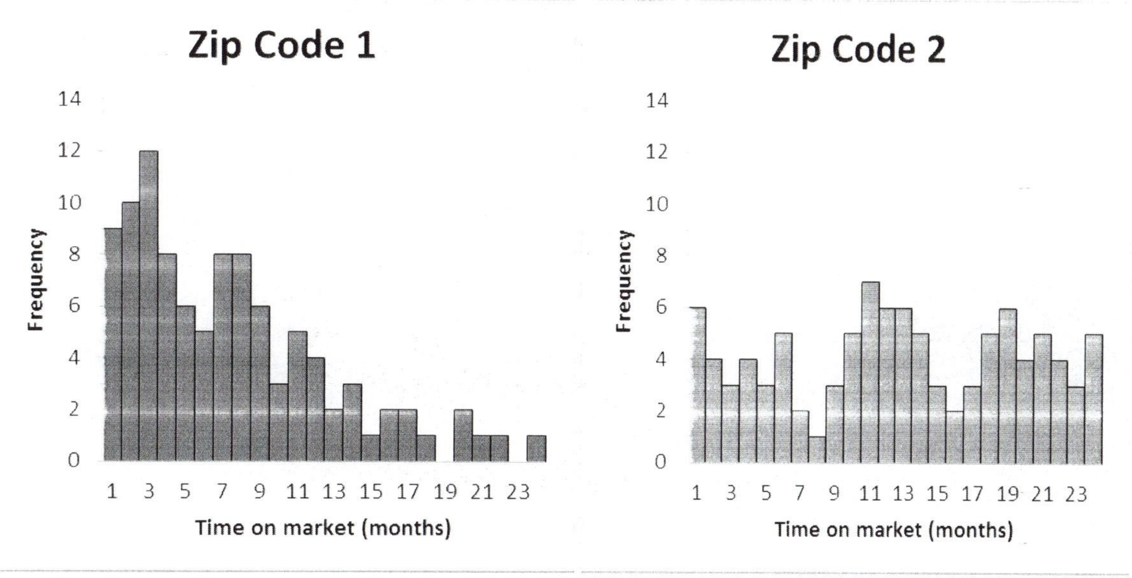

a. The median time a house spends on the market in Zip Code 1 is five months less than Zip Code 2
b. On average, a house spent seven months longer on the market in Zip Code 2 than in Zip Code 1.
c. The mode time on the market is higher for Zip Code 1 than for Zip Code 2.
d. The median time on the market is less than the mean time on the market for Zip Code 1.

134. Attending a summer camp are 12 six-year-olds, 15 seven-year-olds, 14 eight-year-olds, 12 nine-year-olds, and 10 ten-year-olds. If a camper is randomly selected to participate in a special event, what is the probability that he or she is at least eight years old?

a. $\frac{2}{9}$

b. $\frac{22}{63}$

c. $\frac{4}{7}$

d. $\frac{3}{7}$

135. A small company is divided into three departments as shown. Two individuals are chosen at random to attend a conference. What is the approximate probability that two women from the same department will be chosen?

	Department 1	Department 2	Department 3
Women	12	28	16
Men	18	14	15

a. 8.6%
b. 10.7%
c. 11.2%
d. 13.8%

136. A random sample of 90 students at an elementary school were asked these three questions:

Do you like carrots?
Do you like broccoli?
Do you like cauliflower?

The results of the survey are shown below. If these data are representative of the population of students at the school, which of these is most probable?

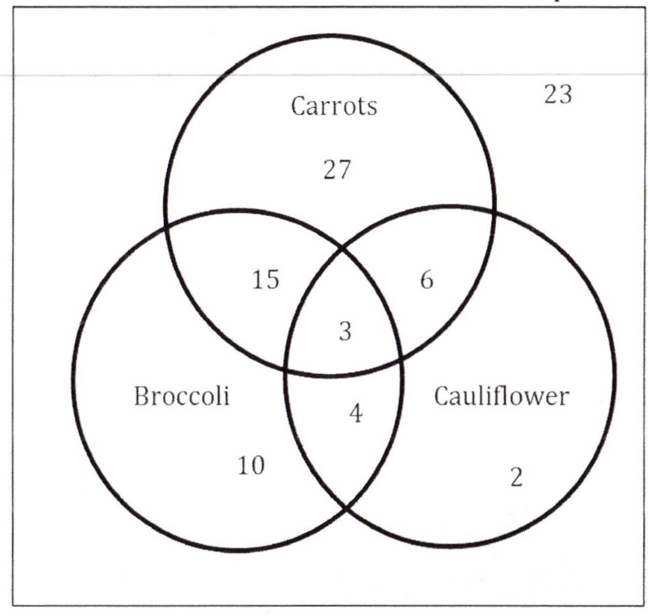

a. A student chosen at random likes broccoli.
b. If a student chosen at random likes carrots, he also likes at least one other vegetable.
c. If a student chosen at random likes cauliflower and broccoli, he also likes carrots.
d. A student chosen at random does not like carrots, broccoli, or cauliflower.

Use the information below to answer questions 137 and 138:

Each day for 100 days, a student tossed a single misshapen coin three times in succession and recorded the number of times the coin landed on heads. The results of his experiment are shown below.

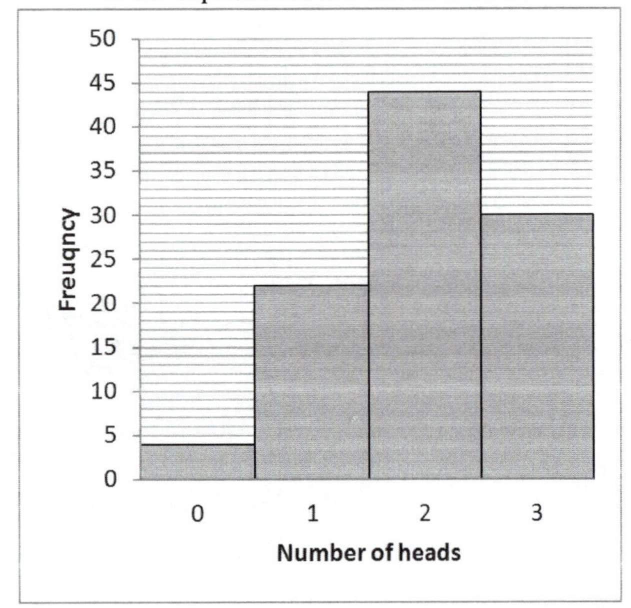

137. Given these experimental data, which of these approximates P(heads) for a single flip of this coin.

a. 0.22
b. 0.5
c. 0.67
d. 0.74

138. Which of these shows the graphs of the probability distributions from ten flips of this misshapen coin and ten flips of a fair coin?

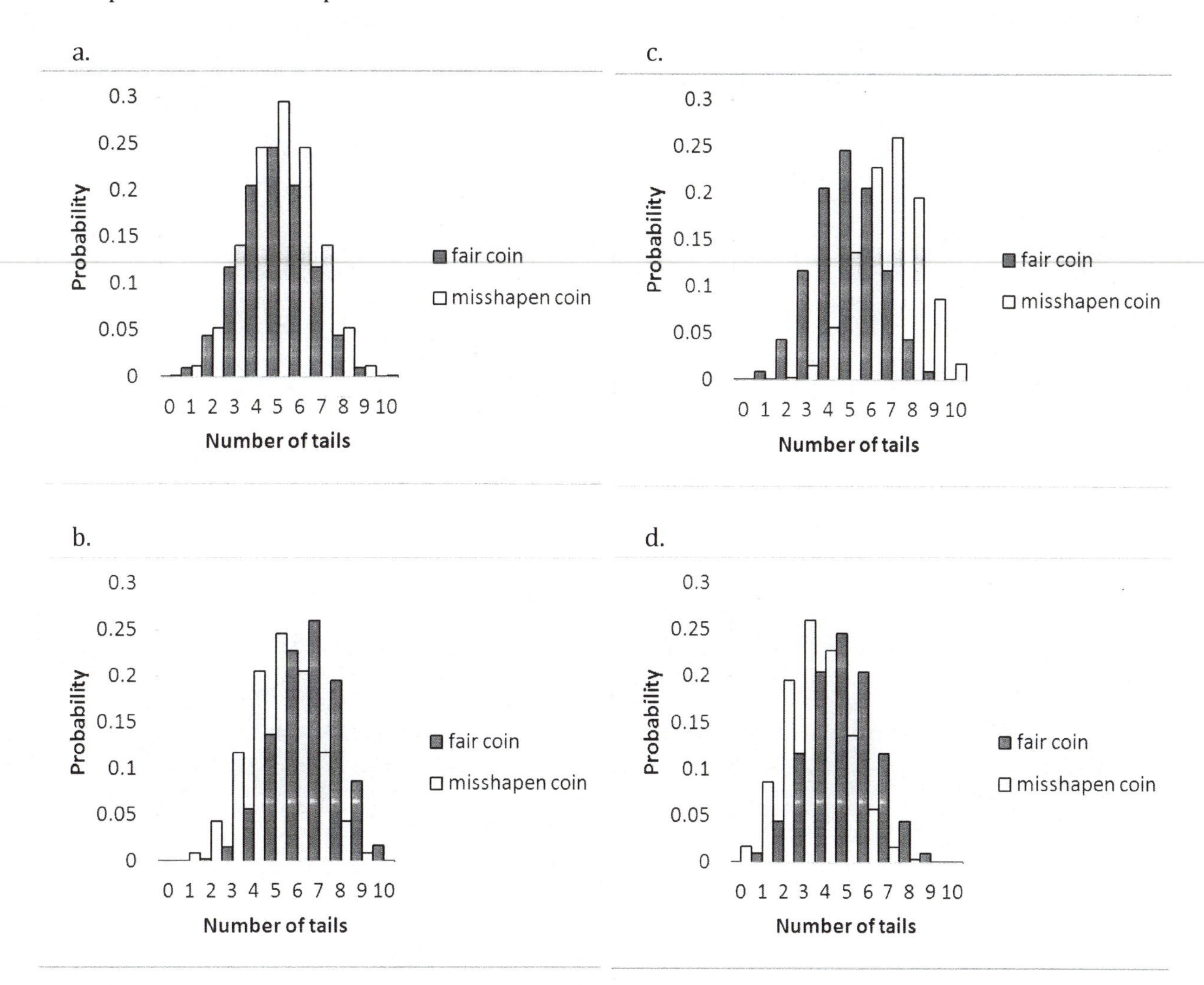

139. Which of these does **NOT** simulate randomly selecting a student from a group of 11 students?

a. Assigning each student a unique card value of A, 1, 2, 3, 4, 5, 6, 7, 8, 9, or J, removing queens and kings from a standard deck of 52 cards, shuffling the remaining cards, and drawing a single card from the deck

b. Assigning each student a unique number 0-10 and using a computer to randomly generate a number within that range

c. Assigning each student a unique number from 2 to 12 ; rolling two dice and finding the sum of the numbers on the dice

d. All of these can be used as a simulation of the event.

140. Gene P has three possible alleles, or gene forms, called a, b and c. Each individual carries two copies of Gene P, one of which is inherited from his or her mother and the other of which is inherited from his or her father. If the two copies of Gene P are of the same form, the individual is homozygous for that allele; otherwise, the individual is heterozygous. A simulation is performed to determine the genotypes, or genetic make-ups, of 500 individuals selected at random from the population. 500 two-digit numbers are generator using a random number generator. Based on the relative frequencies of each allele, the digit 0 is assigned to represent allele a, the digits 1 and 2 to represent allele b, and the digits 3-9 to represent allele c.

28 93 97 37 92 00 27 21 87 13 62 62 15 31 55 09 47 07 54 88 38 88 10
98 34 01 45 14 34 46 38 61 93 22 37 39 57 03 93 50 53 16 28 65 81 60
21 12 13 10 19 91 04 18 49 01 99 30 11 16 00 48 04 63 59 24 02 42 23
06 32 52 19 18 94 94 46 63 87 41 79 39 85 20 43 20 15 03 39 33 77 45
66 77 70 92 25 27 68 71 89 35 98 55 85 47 60 97 12 92 53 44 45 41 51
22 09 23 81 33 04 35 43 48 32 80 36 95 64 56 34 74 55 37 64 84 51 50
25 99 51 94 19 46 10 44 17 25 75 52 47 35 70 65 08 50 98 09 02 24 30
59 00 03 21 40 30 86 16 53 91 28 17 97 58 75 76 73 83 54 40 54 13 38
36 67 74 80 63 12 41 27 96 61 66 05 60 69 96 15 56 82 57 31 83 26 24
78 42 76 49 56 06 57 78 67 02 96 40 82 29 14 07 29 62 90 31 08 26 71
61 18 22 84 23 33 49 29 90 07 08 05 14 59 72 86 44 69 68 99 06 11 95
43 72 58 28 93 97 37 92 00 27 21 87 13 62 62 15 31 55 09 47 07 54 88
38 88 10 98 34 01 45 14 34 46 38 61 93 22 37 39 57 03 93 50 53 16 28
65 81 60 21 12 13 10 19 91 04 18 49 01 99 30 11 16 00 48 04 63 59 24
02 42 23 06 32 52 19 18 94 94 46 63 87 41 79 39 85 20 43 20 15 03 39
33 77 45 66 77 70 92 25 27 68 71 89 35 98 55 85 47 60 97 12 92 53 44
45 41 51 22 09 23 81 33 04 35 43 48 32 80 36 95 64 56 34 74 55 37 64
84 51 50 25 99 51 94 19 46 10 44 17 25 75 52 47 35 70 65 08 50 98 09
02 24 30 59 00 03 21 40 30 86 16 53 91 28 17 97 58 75 76 73 83 54 40
54 13 38 36 67 74 80 63 12 41 27 96 61 66 05 60 69 96 15 56 82 57 31
83 26 24 78 42 76 49 56 06 57 78 67 02 96 40 82 29 14 07 29 62 90 31
08 26 71 61 18 22 84 23 33 49 29 90 07 08 05 14 59

Using the experimental probability that an individual will be homozygous for allele a (light grey) or for allele b (dark grey), predict the number of individuals in a population of 100,000 who will be homozygous for either allele.

a. 2,800
b. 5,000
c. 5,400
d. 9,000

141. The intelligence quotients (IQs) of a randomly selected group of 300 people are normally distributed with a mean IQ of 100 and a standard deviation of 15. In a normal distribution, approximately 68% of values are within one standard deviation of the mean. About how many individuals from the selected group have IQs of at least 85?

a. 96
b. 200
c. 216
d. 252

142. How many different seven-digit telephone numbers can be created in which no digit repeats and in which zero cannot be the first digit?

a. 5,040
b. 35,280
c. 544,320
d. 3, 265,920

143. A teacher wishes to divide her class of twenty students into four groups, each of which will have three boys and two girls. How many possible groups can she form?

a. 248
b. 6,160
c. 73,920
d. 95,040

144. In how many distinguishable ways can a family of five be seated a circular table with five chairs if Tasha and Mac must be kept separated?

a. 6
b. 12
c. 24
d. 60

145. Which of these defines the recursive sequence $a_1 = -1, a_{n+1} = a_n + 2$ explicitly?

a. $a_n = 2n - 3$
b. $a_n = -n + 2$
c. $a_n = n - 2$
d. $a_n = -2n + 3$

146. What is the sum of the series 200 + 100 + 50 + 25 + ...?

a. 300
b. 400
c. 600
d. The sum is infinite.

147. For vector $\boldsymbol{v} = (4, 3)$ and vector $\boldsymbol{w} = (-3,4)$, find $2(\boldsymbol{v} + \boldsymbol{w})$.

a. $(2, 14)$
b. $(14, -2)$
c. $(1,7)$
d. $(7, -1)$

148. Simplify $\begin{bmatrix} 2 & 0 & -5 \end{bmatrix} \left(\begin{bmatrix} 4 \\ 2 \\ -1 \end{bmatrix} - \begin{bmatrix} 3 \\ 5 \\ -5 \end{bmatrix} \right)$.

a. [-18]
b. $\begin{bmatrix} 2 \\ 0 \\ -20 \end{bmatrix}$
c. $\begin{bmatrix} 2 & 0 & -20 \end{bmatrix}$
d. $\begin{bmatrix} 2 & 0 & -5 \\ -6 & 0 & 15 \\ 8 & 0 & -20 \end{bmatrix}$

149. Consider three sets, of which one contains the set of even integers, one contains the factors of twelve, and one contains elements 1, 2, 4, and 9. If each set is assigned the name A, B, or C, and $A \cap B \subseteq B \cap C$, which of these must be set C?

a. The set of even integers
b. The set of factors of 12
c. The set $\{1, 2, 4, 9\}$
d. The answer cannot be determined from the given information.

150. Last year, Jenny tutored students in math, in chemistry, and for the ACT. She tutored ten students in math, eight students in chemistry, and seven students for the ACT. She tutored five students in both math and chemistry, and she tutored four students both in chemistry and for the ACT, and five students both in math and for the ACT. She tutored three students in all three subjects. How many students did Jenny tutor last year?

a. 34
b. 25
c. 23
d. 14

Answers and Explanations

1. C: Because drawing a dodecagon and counting its diagonals is an arduous task, it is useful to employ a different problem-solving strategy. One such strategy is to draw polygons with fewer sides and look for a pattern in the number of the polygons' diagonals.

	3	0
	4	2
	5	5
	6	9
Heptagon	7	14
Octagon	8	20

A quadrilateral has two more diagonals than a triangle, a pentagon has three more diagonals than a quadrilateral, and a hexagon has four more diagonals than a pentagon. Continue this pattern to find that a dodecagon has 54 diagonals.

2. B: The problem does not give any information about the size of the bracelet or the spacing between any of the charms. Nevertheless, creating a simple illustration which shows the order of the charms will help when approaching this problem. For example, the circle below represents the bracelet, and the dotted line between A and B represents the clasp. On the right, the line shows the stretched out bracelet and possible positions of charms C, D, and E based on the parameters.

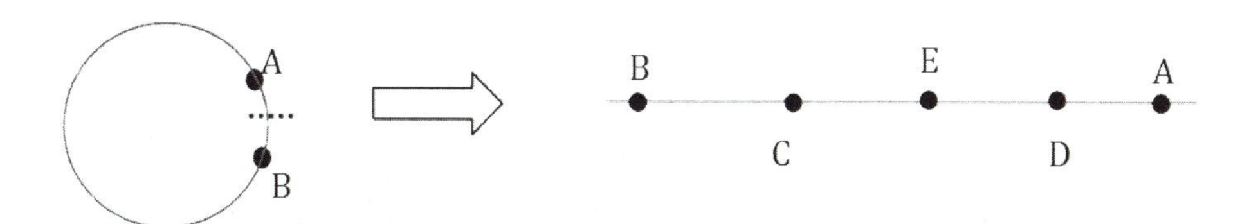

From the drawing above, it appears that statement I is true, but it is not necessarily so. The alternative drawing below also shows the charms ordered correctly, but the distance between B and E is now less than that between D and A.

Statement II must be true: charm E must lie between B and D. Statement III must also be true: the distance between charms E and D must be less than that between C and A, which includes charms E and D in the space between them.

3. B: The population is approximately 36,000, so one quarter of the population consists of about 9,000 individuals under age 35. A third of 9,000 is 3,000, the approximate number of students in grades K-12. Since there are thirteen grades, there are about 230 students in each grade. So, the number of fourth graders is between 200 and 300.

4. A: The final sales price of the rug is $1.08(0.7 \cdot \$296) = \$223.78$ at Store A, $1.08(\$220 - \$10) = \$226.80$ at Store B, and $\$198 + \$35 = \$233$ at Store C.

5. C: The expression representing the monthly charge for Company A is $\$25 + \$0.05m$, where m is the time in minutes spent talking on the phone. Set this expression equal to the monthly charge for Company B, which is $50. Solve for m to find the number of minutes for which the two companies charge the same amount:

$$\$25 + \$0.05m = \$50$$
$$\$0.05m = \$25$$
$$m = 500$$

Notice that the answer choices are given in hours, not in minutes. Since there are 60 minutes in an hour, $m = \frac{500}{60}$ hours = $8\frac{1}{3}$ hours. One-third of an hour is twenty minutes, so m = 8 hours, 20 minutes.

6. D: When the dress is marked down by 20%, the cost of the dress is 80% of its original price; thus, the reduced price of the dress can be written as $\frac{80}{100}x$, or $\frac{4}{5}x$, where x is the original price. When discounted an extra 25%, the dress costs 75% of the reduced price, or $\frac{75}{100}\left(\frac{4}{5}x\right)$, or $\frac{3}{4}\left(\frac{4}{5}x\right)$, which simplifies to $\frac{3}{5}x$. So the final price of the dress is three-fifths of the original price.

7. D: Since there are 100 cm in a meter, on a 1:100 scale drawing, each centimeter represents one meter. Therefore, an area of one square centimeter on the drawing represents one square meter in actuality. Since the area of the room in the scale drawing is 30 cm^2, the room's actual area is 30 m^2.

Another way to determine the area of the room is to write and solve an equation, such as this one:

$$\frac{l}{100} \cdot \frac{w}{100} = 30 \text{ cm}^2 \text{, where } l \text{ and } w \text{ are the dimensions of the actual room}$$
$$\frac{lw}{1000} = 30 \text{ cm}^2$$
$$lw = 300{,}000 \text{ cm}^2$$
$$\text{Area} = 300{,}000 \text{ cm}^2$$

Since this is not one of the answer choices, convert cm^2 to m^2: $300{,}000 \text{ cm}^2 \cdot \frac{1 \text{ m}}{100 \text{ cm}} \cdot \frac{1 \text{ m}}{100 \text{ cm}} = 30 \text{ m}^2$.

8. C: Since the ratio of wages and benefits to other costs is 2:3, the amount of money spent on wages and benefits is $\frac{2}{5}$ of the business's total expenditure. $\frac{2}{5} \cdot \$130{,}000 = \$52{,}000$.

9. A: The height of the ball is a function of time, so the equation can be expressed as $f(t) = -16t^2 + 64t + 5$, and the average rate of change can be found by calculating $\frac{f(3)-f(1)}{3-1}$.

$$\frac{-16(3)^2 + 64(3) + 5 - [-16(1)^2 + 64(1) + 5]}{2} = \frac{-144 + 192 + 5 - (-16 + 64 + 5)}{2} = \frac{0}{2} = 0$$

Alternatively, the rate of change can be determined by finding the slope of the secant line through points $(1, f(1))$ and $(3, f(3))$. Notice that this is a horizontal line, which has a slope of 0.

Height (ft)

Time (sec)

10. B: Since rate in mph $= \frac{\text{distance in miles}}{\text{time in hours}}$, Zeke's driving speed on the way to Atlanta and home from Atlanta in mph can be expressed as d/3 and d/2, respectively, when d=distance between Zeke's house and his destination . Since Zeke drove 20 mph faster on his way home, $\frac{d}{2} - \frac{d}{3} = 20$.

$$6\left(\frac{d}{2} - \frac{d}{3} = 20\right)$$
$$3d - 2d = 120$$
$$d = 120$$

Since the distance between Zeke's house and the store in Atlanta is 120 miles, Zeke drove a total distance of 240 miles in five hours. Therefore, his average speed was $\frac{240 \text{ miles}}{5 \text{ hours}} = 48 \text{ mph}$.

11. C: Aaron ran four miles from home and then back again, so he ran a total of eight miles. Therefore, statement III is false. Statements I and II, however, are both true. Since Aaron ran eight miles in eighty minutes, he ran an average of one mile every ten minutes, or six miles per hour; he ran two miles from point A to B in 20 minutes and four miles from D to E in 40 minutes, so his running speed between both sets of points was the same.

12. D: First, use the table to determine the values of $(a * b)$ and $(c * d)$.

$*$	a	b	c	d
a	d	a	b	c
b	a	b	c	d
c	b	c	d	a
d	c	d	a	b

$(a * b) = a$ and $(c * d) = a$, so $(a * b) * (c * d) = a * a$, which is equal to d.

13. B: When $y = x^3, x = \sqrt[3]{y}$. Similarly, when $y = e^x, x = \ln y$ for $y > 0$. On the other hand, when $y = x + a, x = y - a$; when $y = 1/x, x = 1/y$ for $x, y \neq 0$; and when $y = \sin x, x = \sin^{-1} y$.

14. B: Deductive reasoning moves from one or more general statements to a specific, while inductive reasoning makes a general conclusion based on a series of specific instances or observations. Whenever the premises used in deductive reasoning are true, the conclusion drawn is necessarily true. In inductive reasoning, it is possible for the premises to be true and the conclusion to be false since there may exist an exception to the general conclusion drawn from the observations made.

15. A: The first argument's reasoning is valid, and since its premises are true, the argument is also sound. The second argument's reasoning is invalid; that the premises are true is irrelevant. (For example, consider the true premises "all cats are mammals" and "all dogs are mammals;" it cannot be logically concluded that all dogs are cats.) The third argument's reasoning is valid, but since one of its premises is false, the argument is not sound.

16. C: The logical representation $p \rightarrow q$ means that p implies q. In other words, if p, then q. Unlike the contrapositive (Choice C), neither the converse (choice A) nor the inverse (choice B) is necessarily true. For example, consider this statement: all cats are mammals. This can be written as an if/then statement: if an animal is a cat, then the animal is a mammal. The converse would read, "If an animal is a mammal, then the animal is a cat;" of course, this is not necessarily true since there are many mammals other than cats. The inverse statement, "If an animal is not a cat, then the animal is not a mammal," is false. The contrapositive, "If an animal is not a mammal, then the animal is not a cat" is true since there are no cats which are not mammals.

17. D: The symbol $\wedge$ is the logical conjunction symbol. In order for statement $(p \wedge q)$ to be true, both statements p and q must be true. The $\sim$ symbol means "not," so if $(p \wedge q)$ is true, then $\sim(p \wedge q)$ is false, and if $(p \wedge q)$ is false, then $\sim(p \wedge q)$ is true. The statement $q \leftrightarrow \sim(p \wedge q)$ is true when the value of q is the same as the value of $\sim(p \wedge q)$.

p	q	$(p \wedge q)$	$\sim(p \wedge q)$	$q \leftrightarrow \sim(p \wedge q)$
T	T	T	F	F
T	F	F	T	F
F	T	F	T	T
F	F	F	T	F

18. D: The value "0" means "false," and the value "1" means "true." For the logical disjunction "or," the output value is true if either or both input values are true, else it is false. For the logical conjunction "and," the output value is true only if both input values are true. "Not *A*" is true when *A* is false and is false when *A* is true.

X	Y	Z	not Y	not Z	not Y or not Z	X and (not Y or not Z)
0	0	0	1	1	1	0
0	0	1	1	0	1	0
0	1	0	0	1	1	0
0	1	1	0	0	0	0
1	0	0	1	1	1	1
1	0	1	1	0	1	1
1	1	0	0	1	1	1
1	1	1	0	0	0	0

19. A: The Babylonians used a base-60 numeral system, which is still used in the division of an hour into 60 minutes, a minute into 60 seconds, and a circle into 360 degrees. (The word "algebra" and its development as a discipline separate from geometry are attributed to the Arabic/Islamic civilization. The Greek philosopher Thales is credited with using deductive reasoning to prove geometric concepts. Boolean logic and algebra was introduced by British mathematician George Boole.)

20. C: Leonhard Euler made many important contributions to the field of mathematics. One such contribution, Euler's formula $e^{i\varphi} = \cos\varphi + i\sin\varphi = 0$, can be written as $e^{i\pi} + 1 = 0$ when $\varphi = \pi$. This identity is considered both mathematically remarkable and beautiful, as it links together five important mathematical constants, $e, i, \pi, 0$ and 1.

21. B: The notation $\mathbb{P} \subseteq \mathbb{N} \subseteq \mathbb{Z} \subseteq \mathbb{Q} \subseteq \mathbb{R} \subseteq \mathbb{C}$ means that the set of prime numbers is a subset of the set natural numbers, which is a subset of the set of integers, which is a subset of the set of rational numbers, which is a subset of the set real numbers, which is a subset of the set of complex numbers.

22. A: The set of whole numbers, $\{0, 1, 2, 3, \ldots\}$, does not contain the number -4. Since -4 is an integer, it is also a rational number and a real number.

23. D: In order for a set to be a group under operation $*$,

1. The set must be closed under that operation. In other words, when the operation is performed on any two members of the set, the result must also be a member of that set.
2. The set must demonstrate associativity under the operation: $a * (b * c) = (a * b) * c$
3. There must exist an identity element e in the group: $a * e = e * a = a$
4. For every element in the group, there must exist an inverse element in the group: $a * b = b * a = e$

Note: the group need not be commutative for every pair of elements in the group. If the group demonstrates commutativity, it is called an abelian group.

The set of prime numbers under addition is not closed. For example, 3+5=8, and 8 is not a member of the set of prime numbers. Similarly, the set of negative integers under multiplication is not closed since the product of two negative integers is a positive integer. Though the set of negative integers under addition is closed and is associative, there exists no identity element (the number zero in this case) in the group. The set of positive rational numbers under multiplication is closed and associative; the multiplicative identity 1 is a member of the group, and for each element in the group, there is a multiplicative inverse (reciprocal).

24. A: First, multiply the numerator and denominator by the denominator's conjugate, $4 + 2i$. Then, simplify the result and write the answer in the form $a + bi$.

$$\frac{2+3i}{4-2i} \cdot \frac{4+2i}{4+2i} = \frac{8+4i+12i+6i^2}{16-4i^2} = \frac{8+16i-6}{16+4} = \frac{2+16i}{20} = \frac{1}{10} + \frac{4}{5}i$$

25. D: First, simplify the expression within the absolute value symbol.

$$|(2-3i)^2-(1-4i)|$$
$$|4-12i+9i^2-1+4i|$$
$$|4-12i-9-1+4i|$$
$$|-6-8i|$$

The absolute value of a complex number is its distance from 0 on the complex plane. Use the Pythagorean Theorem (or the 3-4-5 Pythagorean triple and similarity) to find the distance of $-6-8i$ from the origin.

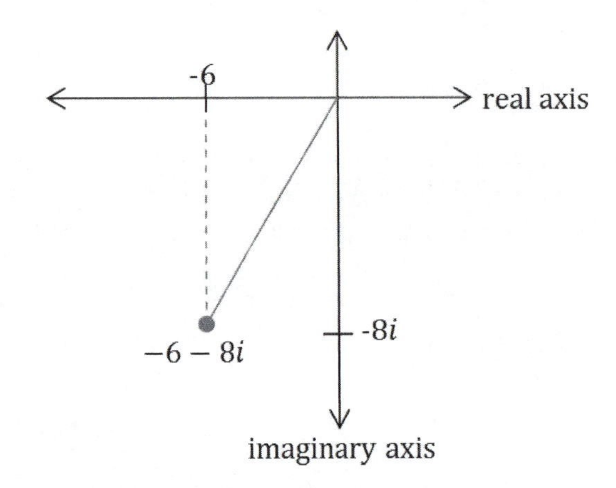

Since the distance from the origin to the point $-6-8i$ is 10, $|-6-8i|=10$.

26. B: In order for a set to be a group under operation $*$,

1. The set must be closed under that operation. In other words, when the operation is performed on any two members of the set, the result must also be a member of that set.
2. The set must demonstrate associativity under the operation: $a*(b*c)=(a*b)*c$
3. There must exist an identity element e in the group: $a*e=e*a=a$
4. For every element in the group, there must exist an inverse element in the group: $a*b=b*a=e$

Choice A can easily be eliminated as the correct answer because the set $\{-i,0,i\}$ does not contain the multiplicative identity 1. Though choices C and D contain the element 1, neither is closed: for example, since $i\cdot i=-1$, -1 must be an element of the group. Choice B is closed, contains the multiplicative identity 1, and the inverse of each element is included in the set as well. Of course, multiplication is an associative operation, so the set $\{-1,1,i,-i\}$ forms a group under multiplication

×	-1	1	i	$-i$
-1	1	-1	$-i$	i
1	-1	1	i	$-i$
i	$-i$	i	-1	1
$-i$	i	$-i$	1	-1

27. D: The identity element is d since $d\#a=a\#d=a, d\#b=b\#d=b, d\#c=c\#d=c$, and $d\#d=d$. The inverse of element c is c since $c\#c=d$, the identity element. The operation # is commutative because $a\#b=b\#a, a\#c=c\#a$, etc. Rather than check that the operation is

commutative for each pair of elements, note that elements in the table display symmetry about the diagonal elements; this indicates that the operation is indeed commutative.

#	a	b	c	d
a	c	d	b	a
b	d	c	a	b
c	b	a	d	c
d	a	b	c	d

28. C: "The square of twice the sum of x and three is equal to the product of twenty-four and x" is represented by the equation $[2(x+3)]^2 = 24x$. Solve for x.

$$[2(x+3)]^2 = 24x$$
$$[2x+6]^2 = 24x$$
$$4x^2 + 24x + 36 = 24x$$
$$4x^2 = -36$$
$$x^2 = -9$$
$$x = \pm\sqrt{-9}$$
$$x = \pm 3i$$

So, $-3i$ is a possible value of x.

29. C: If x is a prime number and that the greatest common factor of x and y is greater than 1, the greatest common factor of x and y must be x. The least common multiple of two numbers is equal to the product of those numbers divided by their greatest common factor. So, the least common multiple of x and y is $\frac{xy}{x} = y$. Therefore, the values in the two columns are the same.

30. D: Since a and b are even integers, each can be expressed as the product of 2 and an integer. So, if we write $a = 2x$ and $b = 2y$, $3(2x)^2 + 9(2y)^3 = c$.

$$3(4x^2) + 9(8y^3) = c$$
$$12x^2 + 72y^3 = c$$
$$12(x^2 + 6y^3) = c$$

Since c is the product of 12 and some other integer, 12 must be a factor of c. Incidentally, the numbers 2, 3, and 6 must also be factors of c since each is also a factor of 12.

31. C: Choice C is the equation for the greatest integer function. A function is a relationship in which for every element of the domain (x), there is exactly one element of the range (y). Graphically, a relationship between x and y can be identified as a function if the graph passes the vertical line test.

The first relation is a parabola on its side, which fails the vertical line test for functions. A circle (Choice B) also fails the vertical line test and is therefore not a function. The relation in Choice D pairs two elements of the range with one of the elements of the domain, so it is also not a function.

32. B: The area of a triangle is $A = \frac{1}{2}bh$, where b and h are the lengths of the triangle's base and height, respectively. The base of the given triangle is x, but the height is not given. Since the triangle

is a right triangle and the hypotenuse is given, the triangle's height can be found using the Pythagorean Theorem.

$$x^2 + h^2 = 6^2$$
$$h = \sqrt{36 - x^2}$$

To find the area of the triangle in terms of x, substitute $\sqrt{36 - x^2}$ for the height and x for the base of the triangle into the area formula.

$$A = \frac{1}{2}bh$$
$$A(x) = \frac{1}{2}(x)(\sqrt{36 - x^2})$$
$$A(x) = \frac{x\sqrt{36 - x^2}}{2}$$

33. A: $[g \circ f\,]x = g(f(x)) = g(2x + 4) = (2x + 4)^2 - 3(2x + 4) + 2 = 4x^2 + 16x + 16 - 6x - 12 + 2 = 4x^2 + 10x + 6$.

34. C: One way to approach the problem is to use the table of values to first write equations for $f(x)$ and $g(x)$: $f(x) = 2x^2$ and $g(x) = 2x + 5$. Then, use those equations to find $f(g(-4))$.

$$g(-4) = 2(-4) + 5 = -3$$
$$f(-3) = 2(-3)^2 = 18$$

So, $f(g(-4)) = 18$.

35. D: By definition, when $f(x)$ and $g(x)$ are inverse functions, $f(g(x)) = g(f(x)) = x$. So, $f(g(4)) = 4$.

36. B: To find the inverse of an equation, solve for x in terms of y; then, exchange the variables x and y. Or, to determine if two functions $f(x)$ and $g(x)$ are inverses, find $f(g(x))$ and $g(f(x))$; if both results are x, then $f(x)$ and $g(x)$ are inverse functions.

For example, to find the inverse of $y = x + 6$, rewrite the equation $x = y + 6$ and solve for y. Since $y = x - 6$, the two given equations given in Choice A are inverses. Likewise, to find the inverse of $y = \frac{2x+3}{x-1}$, rewrite the equation as $x = \frac{2y+3}{y-1}$ and solve for y:

$$xy - x = 2y + 3$$
$$xy - 2y = x + 3$$
$$y(x - 2) = x + 3$$
$$y = \frac{x + 3}{x - 2}$$

The two equations given in Choice C are inverses.

Here, the second method is used to determine if the two equations given in Choices B and D are inverses:

Choice B: $y = 2(2x + 3) - 3 = 4x + 6$. The two given equations are **NOT** inverses. Choice D: $y = \frac{(2x+1)-1}{2} = \frac{2x}{2} = x$ and $y = 2\left(\frac{x-1}{2}\right) + 1 = x - 1 + 1 = x$, so the two given equations are inverses.

37. A: Below is the graph of $g(x)$.

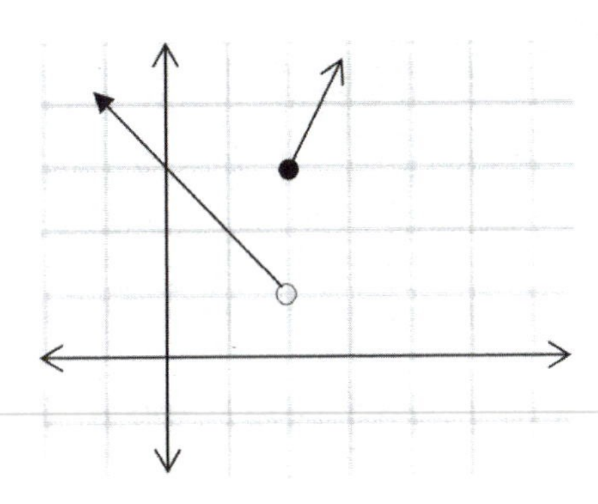

Statement II is true: the graph is indeed discontinuous at $x = 2$. Since $g(3) = 2(3) - 1 = 5$, Statement I is false, and since the range is $y > 1$, Statement III is also false.

38. A: In the range $(-\infty, -1)$, the graph represented is $y = x^2$. In the range $[-1,2)$, the graph is the greatest integer function, $y = [\![x]\!]$. In the range $[-2, \infty)$, the graph is $y = -2x + 6$.

39. B: If $y = a(x + b)(x + c)^2$, the degree of the polynomial is 3. Since the degree of the polynomial is odd and the leading coefficient is positive $(a > 0)$, the end behavior of the graph is below.

$$\swarrow \; \nearrow$$

Therefore, neither Choice A nor Choice C can be a graph of $y = a(x + b)(x + c)^2$. The maximum number of "bumps" (or critical points) in the graph is at most one less than the degree of the polynomial, so Choice D, which has three bumps, cannot be the graph of the function. Choice B displays the correct end behavior and has two bumps, so it is a possible graph of $y = a(x + b)(x + c)^2$.

40. B: $5n + 3s \geq 300$ when $n =$ number of non-student tickets which must be sold and $s =$ number of student tickets which must be sold. The intercepts of this linear inequality are $n = 60$ and $s = 100$. The solid line through the two intercepts represents the minimum number of each type of ticket which must be sold in order to offset production costs. All points above the line represent sales which result in a profit for the school.

41. D: The vertex form of a quadratic equation is $y = a(x - h)^2 + k$, where $x = h$ is the parabola's axis of symmetry and (h, k) is the parabola's vertex. The vertex of the graph is (-1,3), so the equation can be written as $y = a(x + 1)^2 + 3$. The parabola passes through point (1,1), so $1 = a(1 + 1)^2 + 3$. Solve for a:

$$1 = a(1 + 1)^2 + 3$$
$$1 = a(2)^2 + 3$$
$$1 = 4a + 3$$
$$-2 = 4a$$
$$-\frac{1}{2} = a$$

So, the vertex form of the parabola is $y = -\frac{1}{2}(x+1)^2 + 3$. Write the equation in the form $y = ax^2 + bx + c$.

$$y = -\frac{1}{2}(x+1)^2 + 3$$
$$y = -\frac{1}{2}(x^2 + 2x + 1) + 3$$
$$y = -\frac{1}{2}x^2 - x - \frac{1}{2} + 3$$
$$y = -\frac{1}{2}x^2 - x + \frac{5}{2}$$

42. D: There are many ways to solve quadratic equations in the form $ax^2 + bx + c = 0$; however, some methods, such as graphing and factoring, may not be useful for some equations, such as those with irrational or complex roots. Solve this equation by completing the square or by using the Quadratic Formula, $x = \frac{-b \pm \sqrt{b^2 - 4ac}}{2a}$.

$$7x^2 + 6x + 2 = 0; a = 7, b = 6, c = 2$$

$$x = \frac{-b \pm \sqrt{b^2 - 4ac}}{2a}$$
$$x = \frac{-6 \pm \sqrt{6^2 - 4(7)(2)}}{2(7)}$$
$$x = \frac{-6 \pm \sqrt{36 - 56}}{14}$$
$$x = \frac{-6 \pm \sqrt{-20}}{14}$$
$$x = \frac{-6 \pm 2i\sqrt{5}}{14}$$
$$x = \frac{-3 \pm i\sqrt{5}}{7}$$

43. C: A system of linear equations can be solved by using matrices or by using the graphing, substitution, or elimination (also called linear combination) method. The elimination method is shown here:

$$3x + 4y = 2$$
$$2x + 6y = -2$$

In order to eliminate x by linear combination, multiply the top equation by 2 and the bottom equation by –3 so that the coefficients of the x-terms will be additive inverses.

$$2(3x + 4y = 2)$$
$$-3(2x + 6y = -2)$$

Then, add the two equations and solve for y.

$$6x + 8y = 4$$
$$\underline{-6x - 18y = 6}$$
$$-10y = 10$$
$$y = -1$$

Substitute -1 for y in either of the given equations and solve for x.

$$3x + 4(-1) = 2$$
$$3x - 4 = 2$$
$$3x = 6$$
$$x = 2$$

The solution to the system of equations is $(2, -1)$.

44. C: The graph below shows that the lines are parallel and that the shaded regions do not overlap. There is no solution to the set of inequalities given in Choice C.

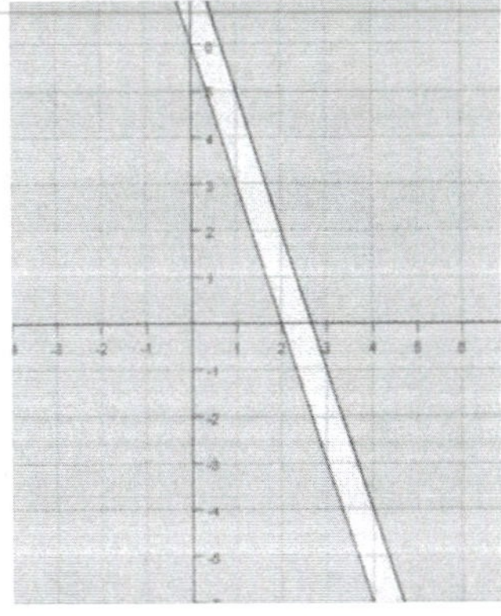

$6x + 2y \leq 12$
$2y \leq -6x + 12$
$y \leq -3x + 6$

$3x \geq 8 - y$
$y \geq -3x + 8$

As in Choice C, the two lines given in Choice A are parallel; however, the shading overlaps between the lines, so that region represents the solution to the system of inequalities.

The shaded regions for the two lines in Choice B do not overlap except at the boundary, but since the boundary is same, the solution to the system of inequalities is the line $y = -2x + 6$.

Choice D contains a set of inequalities which have intersecting shaded regions; the intersection represents the solution to the system of inequalities.

45. A: First, write three equations from the information given in the problem. Since the total number of tickets sold was 810, $\boldsymbol{x + y + z = 810}$. The ticket sales generated \$14,500, so $\boldsymbol{15x + 25y + 20z = 14,500}$. The number of children under ten was the same as twice the number of adults and seniors, so $x = 2(y + z)$, which can be rewritten as $\boldsymbol{x - 2y - 2z = 0}$.

The coefficients of each equation are arranged in the rows of a 3x3 matrix, which, when multiplied by the 3x1 matrix arranging the variables x, y, and z, will give the 3x1 matrix which arranges the constants of the equations.

46. B: There are many ways to solve this system of equations. One is shown below.

1. Multiply the second equation by 2 and combine it with the first equation to eliminate the variable y.
   $$\begin{array}{l} 2x - 4y + z = 10 \\ \underline{-6x + 4y - 8z = -14} \\ -4x \qquad - 7z = -4 \end{array}$$
2. Multiply the third equation by -2 and combine it with the original second equation to eliminate y.
   $$\begin{array}{l} -3x + 2y - 4z = -7 \\ \underline{-2x - 2y + 6z = 2} \\ -5x \qquad + 2z = -5 \end{array}$$
3. Multiply the equation from step one by 5 and the equation from step two by -4 and combine to eliminate x.
   $$\begin{array}{l} -20x - 35z = -20 \\ \underline{20x - 8z = 20} \\ -43z = 0 \\ z = 0 \end{array}$$
4. Substitute 0 for z in the equation from step 2 to find x.
   $$\begin{array}{l} -5x + 2(0) = -5 \\ -5x = -5 \\ x = 1 \end{array}$$
5. Substitute 0 for z and 1 for x into the first original equation to find y.
   $$\begin{array}{l} 2(1) - 4y + (0) = 10 \\ 2 - 4y = 10 \\ -4y = 8 \\ y = -2 \end{array}$$

47. B: One way to solve the equation is to write $x^4 + 64 = 20x^2$ in the quadratic form $(x^2)^2 - 20(x^2) + 64 = 0$. This trinomial can be factored as $(x^2 - 4)(x^2 - 16) = 0$. In each set of parentheses is a difference of squares, which can be factored further: $(x + 2)(x - 2)(x + 4)(x - 4) = 0$. Use the zero product propery to find the solutions to the equation.

$$\begin{array}{cccc} x + 2 = 0 & x - 2 = 0 & x + 4 = 0 & x - 4 = 0 \\ x = -2 & x = 2 & x = -4 & x = 4 \end{array}$$

48. A: First, set the equation equal to zero.

$$3x^3y^2 - 45x^2y = 15x^3y - 9x^2y^2$$
$$3x^3y^2 - 15x^3y + 9x^2y^2 - 45x^2y = 0$$

Then, factor the equation.

$$3x^2y(xy - 5x + 3y - 15) = 0$$
$$3x^2y[x(y - 5) + 3(y - 5)] = 0$$
$$3x^2y[(y - 5)(x + 3)] = 0$$

Use the zero product property to find the solutions.

$$\begin{array}{ccc} 3x^2y = 0 & y - 5 = 0 & x + 3 = 0 \\ x = 0 & y = 5 & x = -3 \\ y = 0 & & \end{array}$$

So, the solutions are $x = \{0, -3\}$ and $y = \{0,5\}$.

49. D: The degree of $f(x)$ is 1, the degree of $g(x)$ is 2, and the degree of $h(x)$ is 3. The leading coefficient for each function is 2. Functions $f(x)$ and $h(x)$ have exactly one real zero ($x = 1$), while $g(x)$ has two real zeros ($x = \pm 1$):

$f(x)$	$g(x)$	$h(x)$
$0 = 2x - 2$	$0 = 2x^2 - 2$	$0 = 2x^3 - 2$
$-2x = -2$	$-2x^2 = -2$	$-2x^3 = -2$
$x = 1$	$x^2 = 1$	$x^3 = 1$
	$x = 1;\ x = -1$	$x = 1$

50. B: The path of a bullet is a parabola, which is the graph of a quadratic function. The path of a sound wave can be modeled by a sine or cosine function. The distance an object travels over time given a constant rate is a linear relationship, while radioactive decay is modeled by an exponential function.

51. B: First, use the properties of logarithms to rewrite $2\log_4 y + \log_4 16 = 3$.

- Since $N\log_a M = \log_a M^N$, $2\log_4 y = \log_4 y^2$. Replacing $2\log_4 y$ by its equivalent in the given equation gives $\log_4 y^2 + \log_4 16 = 3$.
- Since $\log_a M + \log_a N = \log_a MN$, $\log_4 y^2 + \log_4 16 = \log_4 16y^2$. Thus, $\log_4 16y^2 = 3$.
- Since $\log_a M = N$ is equivalent to $a^N = M$, $\log_4 16y^2 = 3$ is equivalent to $4^3 = 16y^2$.

Then, solve for y. (Note that y must be greater than zero.)

$$4^3 = 16y^2$$
$$64 = 16y^2$$
$$4 = y^2$$
$$2 = y$$

Finally, substitute 2 for y in the expression $\log_y 256$ and simplify: $\log_2 256 = 8$ since $2^8 = 256$.

52. B: First, apply the laws of exponents to simplify the expression on the left.

$$\frac{(x^2y)(2xy^{-2})^3}{16x^5y^2} + \frac{3}{xy}$$

$$\frac{(x^2y)(8x^3y^{-6})}{16x^5y^2} + \frac{3}{xy}$$

$$\frac{8x^5y^{-5}}{16x^5y^2} + \frac{3}{xy}$$

$$\frac{1}{2y^7} + \frac{3}{xy}$$

Then, add the two fractions.

$$\frac{1}{2y^7} \cdot \frac{x}{x} + \frac{3}{xy} \cdot \frac{2y^6}{2y^6}$$

$$\frac{x}{2xy^7} + \frac{6y^6}{2xy^7}$$

$$\frac{x + 6y^6}{2xy^7}$$

53. C: If $f(x) = 10^x$ and $f(x) = 5$, then $5 = 10^x$. Since $\log_{10}x$ is the inverse of 10^x, $\log_{10}5 = \log_{10}(10^x) = x$. Therefore, $0.7 \approx x$.

54. C: The graph shown is the exponential function $y = 2^x$. Notice that the graph passes through (-2, 0.25), (0,1), (2,4).

	Choice A	Choice B	Choice C	Choice D
x	x^2	$\sqrt{x}$	2^x	$\log_2 x$
-2	4	undefined in $\mathbb{R}$	0.25	undefined
0	0	0	1	undefined
2	4	$\sqrt{2}$	4	1

55. C: The x-intercept is the point at which $f(x) = 0$. When $0 = \log_b x$, $b^0 = x$; since $b^0 = 1$, the x-intercept of $f(x) = \log_b x$ is always 1. If $f(x) = \log_b x$ and $x = b$, then $f(x) = \log_b b$, which is, by definition, 1. ($b^1 = b$.) If $g(x) = b^x$, then $f(x)$ and g(x) are inverse functions and are therefore symmetric with respect to $y = x$. The statement choice C is not necessarily true since $x < 1$ includes numbers less than or equal to zero, the values for which the function is undefined. The statement $f(x) < 0$ is true only for x values between 0 and 1 ($0 < x < 1$).

56. D: Bacterial growth is exponential. Let x be the number of doubling times and a be the number of bacteria in the colony originally transferred into the broth and y be the number of bacteria in the broth after a doubling times.

Time	Number of doubling times (x)	$a(2^x)$	Number of bacteria (y)
0	0	$a(2^0) = a$	1×10^6
20 minutes	1	$a(2^1)$	2×10^6
40 minutes	2	$a(2^2)$	4×10^6
60 minutes	3	$a(2^3)$	8×10^6

Determine how many bacteria were present in the original colony. Either work backwards by halving the number of bacteria (see gray arrows above) or calculate a:

$$a(2^3) = 8 \times 10^6$$
$$8a = 8 \times 10^6$$
$$a = 10^6$$

The equation for determining the number of bacteria is $y = (2^x) \cdot 10^6$. Since the bacteria double every twenty minutes, they go through three doubling times every hour. So, when the bacteria are allowed to grow for eight hours, they will have gone through 24 doubling times. When $x = 24$, $y = (2^{24}) \cdot 10^6 = 16777216 \times 10^6$, which is approximately 1.7×10^{13}.

57. C: Since the pH scale is a base–10 logarithmic scale, a difference in pH of 1 indicates a ratio between strengths of 10. So, an acid with a pH of 3 is 100 times stronger than an acid with a pH of 5.

58. A:

$$\sqrt{\frac{-28x^6}{27y^5}} = \frac{2x^3 i\sqrt{7}}{3y^2\sqrt{3y}} \cdot \frac{\sqrt{3y}}{\sqrt{3y}} = \frac{2x^3 i\sqrt{21y}}{9y^2}$$

59. C:

$-4 \le 2 + 3(x-1) \le 2$ $-6 \le 3(x-1) \le 0$ $-2 \le x - 1 \le 0$ $-1 \le x \le 1$	$-2x^2 + 2 \ge x^2 - 1$ $-3x^2 \ge -3$ $x^2 \le 1$ $-1 \le x \le 1$	$\frac{11 - \lvert 3x \rvert}{7} \ge 2$ $11 - \lvert 3x \rvert \ge 14$ $-\lvert 3x \rvert \ge 3$ $\lvert 3x \rvert \le -1$ No solution	$3\lvert 2x \rvert + 4 \le 10$ $3\lvert 2x \rvert \le 6$ $\lvert 2x \rvert \le 2$ $-2 \le 2x \le 2$ $-1 \le x \le 1$

60. D: When solving radical equations, check for extraneous solutions.

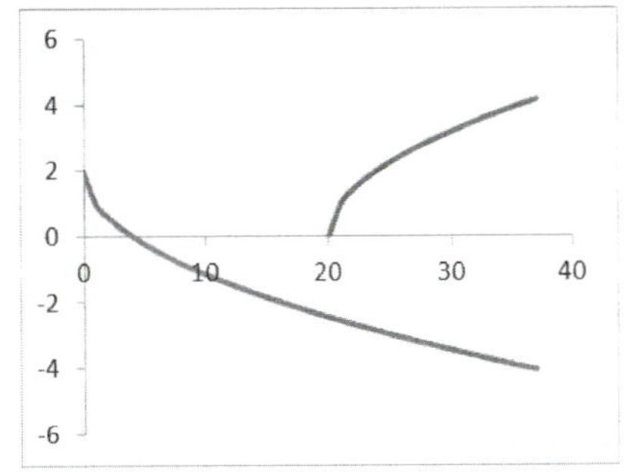

$2 - \sqrt{x} = \sqrt{x - 20}$
$(2 - \sqrt{x})^2 = (\sqrt{x - 20})^2$
$4 - 4\sqrt{x} + x = x - 20$
$-4\sqrt{x} = -24$
$\sqrt{x} = 6$
$\sqrt{x}^2 = 6^2$
$x = 36$

$2 - \sqrt{36} = \sqrt{36 - 20}$
$2 - 6 = \sqrt{16}$
$-4 \ne 4$

Since the solution does not check, there is no solution. Notice that the graphs $y = 2 - \sqrt{x}$ and $y = \sqrt{x - 20}$ do not intersect, which confirms there is no solution.

61. B: Notice that choice C cannot be correct since $x \neq 1$. ($x = 1$ results in a zero in the denominator.)

$$\frac{x-2}{x-1} = \frac{x-1}{x+1} + \frac{2}{x-1}$$
$$(x-1)(x+1)\left(\frac{x-2}{x-1} = \frac{x-1}{x+1} + \frac{2}{x-1}\right)$$
$$(x+1)(x-2) = (x-1)^2 + 2(x+1)$$
$$x^2 - x - 2 = x^2 - 2x + 1 + 2x + 2$$
$$x^2 - x - 2 = x^2 + 3$$
$$-x = 5$$
$$x = -5$$

62. A: The denominator of a fraction cannot equal zero. Therefore, for choices A and B,.

$$x^2 - x - 2 \neq 0$$
$$(x+1)(x-2) \neq 0$$
$$x + 1 \neq 0 \quad x - 2 \neq 0$$
$$x \neq -1 \quad x \neq 2.$$

Since choice A is in its simplest form, there are vertical asymptotes at $x = -1$ and $x = 2$. However, for choice B,

$$\frac{3x+3}{x^2-x-2} = \frac{3(x+1)}{(x+1)(x-2)} = \frac{3}{x-2}.$$

So, at $x = -2$ there is an asymptote, while at $x = -1$, there is simply a hole in the graph. So, choice B does not match the given graph. For choice C, there are asymptotes at $x = -1$ and $x = 2$; however, notice that it is possible for the graph of choice C to intersect the x-axis since it is possible that $y = 0$ (when $x = 0.5$). Since the given graph does not have an x-intercept, choice C is incorrect. For choice A, it is not possible that y=0, so it is a possible answer. Check a few points on the graph to make sure they satisfy the equation.

x	y
-2	$\frac{3}{4}$
0	$-\frac{3}{2}$
$\frac{1}{2}$	$-\frac{4}{3}$
1	$-\frac{3}{2}$
3	$\frac{3}{4}$

The points $\left(-2, \frac{3}{4}\right), \left(0, -\frac{3}{2}\right), \left(\frac{1}{2}, -\frac{4}{3}\right), \left(1, -\frac{3}{2}\right)$, and $(3, \frac{3}{4})$ are indeed points on the graph.

63. A: An easy way to determine which is the graph of $f(x) = -2|-x + 4| - 1$ is to find $f(x)$ for a few values of x. For example, $f(x) = -2|0 + 4| - 1 = -9$. Graphs A and B pass through (0, -9), but graphs C and D do not. $f(4) = -2|-4 + 4| - 1 = -1$. Graphs A and D pass through (4, -1), but graphs B and C do not. Graph A is the correct graph. $f(x) = -2|-x + 4| - 1$ shifts the graph of $y = |x|$ to the left four units, reflects it across the y-axis, inverts it, makes it narrower, and shifts it down one unit.

64. C: The first function shifts the graph of $y = \frac{1}{x}$ to the right one unit and up one unit. The domain and range of $y = \frac{1}{x}$ are $\{x: x \neq 0\}$ and $\{y: y \neq 0\}$, so the domain and range of $y = \frac{1}{x-1} + 1$ are $\{x: x \neq 1\}$ and $\{y: y \neq 1\}$. The element 1 is not in its domain.

The second function inverts the graph of $y = \sqrt{x}$ and shifts it to the left two units and down one unit. The domain and range of $y = \sqrt{x}$ are $\{x: x \geq 0\}$ and $\{y: y \geq 0\}$, so the domain and range of $y = -\sqrt{x+2} - 1$ are $\{x: x \geq -2\}$ and $\{y: y \leq -1\}$. The range does not contain the element 2.

The third function shifts the graph of $y = |x|$ to the left two units and down three units. The domain of $y = |x|$ the set of all real numbers and range is $\{y: y \geq 0\}$, so the domain of $y = |x+2| - 3$ is the set of all real numbers and the range is $\{y: y \geq -3\}$. The domain contains the element 1 and the range contains the element 2.

This is the graph of the fourth function. The domain of this piece-wise function is the set of all real numbers, and the range is $\{y: y \leq -1\}$. The range does not contain the element 2.

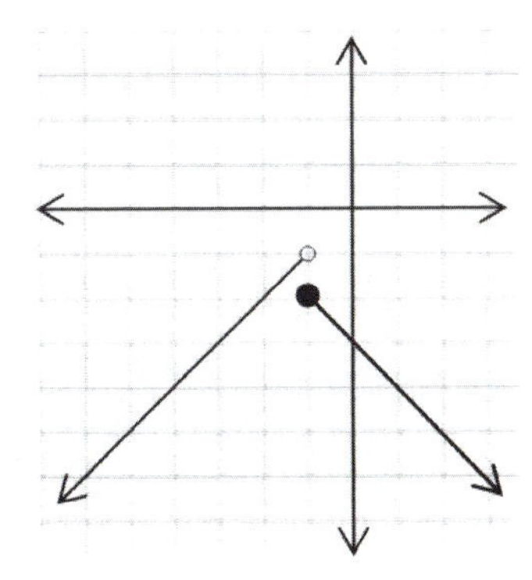

65. B: First, state the exclusions of the domain.

$$x^3 + 2x^2 - x - 2 \neq 0$$
$$(x+2)(x-1)(x+1) \neq 0$$
$$x + 2 \neq 0 \quad x - 1 \neq 0 \quad x + 1 \neq 0$$
$$x \neq -2 \quad x \neq 1 \quad x \neq -1$$

To determine whether there are asymptotes or holes at these values of x, simplify the expression $\frac{x^2-x-6}{x^3+2x^2-x-2}$.

$$\frac{(x-3)(x+2)}{(x+2)(x-1)(x+1)} = \frac{x-3}{(x-1)(x+1)}$$

There are asymptotes at $x = 1$ and at $x = -1$ and a hole at $x = 2$. Statement I is false.

To find the x-intercept of $f(x)$, solve $f(x) = 0$. $f(x) = 0$ when the numerator is equal to zero. The numerator equals zero when $x = 2$ and $x = 3$; however, 2 is excluded from the domain of $f(x)$, so the x-intercept is 3. To find the y-intercept of $f(x)$, find $f(0)$. $\frac{0^2-0-6}{0^3+2(0)^2-0-2} = \frac{-6}{-2} = 3$. The y-intercept is 3. Statement II is true.

66. C: The period of the pendulum is a function of the square root of the length of its string, and is independent of the mass of the pendulum or the angle from which it is released. If the period of

Pendulum 2's swing is four times the period of Pendulum 1's swing, then the length of Pendulum 1's string must be 16 times the length of Pendulum 2's swing since all other values besides L in the expression $2\pi\sqrt{\frac{L}{g}}$ remain the same.

67. D: There are many ways Josephine may have applied her knowledge to determine how to approximately measure her medicine using her plastic spoon. The only choice which correctly uses dimensional analysis is choice D: the dosage $\approx 25 \text{ cc} \cdot \frac{1 \text{ ml}}{1 \text{ cc}} \cdot \frac{1\text{L}}{1000\text{ml}} \cdot \frac{0.5 \text{ gal}}{2\text{L}} \cdot \frac{16\text{c}}{1 \text{ gal}} \cdot \frac{48\text{t}}{1\text{c}} \cdot \frac{1 \text{ spoonful}}{1\text{t}}$
$\rightarrow \frac{25}{1000} \cdot \frac{1}{4} \cdot 16 \cdot 48 \approx 5$.

68. C: If 1" represents 60 feet, 10" represents 600 ft, which is the same as 200 yards.

69. D: If the distance between the two houses is 10 cm on the map, then the actual distance between the houses is 100 m.

To find x, use the Pythagorean Theorem:

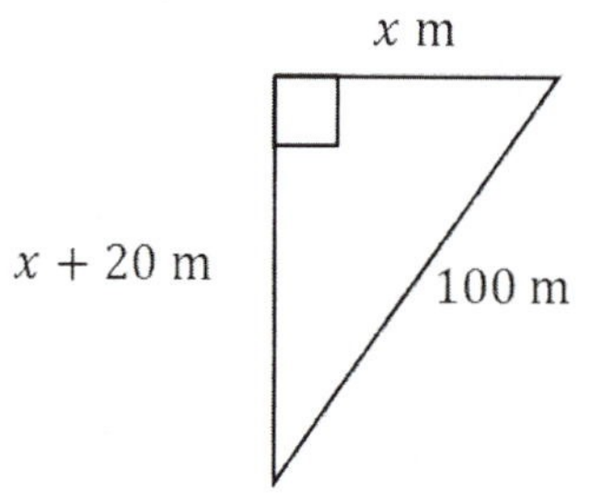

$x^2 + (x + 20)^2 = (100)^2$
$x^2 + x^2 + 40x + 400 = 10000$
$2x^2 + 40x - 9600 = 0$
$2(x^2 + 20x - 4800) = 0$
$2(x - 60)(x + 80) = 0$
$x = 60 \quad x = -80$

Since x represents a distance, it cannot equal –80. Since $x = 60$, $x + 20 = 80$. Roxana walks a total of 140 m to get to her friend's house.

70. D: ΔABC is similar to the smaller triangle with which it shares vertex A. $AB = (2x - 1) + (x + 7) = 3x + 6$. $AC = 4 + 8 = 12$. Set up a proportion and solve for x:

$$\frac{3x + 6}{12} = \frac{2x - 1}{4}$$
$$12x + 24 = 24x - 12$$
$$36 = 12x$$
$$3 = x$$

So, $AB = 3x + 6 = 3(3) + 6 = 15$.

71. B: Percent error $= \frac{|\text{actual value} - \text{measured value}|}{\text{actual value}} \times 100\%$, and the average percent error is the sum of the percent errors for each trial divided by the number of trials.

	% error Trial 1	% error Trial 2	% error Trial 3	% error Trial 4	Average percent error
Scale 1	0.1%	0.2%	0.2%	0.1%	0.15%
Scale 2	2.06%	2.09%	2.10%	2.08%	2.08%

The percent error for Scale 1 is less than the percent error for Scale 2, so it is more accurate. The more precise scale is Scale 2 because its range of values, 10.210 g − 10.206 g = 0.004 g, is smaller than the Scale 2's range of values, 10.02 g − 9.98 g = 0.04 g.

72. C: If l and w represent the length and width of the enclosed area, its perimeter is equal to $2l + 2w$; since the fence is positioned x feet from the lot's edges on each side, the perimeter of the lot is $2(l + 2x) + 2(w + 2x)$. Since the amount of money saved by fencing the smaller are is \$432, and since the fencing material costs \$12 per linear foot, 36 fewer feet of material are used to fence around the playground than would have been used to fence around the lot. This can be expressed as the equation $2(l + 2x) + 2(w + 2x) - (2l + 2w) = 36$.

$$2(l + 2x) + 2(w + 2x) - (2l + 2w) = 36$$
$$2l + 4x + 2w + 4x - 2l - 2w = 36$$
$$8x = 36$$
$$x = 4.5 \text{ ft}$$

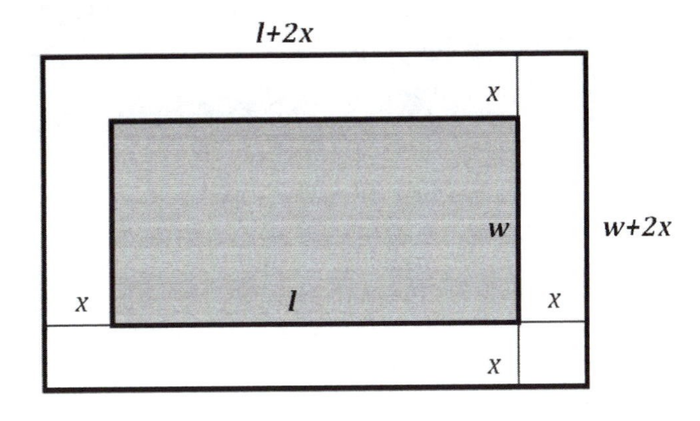

The difference in the area of the lot and the enclosed space is 141 yd^2, which is the same as 1269 ft^2. So, $(l + 2x)(w + 2x) - lw = 1269$. Substituting 4.5 for x,

$$(l + 9)(w + 9) - lw = 1269$$
$$lw + 9l + 9w + 81 - lw = 1269$$
$$9l + 9w = 1188$$
$$9(l + w) = 1188$$
$$l + w = 132 \text{ ft}$$

Therefore, the perimeter of the enclosed space, $2(l + w)$, is $2(132) = 264$ ft. The cost of 264 ft of fencing is $264 \cdot \$12 = \$3{,}168$.

73. B: The volume of Natasha's tent is $\frac{x^2h}{3}$. If she were to increase by 1 ft the length of each side of the square base, the tent's volume would be $\frac{(x+1)^2h}{3} = \frac{(x^2+2x+1)(h)}{3} = \frac{x^2h+2xh+h}{3} = \frac{x^2h}{3} + \frac{2xh+h}{3}$. Notice this is the volume of Natasha's tent, $\frac{x^2h}{3}$, increased by $\frac{2xh+h}{3}$, or $\frac{h(2x+1)}{3}$.

74. A: The area of a circle is πr^2, so the area of a semicircle is $\frac{\pi r^2}{2}$. Illustrated below is a method which can be used to find the area of the shaded region.

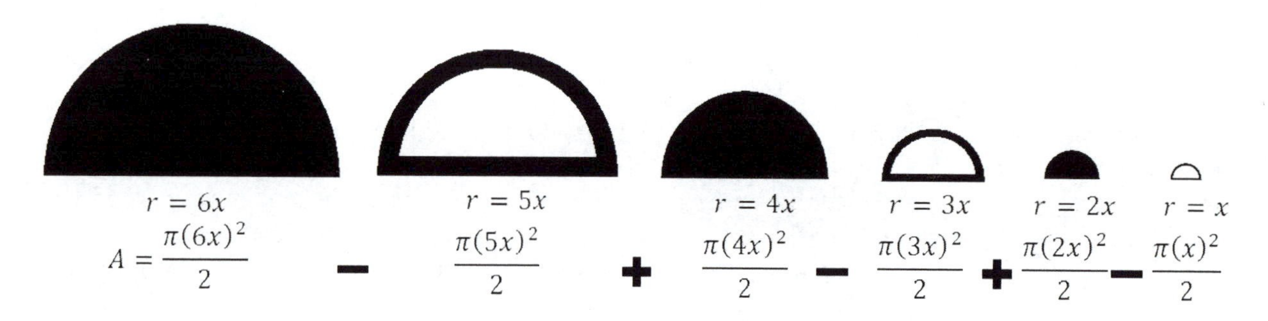

The area of the shaded region is $\frac{\pi(36x^2-25x^2+16x^2-9x^2+4x^3-x^2)}{2} = \frac{(21x^2)\pi}{2}$.

75. B. Euclidean geometry is based on the flat plane. One of Euclid's five axioms, from which all Euclidean geometric theorems are derived, is the parallel postulate, which states that in a plane, for any line *l* and point *A* not on *l*, exactly one line which passes through *A* does not intersect *l*.

Non-Euclidean geometry considers lines on surfaces which are not flat. For instance, on the Earth's surface, if point *A* represents the North Pole and line *l* represents the equator (which does not pass through *A*), all lines of longitude pass through point *A* and intersect line *l*. In elliptical geometry, there are infinitely many lines which pass though *A* and intersect *l*, and there is no line which passes through *A* which does not also intersect *l*. In hyperbolic geometry, the opposite is true. When *A* is not on *l*, all lines which pass through A diverge from *l*, so none of the lines through *A* intersect *l*.

76. B: When four congruent isosceles trapezoids are arranged in an arch, the bases of the trapezoid come together to form regular octagons, the smaller of which is shown to the right. The measure of each angle of a regular octagon is 135°. $\left(\frac{(8-2)(180°)}{8} = 135°.\right)$ From the relationship of two of the trapezoid's base angles with one of the octagon's interior angles, write and solve an equation:

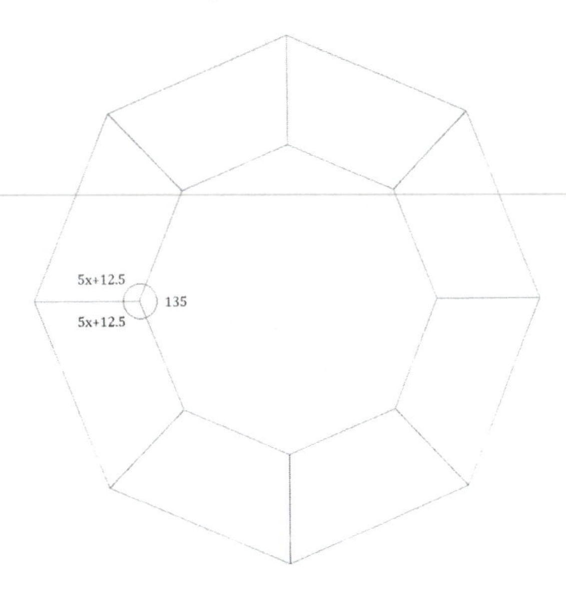

$(5x + 12.5) + (5x + 12.5) + 135 = 360$
$10x + 160 = 360$
$10x = 200$
$x = 20$

77. C: Sketch a diagram (this one is not to scale) and label the known segments. Use the property that two segments are congruent when they originate from the same point outside of a circle and are tangent to the circle.

The point of tangency of $\overline{CB}$ divides the segment into two pieces measuring 4 and 6; the point of tangency of $\overline{BA}$ divides the segment into two pieces measuring 6 and 8; the point of tangency of $\overline{AD}$ divides the segment into two pieces measuring 8 and 4. Therefore $AD = 8 + 4 = 12$.

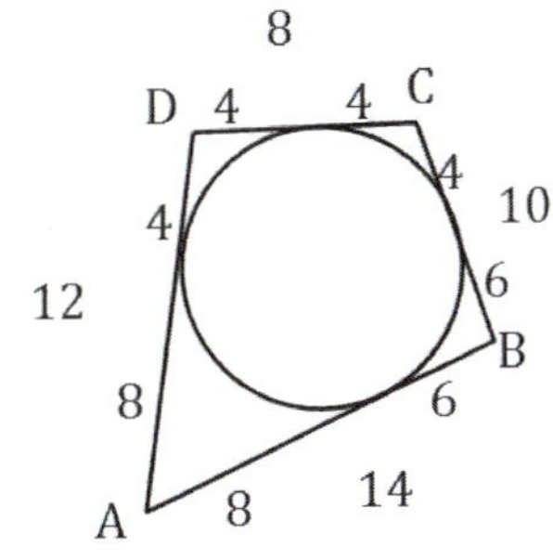

78. D: Let b represent the base of the triangle. The height h of the triangle is the altitude drawn from the vertex opposite of b to side b.

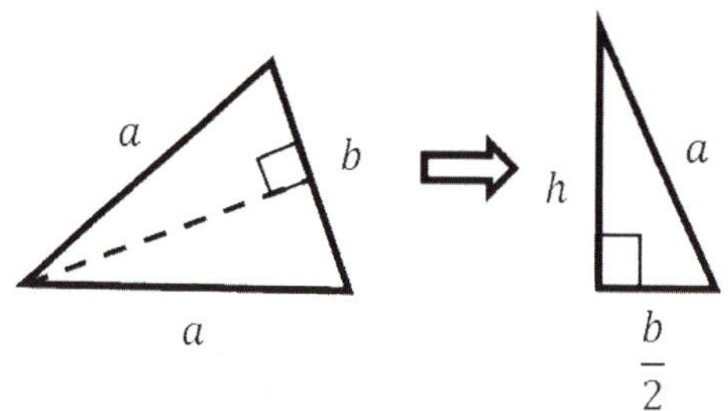

The height of the triangle can be found in terms of a and b by using the Pythagorean theorem:

$$h^2 + \left(\frac{b}{2}\right)^2 = a^2$$

$$h = \sqrt{a^2 - \frac{b^2}{4}} = \sqrt{\frac{4a^2 - b^2}{4}} = \frac{\sqrt{4a^2 - b^2}}{2}$$

The area of a triangle is $A = \frac{1}{2}bh$, so $A = \frac{1}{2}b\left(\frac{\sqrt{4a^2-b^2}}{2}\right) = \frac{b\sqrt{4a^2-b^2}}{4}$.

79. B: Since $\angle ADC$ is a right triangle with legs measuring 5 and 12, its hypotenuse measures 13. (5-12-13 is a Pythagorean triple.)

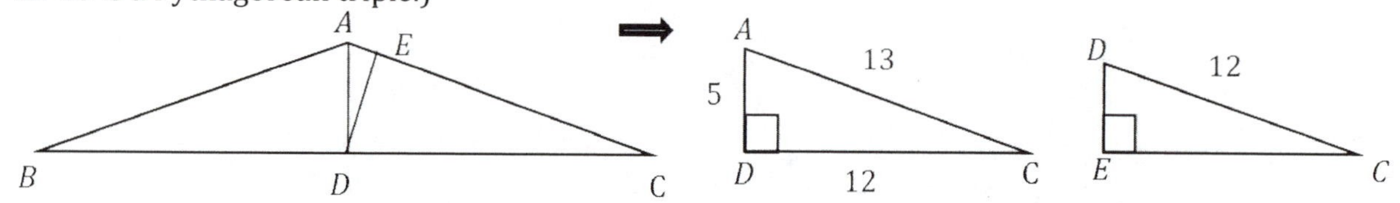

$\angle ADC$ and $\angle DEC$ are both right triangles which share vertex C. By the AA similarity theorem $\angle ADC \sim \angle DEC$. Therefore, a proportion can be written and solved to find DE.

$$\frac{5}{DE} = \frac{13}{12}$$
$$DE = 4.6$$

80. C: The center of the sphere is shared by the center of the cube, and each of the corners of the cube touches the surface of the sphere. Therefore, the diameter of the sphere is the line which passes through the center of the cube and connects one corner of the cube to the opposite corner on the opposite face. Notice in the illustration below that the diameter d of the sphere can be represented as the hypotenuse of a right triangle with a short leg measuring 4 units. (Since the volume of the cube is 64 cubic units, each of its sides measures $\sqrt[3]{64} = 4$ units.) The long leg of the triangle is the diagonal of the base of the cube. Its length can be found using the Pythagorean theorem: $4^2 + 4^2 = x^2; x = \sqrt{32} = 4\sqrt{2}$.

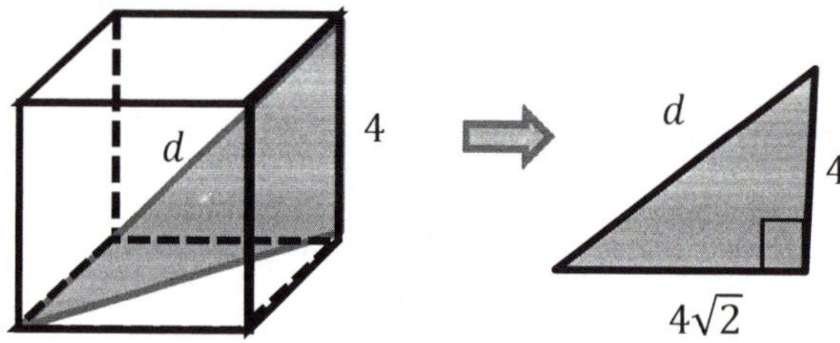

Use the Pythagorean theorem again to find d, the diameter of the sphere: $d^2 = \left(4\sqrt{2}\right)^2 + 4^2$; $d = \sqrt{48} = 4\sqrt{3}$. To find the volume of the sphere, use the formula $V = \frac{4}{3}\pi r^3$. Since the radius r of the sphere is half the diameter, $r = 2\sqrt{3}$, and $V = \frac{4}{3}\pi(2\sqrt{3})^3 = \frac{4}{3}\pi\left(24\sqrt{3}\right) = 32\pi\sqrt{3}$ cubic units.

81. D. Since it is given that $\overline{FD} \cong \overline{BC}$ and $\overline{AB} \cong \overline{DE}$, step 2 needs to establish either that $\overline{AC} \cong \overline{EF}$ or that $\Delta ABC \cong \Delta FDE$ in order for step 5 to show that $\Delta ABC \cong \Delta EDF$. The statement $\overline{AC} \cong \overline{EF}$ cannot be shown directly from the given information. On the other hand, $\Delta ABC \cong \Delta FDE$ can be determined: when two parallel lines ($\overline{BC} \| \overline{FG}$) are cut by a transversal ($\overline{AE}$), alternate exterior angles ($\Delta ABC, \Delta FDE$) are congruent. Therefore, $\Delta ABC \cong \Delta EDF$ by the side-angle-side (SAS) theorem.

82. A: Step 5 established that $\Delta ABC \cong \Delta EDF$. Because corresponding parts of congruent triangles are congruent (CPCTC), $\angle BAC \cong \angle DEF$. This is useful to establish when trying to prove $\overline{FE} \| \overline{AG}$: when two lines ($\overline{FE}$ and $\overline{AG}$) are cut by a transversal ($\overline{AE}$) and alternate interior angles ($\angle BAC, \angle DEF$) are congruent, then the lines are parallel. The completed proof is shown immediately following.

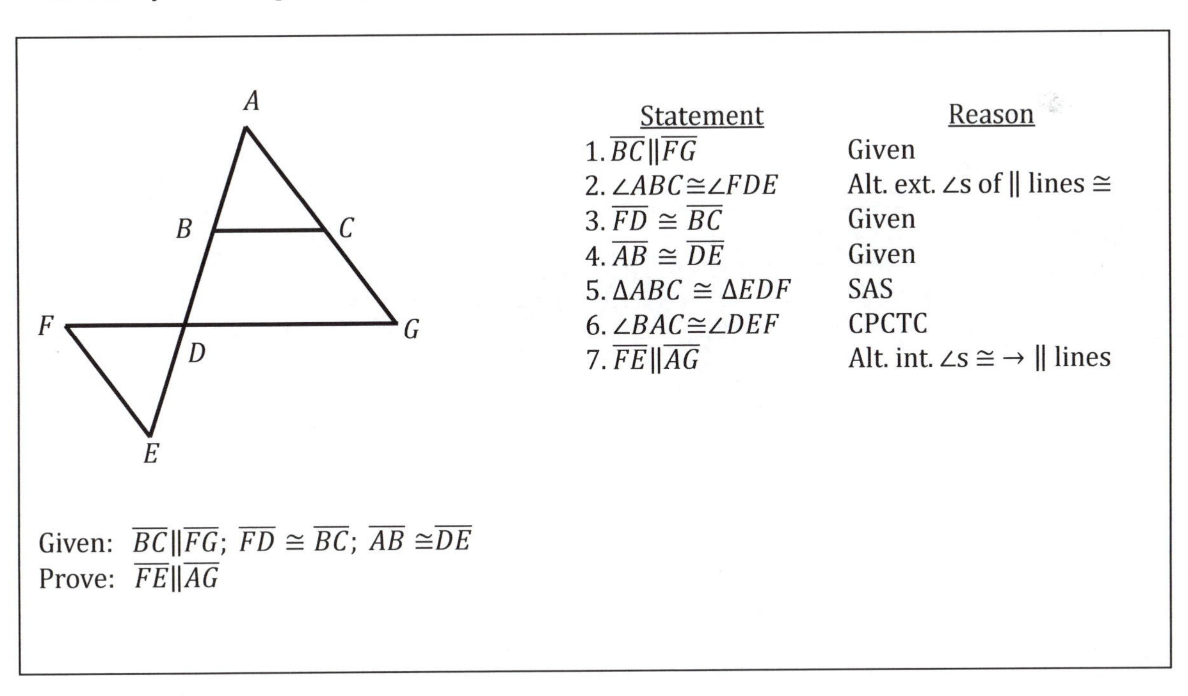

Statement	Reason
1. $\overline{BC} \| \overline{FG}$	Given
2. $\angle ABC \cong \angle FDE$	Alt. ext. $\angle$s of $\|$ lines $\cong$
3. $\overline{FD} \cong \overline{BC}$	Given
4. $\overline{AB} \cong \overline{DE}$	Given
5. $\Delta ABC \cong \Delta EDF$	SAS
6. $\angle BAC \cong \angle DEF$	CPCTC
7. $\overline{FE} \| \overline{AG}$	Alt. int. $\angle$s $\cong \rightarrow \|$ lines

Given: $\overline{BC} \| \overline{FG}$; $\overline{FD} \cong \overline{BC}$; $\overline{AB} \cong \overline{DE}$
Prove: $\overline{FE} \| \overline{AG}$

83. B: A cube has six square faces. The arrangement of these faces in a two-dimensional figure is a net of a cube if the figure can be folded to form a cube. Figures A, C, and D represent three of the eleven possible nets of a cube. If choice B is folded, however, the bottom square in the second column will overlap the fourth square in the top row, so the figure does not represent a net of a cube.

84. D: The cross-section is a hexagon.

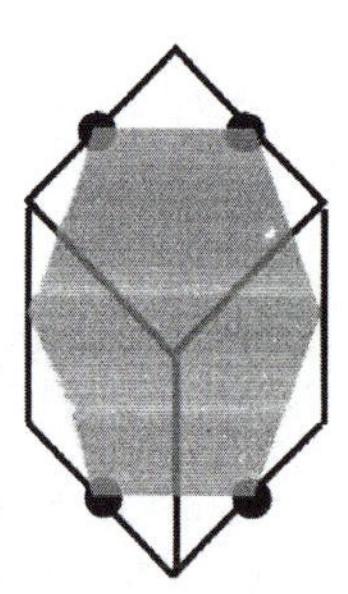

85. A: Use the formula for the volume of a sphere to find the radius of the sphere:

$$V = \frac{4}{3}\pi r^3$$
$$36\pi = \frac{4}{3}\pi r^3$$
$$36 = \frac{4}{3}r^3$$
$$36 = \frac{4}{3}r^3$$
$$27 = r^3$$
$$3 = r$$

Then, substitute the point $(h, k, l) = (1, 0, -2)$ and the radius $r = 3$ into the equation of a sphere:

$$(x-h)^2 + (y-k)^2 + (z-l)^2 = r^2$$
$$(x-1)^2 + y^2 + (z+2)^2 = 3^2$$
$$(x-1)^2 + y^2 + (z+2)^2 = 9$$
$$x^2 - 2x + 1 + y^2 + z^2 + 4z + 4 = 9$$
$$x^2 + y^2 + z^2 - 2x + 4z = 4$$

86. B: The triangle is a right triangle with legs 3 and 4 units long.

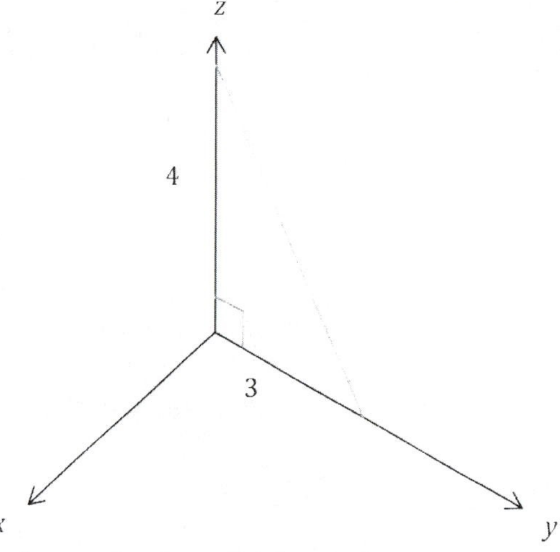

If the triangle is rotated about the z-axis, the solid formed is a cone with a height of 4 and a radius of 3; this cone has volume $V = \frac{1}{3}\pi r^2 h = \frac{1}{3}\pi 3^2 4 = 12\pi$ cubic units. If the triangle is rotated about the y-axis, the solid formed is a cone with a height of 3 and a radius of 4. This cone has volume

$V = \frac{1}{3}\pi r^2 h = \frac{1}{3}\pi 4^2 3 = 16\pi$ cubic units. The difference in the volumes of the two cones is $16\pi - 12\pi = 4\pi$ cubic units.

87. D: The point $(5, -5)$ lies on the line which has a slope of -2 and which passes through $(3, -1)$. If $(5, -5)$ is one of the endpoints of the line, the other would be $(1,3)$.

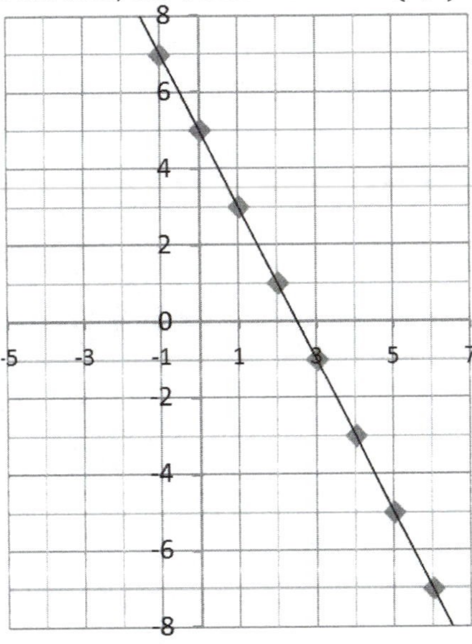

88. D: Since all of the answer choices are parallelograms, determine whether the parallelogram is also a rhombus or a rectangle or both. One way to do this is by examining the parallelogram's diagonals. If the parallelogram's diagonals are perpendicular, then the parallelogram is a rhombus. If the parallelogram's diagonals are congruent, then the parallelogram is a rectangle. If a parallelogram is both a rhombus and a rectangle, then it is a square.

To determine whether the diagonals are perpendicular, find the slopes of the diagonals of the quadrilateral:

- Diagonal 1: $\frac{6-2}{-5-3} = \frac{4}{-8} = -\frac{1}{2}$
- Diagonal 2: $\frac{0-8}{-3-1} = -\frac{8}{-4} = 2$

The diagonals have opposite inverse slopes and are therefore perpendicular. Thus, the parallelogram is a rhombus.

To determine whether the diagonals are congruent, find the lengths of the diagonals of the quadrilateral:

- Diagonal 1: $\sqrt{(6-2)^2 + (-5-3)^2} = \sqrt{(4)^2 + (-8)^2} = \sqrt{16+64} = \sqrt{80} = 4\sqrt{5}$
- Diagonal 2: $\sqrt{(0-8)^2 + (-3-1)\text{^}2} = \sqrt{(-8)^2 + (-4)\text{^}2} = \sqrt{64+16} = \sqrt{80} = 4\sqrt{5}$

The diagonals are congruent, so the parallelogram is a rectangle.

Since the polygon is a rhombus and a rectangle, it is also a square.

89. A: The equation of the circle is given in general form. When the equation is written in the standard form $(x-h)^2+(y-k)^2=r^2$, where (h,k) is the center of the circle and r is the radius of the circle, the radius is easy to determine. Putting the equation into standard form requires completing the square for x and y:

$$x^2-10x+y^2+8y=-29$$
$$(x^2-10x+25)+(y^2+8y+16)=-29+25+16$$
$$(x-5)^2+(y+4)^2=12$$

Since $r^2=12$, and since r must be a positive number, $r=\sqrt{12}=2\sqrt{3}$.

90. D: One way to determine whether the equation represents an ellipse, a circle, a parabola, or a hyperbola is to find the determinant b^2-4ac of the general equation form of a conic section, $ax^2+bxy+cy^2+dx+ey+f=0$, where $a,b,c,d,e,$ and f are constants. Given that the conic section is non-degenerate, if the determinant is positive, then the equation is a hyperbola; if the determinant is negative, then the equation is a circle (when $a=c$ and $b=0$) or an ellipse; and if the determinant is zero, then the equation is a parabola. For $2x^2-3y^2-12x+6y-15=0$, $a=2,\ b=0,\ c=-3,\ d=-12,\ e=6,$ and $f=-15$. The determinant b^2-4ac is equal to $0^2-4(2)(-3)=24$. Since the determinant is positive, the graph is hyperbolic.

Another way to determine the shape of the graph is to look at the coefficients for the x^2 and y^2 terms in the given equation. If one of the coefficients is zero (in other words, if there is either an x^2 or a y^2 term in the equation but not both), then the equation is a parabola; if the coefficients have the same sign, then the graph is an ellipse or circle; and if the coefficients have opposite signs, then the graph is a hyperbola. Since the coefficient of x^2 is 2 and the coefficient of y^2 is -3, the graph is a hyperbola. That the equation can be written in the standard form for a hyperbola, $\frac{(x-h)^2}{a^2}-\frac{(y-k)^2}{b^2}=1$, confirms the conclusion.

$$2x^2-3y^2-12x+6y-15=0$$
$$2x^2-12x-3y^2+6y=15$$
$$2(x^2-6x)-3(y^2-2y)=15$$
$$2(x^2-6x+9)-3(y^2-2y+1)=15+2(9)-3(1)$$
$$2(x-3)^2-3(y-1)^2=30$$
$$\frac{(x-3)^2}{15}-\frac{(y-1)^2}{10}=1$$

91. B: The graph of $f(x)$ is a parabola with a focus of (a,b) and a directrix of $y=-b$. The axis of symmetry of a parabola passes through the focus and vertex and is perpendicular to the directrix. Since the directrix is a horizontal line, the axis of symmetry is $x=a$; therefore, the x-coordinate of the parabola's vertex must be a. The distance between a point on the parabola and the directrix is equal to the distance between that point and the focus, so the y-coordinate of the vertex must be $y=\frac{-b+b}{2}=0$. So, the vertex of the parabola given by $f(x)$ is $(a,0)$.

If $g(x)$ were a translation of $f(x)$, as is the case for choices A, C, and D, the vertices of $f(x)$ and $g(x)$ would differ. Since the vertex of the graph of $g(x)$ is $(a,0)$, none of those choices represent the correct response. However, if $g(x)=-f(x)$, the vertices of the graphs of both functions would be the same; therefore, this represents a possible relation between the two functions.

92. C: When a figure is reflected twice over non-parallel lines, the resulting transformation is a rotation about the point of intersection of the two lines of reflection. The two lines of reflection $y=x+2$ and $x=0$ intersect at (0,2). So, $\Delta A''B''C''$ represents a rotation of ΔABC about the point

(0,2). The angle of rotation is equal to twice the angle between the two lines of reflection when measured in a clockwise direction from the first to the second line of reflection. Since the angle between the lines or reflection measures 135°, the angle of rotation which is the composition of the two reflections measures 270°. All of these properties can be visualized by drawing ΔABC, $\Delta A'B'C'$, and $\Delta A''B''C''$.

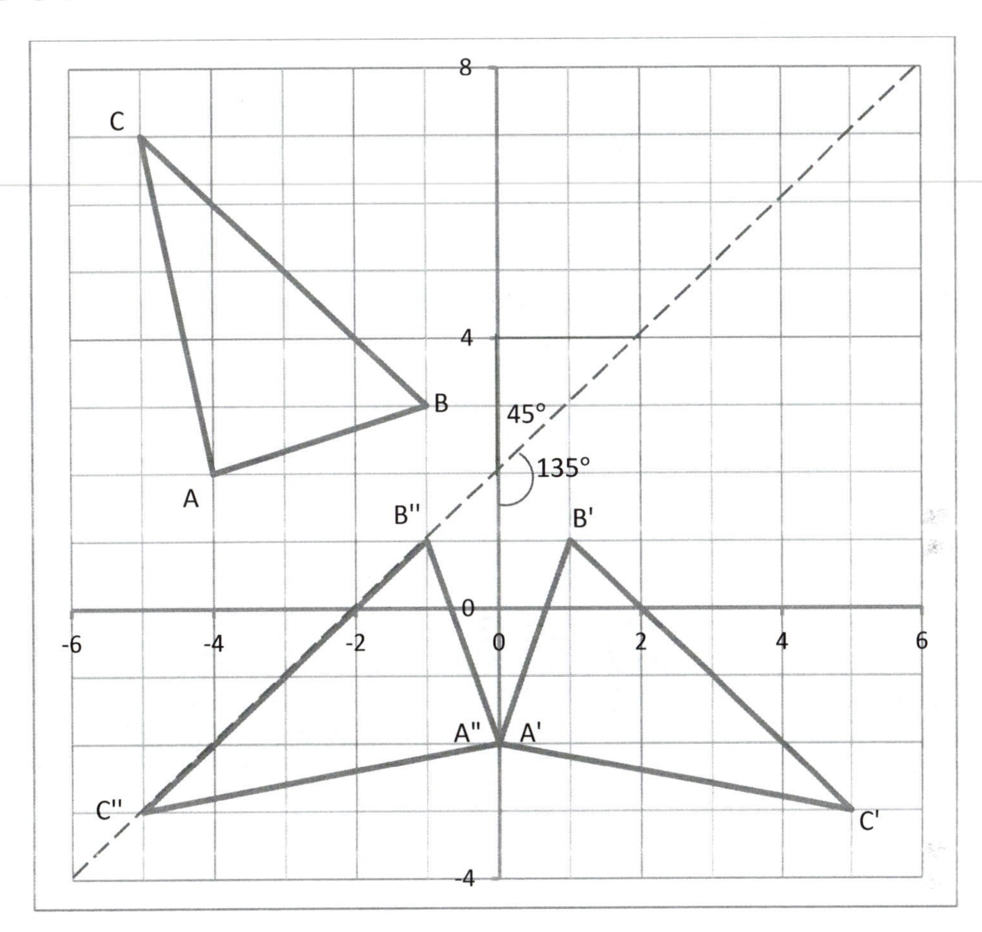

93. B: All regular polygons have rotational symmetry. The angle of rotation is the smallest angle by which the polygon can be rotated such that it maps onto itself; any multiple of this angle will also map the polygon onto itself. The angle of rotation for a regular polygon is the angle formed between two lines drawn from consecutives vertices to the center of the polygon. Since the vertices of a regular polygon lie on a circle, for a regular polygon with n sides, the angle of rotation measures $\frac{360°}{n}$.

Number of sides of regular polygon	Angle of rotation	Angles ≤ 360° which map the polygon onto itself
4	$\frac{360}{4} = 90°$	90°, 180°, 270°, 360°
6	$\frac{360}{6} = 60°$	60°, 120°, 180°, 240°, 300°, 360°
8	$\frac{360}{8} = 45°$	45°, 90°, 135°, 180°, 225°, 270°, 315°, 316°
10	$\frac{360}{10} = 36°$	36°, 72°, 108°, 144°, 180°, 216°, 252°, 288°, 324°, 360°

94. A: Since the y-coordinates of points P and Q are the same, line segment $\overline{PQ}$ is a horizontal line segment whose length is the difference in the x-coordinates a and c. Because the length of a line cannot be negative, and because it is unknown whether $a > c$ or $a < c$, $PQ = |a - c|$ or $|c - a|$. Since the x-coordinates of Q and Q' are the same, line segment $\overline{P'Q}$ is a vertical line segment whose length is $|d - b|$or $|b - d|$. The quadrilateral formed by the transformation of $\overline{PQ}$ to $\overline{P'Q'}$ is a parallelogram. If the base of the parallelogram is $\overline{PQ}$, then the height is $\overline{P'Q}$ since $\overline{PQ} \perp \overline{P'Q}$. For a parallelogram, $A = bh$, so $A = |a - c| \cdot |b - d|$.

95. B: Since $\tan B = \frac{opposite}{adjacent} = \frac{b}{a}$, choice A is incorrect.

$\cos B = \frac{adjacent}{hypotenuse}$. The hypotenuse of a right triangle is equal to the square root of the sum of the squares of the legs, so $\cos B = \frac{adjacent}{hypotenuse} = \frac{a}{\sqrt{a^2+b^2}}$. Rationalize the denominator: $\frac{a}{\sqrt{a^2+b^2}} \cdot \frac{\sqrt{a^2+b^2}}{\sqrt{a^2+b^2}} = \frac{a\sqrt{a^2+b^2}}{a^2+b^2}$. Choice B is correct.

$\sec B = \frac{hypotenuse}{adjacent} = \frac{\sqrt{a^2+b^2}}{a}$, and csc B = $\frac{\sqrt{a^2+b^2}}{b}$, so choices C and D are incorrect.

96. C: Find the missing angle measures in the diagram by using angle and triangle properties. Then, use the law of sines to find the distance y between the window and the wife's car: $\frac{60}{\sin 15°} = \frac{y}{\sin 45°}$, so $y = \frac{60 \sin 45°}{\sin 15} \approx 163.9$ ft. Use this number in a sine or cosine function to find x: $\sin 30° \approx \frac{x}{163.9}$, so $x \approx 163.9 \sin 30° \approx 82$. Therefore, the man's wife is parked approximately 82 feet from the building.

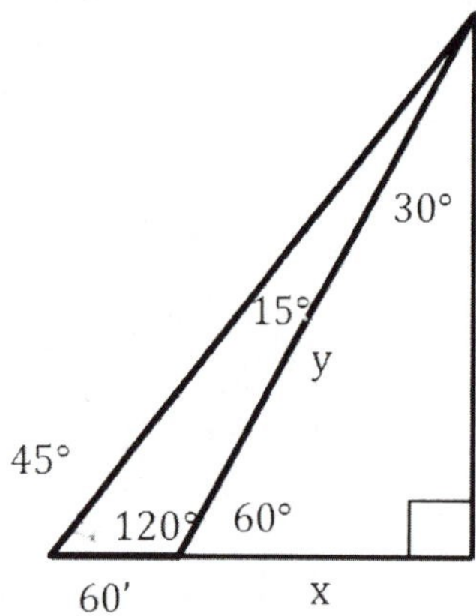

Alternatively, notice that when the man is looking down at a 45 degree angle, the triangle that is formed is an isosceles triangle, meaning that the height of his office is the same as the distance from the office to his car, or x + 60 feet. With this knowledge, the problem can be modeled with a single equation:

$$\frac{x + 60}{x} = \tan 60° \quad or \quad x = \frac{60}{\tan 60° - 1}$$

97. A: The reference angle for $-\frac{2\pi}{3}$ is $2\pi - \frac{2\pi}{3} = \frac{4\pi}{3}$, so $\tan(-\frac{2\pi}{3}) = \tan\left(\frac{4\pi}{3}\right) = \frac{sin\left(\frac{4\pi}{3}\right)}{\cos\left(\frac{4\pi}{3}\right)}$. From the unit circle, the values of $\sin\left(\frac{4\pi}{3}\right)$ and $\cos\left(\frac{4\pi}{3}\right)$ are $-\frac{\sqrt{3}}{2}$ and $-\frac{1}{2}$, respectively. Therefore, $\tan(-\frac{2\pi}{3}) = \frac{-\frac{\sqrt{3}}{2}}{-\frac{1}{2}} = \sqrt{3}$.

98. D: On the unit circle, $\sin\theta = \frac{1}{2}$ when $\theta = \frac{\pi}{6}$ and when $\theta = \frac{5\pi}{6}$. Since only $\frac{5\pi}{6}$ is in the given range of $\frac{\pi}{2} < \theta < \pi, \theta = \frac{5\pi}{6}$.

99. C: Use trigonometric equalities and identities to simplify. $\cos\theta \cot\theta = \cos\theta \cdot \frac{\cos\theta}{\sin\theta} = \frac{\cos^2\theta}{\sin\theta} = \frac{1-\sin^2\theta}{\sin\theta} = \frac{1}{\sin\theta} - \sin\theta = \csc\theta - \sin\theta$.

100. B: The trigonometric identity $\sec^2\theta = \tan^2\theta + 1$ can be used to rewrite the equation $\sec^2\theta = 2\tan\theta$ as $\tan^2\theta + 1 = 2\tan\theta$, which can then be rearranged into the form $\tan^2\theta - 2\tan\theta + 1 = 0$. Solve by factoring and using the zero product property:

$$\tan^2\theta - 2\tan\theta + 1 = 0$$
$$(\tan\theta - 1)^2 = 0$$
$$\tan\theta - 1 = 0$$
$$\tan\theta = 1.$$

Since $\tan\theta = 1$ when $\sin\theta = \cos\theta$, for $0 < \theta \leq 2\pi$, $\theta = \frac{\pi}{4}$ or $\frac{5\pi}{4}$.

101. A: Since the graph shows a maximum height of 28 inches above the ground, and since the maximum distance from the road the pebble reaches is when it is at the top of the tire, the diameter of the tire is 28 inches. Therefore, its radius is 14 inches. From the graph, it can be observed that the tire makes 7.5 rotations in 0.5 seconds. Thus, the tire rotates 15 times in 1 second, or $15 \cdot 60 = 900$ times per minute.

102. C: The dashed line represents the sine function (x) , and the solid line represents a cosine function $g(x)$. The amplitude of $f(x)$ is 4, and the amplitude of $g(x)$ is 2. The function $y = \sin x$ has a period of 2π, while the graph of function $f(x) = a_1 \sin(b_1 x)$ has a period of 4π; therefore, $b_1 = \frac{2\pi}{4\pi} = 0.5$, which is between 0 and 1. The graph of $g(x) = a_2 \cos(b_2 x)$ has a period of π, so $b_2 = \frac{2\pi}{\pi} = 2$.

103. B: The graph of $f(x)$ is stretched vertically by a factor of 4 with respect to $y = \sin x$, so $a_1 = 4$. The graph of $g(x)$ is stretched vertically by a factor of two and is inverted with respect to the graph of $y = \cos x$, so $a_2 = -2$. Therefore, the statement $a_2 < 0 < a_1$ is true.

104. A: The graph to the right shows the height h in inches of the weight on the spring above the table as a function of time t in seconds. Notice that the height is 3 in above the table at time 0 since the weight was pulled down two inches from its starting position 5 inches above the table. The spring fluctuates 2 inches above and below its equilibrium point, so its maximum height is 7 inches above the table. The graph represents a cosine curve which has been inverted, stretched vertically by a factor of 2, and shifted up five units; also, the graph has been compressed horizontally, with a period of 1 rather than 2π. So, the height of the weight on the spring as a function of time is $h = -2\cos(2\pi t) + 5$.

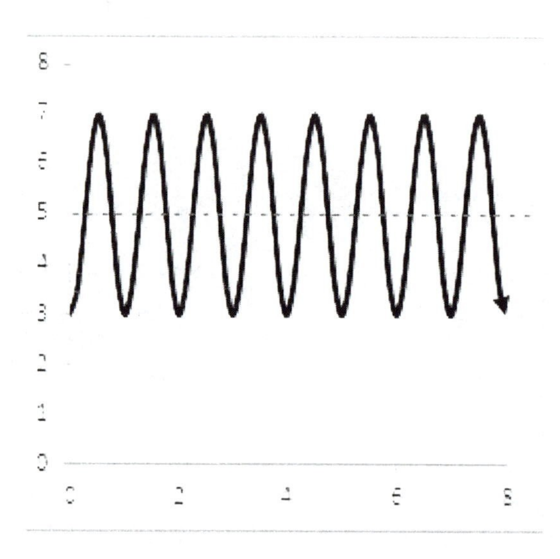

105. C: Since evaluating $\frac{x^3+3x^2-x-3}{x^2-9}$ at $x = -3$ produces a fraction with a zero denominator, simplify the polynomial expression before evaluating the limit:

$$\frac{x^3+3x^2-x-3}{x^2-9} = \frac{x^2(x+3)-1(x+3)}{(x+3)(x-3)} = \frac{(x+3)(x^2-1)}{(x+3)(x-3)} = \frac{(x+1)(x-1)}{x-3}$$
$$\lim_{x\to -3} \frac{(x+1)(x-1)}{x-3} = \frac{(-3+1)(-3-1)}{-3-3} = -\frac{8}{-6} = -\frac{4}{3}.$$

106. B: To evaluate the limit, divide the numerator and denominator by x^2 and use these properties of limits: $\lim_{x\to\infty} \frac{1}{x} = 0$; the limit of a sum of terms is the sum of the limits of the terms; and the limit of a product of terms is the product of the limits of the terms.

$$\lim_{x\to\infty} \frac{x^2+2x-3}{2x^2+1} = \lim_{x\to\infty} \frac{\frac{x^2}{x^2}+\frac{2x}{x^2}-\frac{3}{x^2}}{\frac{2x^2}{x^2}+\frac{1}{x^2}} = \lim_{x\to\infty} \frac{1+\frac{2}{x}-\frac{3}{x^2}}{2+\frac{1}{x^2}} = \frac{1+0-0}{2+0} = \frac{1}{2}.$$

107. B: Evaluating $\frac{|x-3|}{3-x}$ when $x = 3$ produces a fraction with a zero denominator. To find the limit as x approaches 3 from the right, sketch a graph or make a table of values.

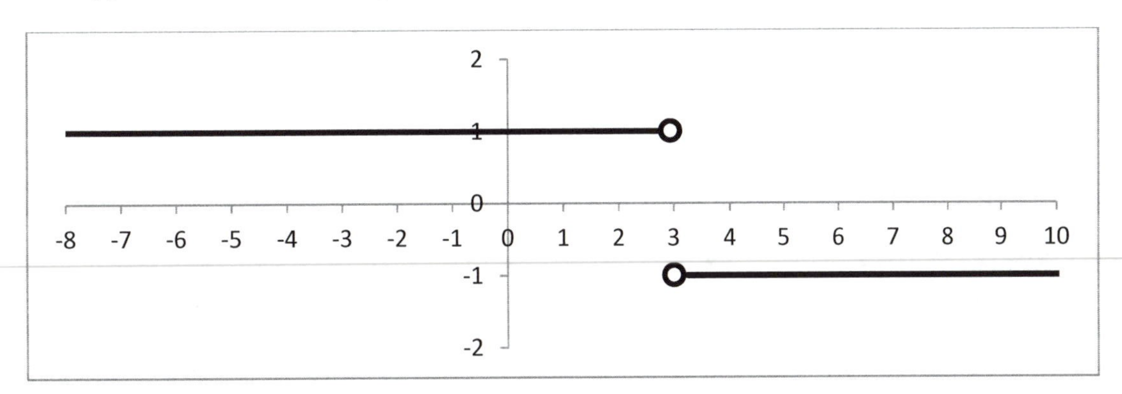

The value of the function approaches -1 as x approaches three from the right, so $\lim_{x\to 3^+} \frac{|x-3|}{3-x} = -1$.

108. C: The slope of the line tangent to the graph of a function f at $x = a$ is $f'(a)$. Since $f(x) = \frac{1}{4}x^2 - 3$, $f'(x) = 2\left(\frac{1}{4}\right)x^{(2-1)} - 0 = \frac{1}{2}x$. So, the slope at $x = 2$ is $f'(2) = \frac{1}{2}(2) = 1$.

109. D: The definition of the derivative of f at 2, or $f'(2)$, is the limit of the difference quotient $\lim_{h\to 0} \frac{f(2+h)-f(2)}{h}$. Rather than find the limit, simply evaluate the derivative of the function at $x = 2$:

$$f(x) = 2x^3 - 3x^2 + 4$$
$$f'(x) = 6x^2 - 6x$$
$$f'(2) = 6(2)^2 - 6(2)$$
$$f'(2) = 12$$

110. D: To find the derivative of $y = e^{3x^2-1}$, use the Chain Rule. Let $u = 3x^2 - 1$. Thus, $y = e^u$, and $\frac{dy}{du} = e^u$. Since $\frac{dy}{dx} = \frac{dy}{du} \cdot \frac{du}{dx}$, and since $\frac{du}{dx} = 6x$, $\frac{dy}{dx} = e^{3x^2-1} \cdot 6x = 6x\, e^{3x^2-1}$.

111. C: To find the derivative of $y = \ln(2x + 1)$, use the Chain Rule. Let $u = 2x + 1$. Thus, $y = \ln u$, and $\frac{dy}{du} = \frac{1}{u}$. Since $\frac{dy}{dx} = \frac{dy}{du} \cdot \frac{du}{dx}$, and since $\frac{du}{dx} = 2$, $\frac{dy}{dx} = \left(\frac{1}{2x+1}\right)(2) = \frac{2}{2x+1}$.

112. A: If $\lim_{x\to a^+} f(x) = \lim_{x\to a^-} f(x)$, then $\lim_{x\to a^+} f(x) = \lim_{x\to a^-} f(x) = \lim_{x\to a} f(x)$. Otherwise, $\lim_{x\to a} f(x)$ does not exist. If $\lim_{x\to a} f(x)$ exists, and if $\lim_{x\to a} f(x) = f(a)$, then the function is continuous at a. Otherwise, f is discontinuous at a.

113. A: To find the second derivative of the function, take the derivative of the first derivative of the function:

$$f(x) = 2x^4 - 4x^3 + 2x^2 - x + 1$$
$$f'(x) = 8x^3 - 12x^2 + 4x - 1$$
$$f''(x) = 24x^2 - 24x + 4.$$

114. A: The critical points of the graph occur when $f'(x) = 0$.

$$f(x) = 4x^3 - x^2 - 4x + 2$$
$$f'(x) = 12x^2 - 2x - 4$$
$$= 2(6x^2 - x - 2)$$
$$= 2(3x - 2)(2x + 1)$$

$$0 = 2(3x - 2)(2x + 1)$$
$$3x - 2 = 0 \quad 2x + 1 = 0$$
$$x = \frac{2}{3} \quad x = -\frac{1}{2}$$

If $f''(x) > 0$ for all x in an interval, the graph of the function is concave upward on that interval, and if $f''(x) < 0$ for all x in an interval, the graph of the function is concave upward on that interval. Find the second derivative of the function and determine the intervals in which $f''(x)$ is less than zero and greater than zero:

$$f''(x) = 24x - 2$$
$$24x - 2 < 0 \quad 24x - 2 > 0$$
$$x < \frac{1}{12} \quad x > \frac{1}{12}$$

The graph of f is concave downward on the interval $\left(-\infty, -\frac{1}{12}\right)$ and concave upward on the interval $\left(-\frac{1}{12}, \infty\right)$. The inflection point of the graph is $\left(\frac{1}{12}, f\left(\frac{1}{12}\right)\right) = \left(\frac{1}{12}, \frac{359}{216}\right)$. The point $\left(\frac{2}{3}, f\left(\frac{2}{3}\right)\right) = \left(\frac{2}{3}, \frac{2}{27}\right)$ is a relative minimum and the point $\left(-\frac{1}{2}, f\left(-\frac{1}{2}\right)\right) = \left(-\frac{1}{2}, 3\frac{1}{4}\right)$ is a relative maximum.

115. D: The velocity v of the ball at any time t is the slope of the line tangent to the graph of h at time t. The slope of a line tangent to the curve $h = -16t^2 + 50t + 3$ is h'.

$$h' = v = -32t + 50$$

When $t = 2$, the velocity of the ball is $-32(2) + 50 = -14$. The velocity is negative because the slope of the tangent line at $t = 2$ is negative; velocity has both magnitude and direction, so a velocity of -14 means that the velocity is 14 ft/s downward.

116. B: The manufacturer wishes to minimize the surface area A of the can while keeping its volume V fixed at $0.5 \text{ L} = 500 \text{ mL} = 500 \text{ cm}^3$. The formula for the surface area of a cylinder is $A = 2\pi rh + 2\pi r^2$, and the formula for volume is $V = \pi r^2 h$. To combine the two formulas into one, solve the volume formula for r or h and substitute the resulting expression into the surface area formula for r or h. The volume of the cylinder is 500 cm³, so $500 = \pi r^2 h \rightarrow h = \frac{500}{\pi r^2}$. Therefore, $A = 2\pi rh + 2\pi r^2 \rightarrow 2\pi r\left(\frac{500}{\pi r^2}\right) + 2\pi r^2 = \frac{1000}{r} + 2\pi r^2$. Find the critical point(s) by setting the first derivative equal to zero and solving for r. Note that r represents the radius of the can and must therefore be a positive number.

$$A = 1000r^{-1} + 2\pi r^2$$
$$A' = -1000r^{-2} + 4\pi r$$
$$0 = -\frac{1000}{r^2} + 4\pi r$$
$$\frac{1000}{r^2} = 4\pi r$$
$$1000 = 4\pi r^3$$
$$\sqrt[3]{\frac{1000}{4\pi}} = r$$

So, when r≈4.3 cm, the minimum surface area is obtained. When the radius of the can is 4.30 cm, its height is $h \approx \frac{500}{\pi(4.30)^2} \approx 8.6$ cm, and the surface area is approximately $\frac{1000}{4.3} + 2\pi(4.3)^2 \approx 348.73 \text{ cm}^2$. Confirm that the surface area is greater when the radius is slightly smaller or larger than 4.3 cm. For instance, when r=4 cm, the surface area is approximately 350.5 cm², and when r=4.5 cm, the surface area is approximately 349.5 cm².

117. C: Partitioned into rectangles with length of 1, the left Riemann sum is 20+25+28+30+29+26+22+16+12+10+10+13=241 square units, and the right Riemann sum is 25+28+30+29+26+22+16+12+10+10+13+17=238 square units.

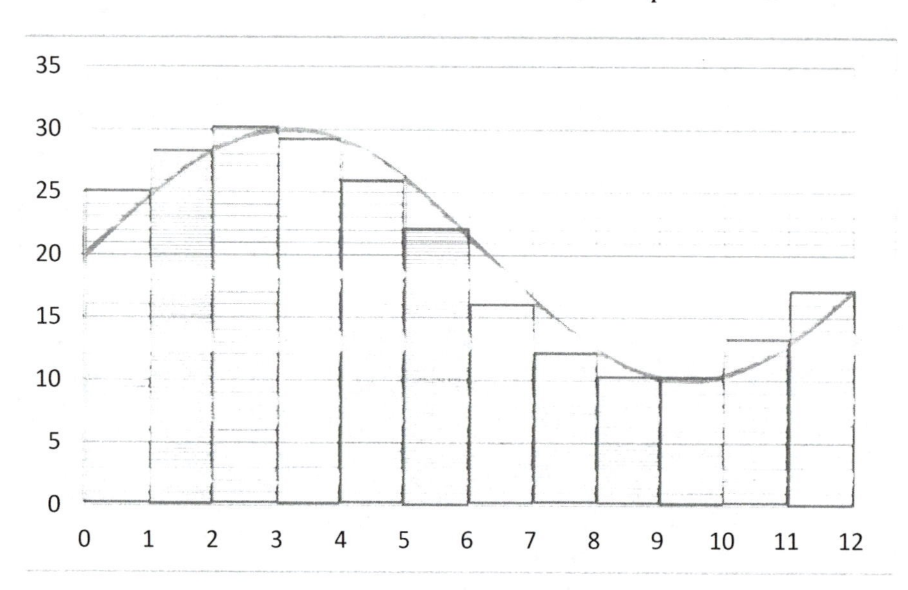

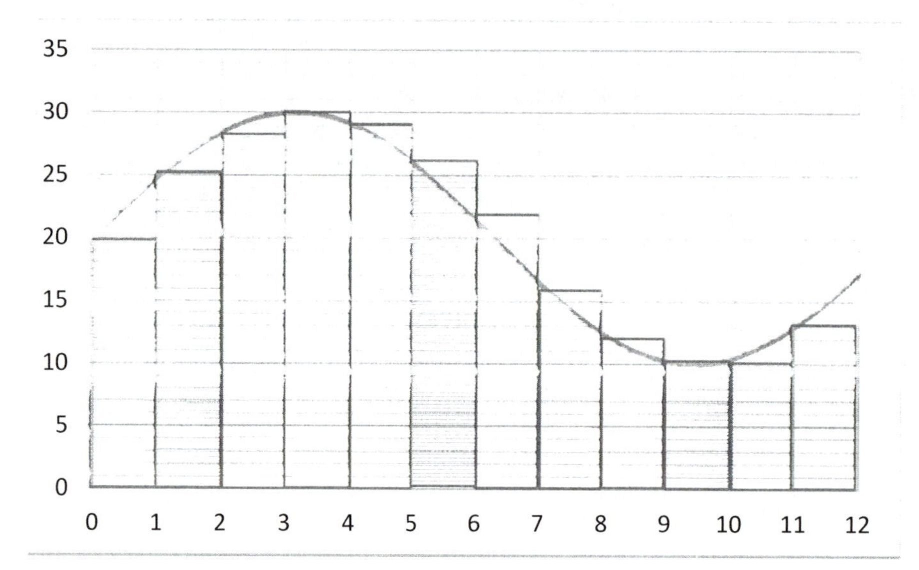

118. B: The area under curve $f(x)$ is $\int_1^2 \frac{1}{x} = [\ln(2)] - [\ln(1)] \approx 0.69$.

119. A: $\int 3x^2 + 2x - 1 = \frac{3}{2+1}x^{2+1} + \frac{2}{1+1}x^{1+1} - x + c = x^3 + x^2 - x + c$.

120. B: To calculate $\int 3x^2 e^{x^3}\,dx$, let $u = x^3$. Since $du = 3x^2dx$, $\int 3x^2e^{x^3}\,dx = \int e^u\,du \to e^u + c \to e^{x^3} + c$.

121. B: Find the points of intersection of the two graphs:

$$x^2 - 4 = -x + 2$$
$$x^2 + x - 6 = 0$$
$$(x + 3)(x - 2) = 0$$
$$x = -3 \quad x = 2$$

The finite region is bound at the top by the line $y = -x + 2$ and at the bottom by $y = x^2 - 4$, so the area is between the graphs on [-3,2], and the height of the region at point x is defined by $[(-x + 2) - (x^2 - 4)]$. Thus, the area of the region is

$$A = \int_{-3}^{2} [(-x + 2) - (x^2 - 4)]dx$$

$$= \int_{-3}^{2} (-x^2 - x + 6)\, dx$$

$$= \left[-\frac{1}{3}(2)^3 - \frac{1}{2}(2)^2 + 6(2)\right] - \left[-\frac{1}{3}(-3)^3 - \frac{1}{2}(-3)^2 + 6(-3)\right]$$

$$= \left[-\frac{8}{3} - 2 + 12\right] - \left[9 - \frac{9}{2} - 18\right] = \frac{22}{3} - \left(-\frac{27}{2}\right) = \frac{125}{6}$$

122. C: The acceleration a of an object at time t is the derivative of the velocity v of the object at time t, which is the derivative of the position x of the object at time t. So, given the velocity of an object at time t, $x(t)$ can be found by taking the integral of the $v(t)$, and $a(t)$ can be found by taking the derivative of $v(t)$.

$x(t) = \int v(t)dt = \int(12t - t^2)dt = 6t^2 - \frac{1}{3}t^3 + c$. Since the position of the car at time 0 is 0, $v(0) = 0 = 6(0)^2 - \frac{1}{3}(0)^3 + c \rightarrow 0 = 0 - 0 + c \rightarrow c = 0$. Therefore, $x(t) = 6t^2 - \frac{1}{3}t^3$.

$a(t) = v'(t) = 12 - 2t$.

Find the time at which the acceleration is equal to 0: $0 = 12 - 2t \rightarrow t = 6$. Then, find $x(6)$ to find the position of the car when the velocity is 0: $6(6)^2 - \frac{1}{3}(6)^3 = 216 - 72 = 144$.

123. D: To draw a box-and-whisker plot from the data, find the median, quartiles, and upper and lower limits.

Stem	Leaves
3	6 7 9 9
4	2 3 8 8 9
5	0 1 1 1 5 7
6	0 0 1 2 3

Key
3|6 = 36

The median is $\frac{50+51}{2} = 50.5$, the lower quartile is $\frac{22+23}{2} = 22.5$, and the upper quartile is $\frac{57+60}{2} = 58.5$. The box of the box-and-whisker plot goes through the quartiles, and a line through the box represents the median of the data. The whiskers extend from the box to the lower and upper limits, unless there are any outliers in the set. In this case, there are no outliers, so the box-and-whisker plot in choice A correctly represents the data set.

To draw a pie chart, find the percentage of data contained in each of the ranges shown. There are four out of twenty numbers between 30 and 39, inclusive, so the percentage shown in the pie chart for that range of data is $\frac{4}{20} \cdot 100\% = 20\%$; there are five values between 40 to 49, inclusive, so the percentage of data for that sector is $\frac{5}{20} \cdot 100\% = 25\%$; $\frac{6}{20} \cdot 100\% = 30\%$ of the data is within the range of 50-59, and $\frac{5}{20} \cdot 100\% = 25\%$ is within the range of 60-69. The pie chart shows the correct percentage of data in each category.

To draw a cumulative frequency histogram, find the cumulative frequency of the data.

Range	Frequency	Cumulative frequency
30-39	4	4
40-49	5	9
50-59	6	15
60-69	5	20

The histogram shows the correct cumulative frequencies.

Therefore, all of the graphs represent the data set.

124. B: A line graph is often used to show change over time. A Venn diagram shows the relationships among sets. A box and whisker plot shows displays how numeric data are distributed throughout the range. A pie chart shows the relationship of parts to a whole.

125. B: In choice A, the teacher surveys all the members of the population in which he is interested. However, since the response is voluntary, the survey is biased: the participants are self-selected rather than randomly selected. It may be that students who have a strong opinion are more likely to respond than those who are more neutral, and this would give the teacher a skewed perspective of student opinions. In choice B, students are randomly selected, so the sampling technique is not biased. In choice C, the student uses convenience sampling, which is a biased technique. For example, perhaps the student is in an honors class; his sampling method would not be representative of the entire class of eleventh graders, which includes both students who take and who do not take honors classes. Choice D also represents convenience sampling; only the opinions of parents in the PTA are examined, and these parents' opinions may not reflect the opinions of all parents of students at the school.

126. A: Nominal data are data that are collected which have no intrinsic quantity or order. For instance, a survey might ask the respondent to identify his or her gender. While it is possible to compare the relative frequency of each response (for example, "most of the respondents are women"), it is not possible to calculate the mean, which requires data to be numeric, or median, which requires data to be ordered. Interval data are both numeric and ordered, so mean and median can be determined, as can the mode, the interval within which there are the most data. Ordinal data has an inherent order, but there is not a set interval between two points. For example, a survey might ask whether the respondent whether he or she was very dissatisfied, dissatisfied, neutral, satisfied, or very satisfied with the customer service received. Since the data are not

numeric, the mean cannot be calculated, but since ordering the data is possible, the median has context.

127. A: The average number of male students in the 11th and 12th grades is 134 males. The number of Hispanic students at the school is 10% of 1219, which is 122 students. The difference in the number of male and female students at the school is $630 - 589 = 41$, and the difference in the number of 9th and 12th grade students at the school is 354 - 255 = 99.

128. C: 52% of the student population is white. There are 630 female students at the school out of 1219 students, so the percentage of female students is $\frac{630}{1219} \cdot 100\% \approx 52\%$. The percentages rounded to the nearest whole number are the same.

129. D: 131 of 283 eleventh graders are male. Given that an 11th grader is chosen to attend the conference, the probability that a male is chosen is $\frac{\text{number of males}}{\text{number of 11th graders}} = \frac{131}{283} \approx 0.46$. Note that this is **NOT** the same question as one which asks for the probability of selecting at random from the school a male student who is in eleventh grade, which has a probability of $\frac{131}{1219} \approx 0.11$.

130. A: The range is the spread of the data. It can be calculated for each class by subtracting the lowest test score from the highest, or it can be determined visually from the graph. The difference between the highest and lowest test scores in class A is 98-23=75 points. The range for each of the other classes is much smaller.

131. D: 75% of the data in a set is above the first quartile. Since the first quartile for this set is 73, there is a 75% chance that a student chosen at random from class 2 scored above a 73.

132. C: The line through the center of the box represents the median. The median test score for classes 1 and 2 is 82.

Note that for class 1, the median is a better representation of the data than the mean. There are two outliers (points which lie outside of two standard deviations from the mean) which bring down the average test score. In cases such as this, the mean is not the best measure of central tendency.

133. D: Since there are 100 homes' market times represented in each set, the median time a home spends on the market is between the 50th and 51st data point in each set. The 50th and 51st data points for Zip Code 1 are six months and seven months, respectively, so the median time a house in Zip Code 1 spends on the market is between six and seven months (6.5 months), which by the realtor's definition of market time is a seven month market time. The 50th and 51st data points for Zip Code 2 are both thirteen months, so the median time a house in Zip Code 2 spends on the market is thirteen months.

To find the mean market time for 100 houses, find the sum of the market times and divide by 100. If the frequency of a one month market time is 9, the number 1 is added nine times (1·9), if frequency of a two month market time is 10, the number 2 is added ten times (2·10), and so on. So, to find the average market time, divide by 100 the sum of the products of each market time and its corresponding frequency. For Zip Code 1, the mean market time is 7.38 months, which by the realtor's definition of market time is an eight month market time. For Zip Code 2, the mean market time is 12.74, which by the realtor's definition of market time is a thirteen month market time.

The mode market time is the market time for which the frequency is the highest. For Zip Code 1, the mode market time is three months, and for Zip Code 2, the mode market time is eleven months.

The statement given in choice D is true. The median time a house spends on the market in Zip Code 1 is less than the mean time a house spends on the market in Zip Code 1.

Time on market	Frequency for Zip Code 1	Frequency for Zip Code 2	Time·Frequency for Zip Code 1	Time·Frequency for Zip Code 1
1	9	6	9	6
2	10	4	20	8
3	12	3	36	9
4	8	4	32	16
5	6	3	30	15
6	5	5	30	30
7	8	2	56	14
8	8	1	64	8
9	6	3	54	27
10	3	5	30	50
11	5	7	55	77
12	4	6	48	72
13	2	6	26	78
14	3	5	42	70
15	1	3	15	45
16	2	2	32	32
17	2	3	34	51
18	1	5	18	90
19	0	6	0	114
20	2	4	40	80
21	1	5	21	105
22	1	4	22	88
23	0	3	0	69
24	1	5	24	120
SUM	100	100	738	1274

134. C: The probability of an event is the number of possible occurrences of that event divided by the number of all possible outcomes. A camper who is at least eight years old can be eight, nine, or ten years old, so the probability of randomly selecting a camper at least eight years old is $\frac{\text{number of eight-, nine-, and ten-year old campers}}{\text{total number of campers}} = \frac{14+12+10}{12+15+14+12+10} = \frac{36}{63} = \frac{4}{7}$.

135. B: There are three ways in which two women from the same department can be selected: two women can be selected from the first department, or two women can be selected from the second department, or two women can be selected from the third department.

The probability that two women are selected from Department 1 is $\frac{12}{103} \times \frac{11}{102} = \frac{132}{10506}$, the probability that two women are selected from Department 2 is $\frac{28}{103} \times \frac{27}{102} = \frac{756}{10506}$, and the probability that two women are selected from Department 3 is $\frac{16}{103} \times \frac{15}{102} = \frac{240}{10506}$. Since any of these is a discrete possible outcome, the probability that two women will be selected from the same department is the sum of these outcomes: $\frac{132}{10506} + \frac{756}{10506} + \frac{240}{10506} \approx 0.107$, or 10.7%.

	Department 1	Department 2	Department 3	Total
Women	12	28	16	56
Men	18	14	15	47
Total	30	42	31	103

136. B: The number of students who like broccoli is equal to the number of students who like all three vegetables plus the number of students who like broccoli and carrots but not cauliflower plus the number of students who like broccoli and cauliflower but not carrots plus the number of students who like broccoli but no other vegetable: $3 + 15 + 4 + 10 = 32$. These students plus the numbers of students who like just cauliflower, just carrots, cauliflower and carrots, or none of the vegetables represents the entire set of students sampled: $32 + 2 + 27 + 6 + 23 = 90$. So, the probability that a randomly chosen student likes broccoli is $\frac{32}{90} \approx 0.356$.

The number of students who like carrots and at least one other vegetable is $15 + 6 + 3 = 24$. The number of students who like carrots is $24 + 27 = 51$. So, the probability that a student who likes carrots will also like at least one other vegetable is $\frac{24}{51} \approx 0.471$. The number of students who like cauliflower and broccoli is $4 + 3 = 7$. The number of students who like all three vegetables is 3. So, the probability that a student who likes cauliflower and broccoli will also like carrots is $\frac{3}{7} \approx 0.429$.

The number of students who do not like carrots, broccoli, or cauliflower is 23. The total number of students surveyed is 90. So, the probability that a student does not like any of the three vegetables is $23/90 \approx 0.256$.

137. C: Since each coin toss is an independent event, the probability of the compound event of flipping the coin three times is equal to the product of the probabilities of the individual events. For example, $P(HHH) = P(H) \cdot P(H) \cdot P(H)$, $P(HHT) = P(H) \cdot P(H) \cdot P(T)$, etc. When a coin is flipped three times, all of the possible outcomes are HHH, HHT, HTH, HTT, THH, THT, TTH, and TTT. Since the only way to obtain three heads is by the coin landing on heads three times,

$$P(three\ heads) = P(HHH) = P(H)P(H)P(H).$$

Likewise,

$$P(no\ heads) = P(T)P(T)P(T).$$

Since there are three ways to get one head,

$$P(one\ head) = P(HTT) + P(THT) + P(TTH) = P(H)P(T)P(T) + P(T)P(H)P(T) + P(T)P(T)P(H)$$
$$= P(H)[(3P(T)^2],$$

And since there are three ways to get two heads,

$$P(two\ heads) = P(HHT) + P(HTH) + P(THH)$$
$$= P(H)P(H)P(T) + P(H)P(T)P(H) + P(T)P(H)P(H) = P(H)^2[3P(T)]$$

Use these properties to calculate the experimental probability P(H):

30 out of 100 coin tosses resulted in three heads, and $P(three\ heads) = P(H)P(H)P(H) = P(H)^3$. So, experimental P(H) can be calculated by taking the cube root of $\frac{30}{100}$. $\sqrt[3]{0.3} \approx 0.67$.
Similarly, $P(no\ heads) = P(T)P(T)P(T) = \frac{4}{100}$. $P(T) = \sqrt[3]{0.04} \approx 0.34$. $P(H) + P(T) = 1$, $P(T) = 1 - P(H)$. Thus, $P(H) = 1 - P(T) \approx 0.66$.

Notice that these calculated values of P(H) re approximately the same, Since 100 is a fairly large sample size for this kind of experiment, the approximation for $P(H)$ ought to consistent for the compiled data set. Rather than calculating $P(H)$ using the data for one head and two heads, use the average calculated probability to confirm that the number of expected outcomes of one head and two head matches the number of actual outcomes.

The number of expected outcomes of getting one head in three coin flips out of 100 trials $100\{0.665[3(1 - 0.665)^2]\} \approx 22$, and the expected outcome getting of two heads in three coin flips out of 100 trials three flips is $100\{0.665^2[3(1 - 0.665)]\} \approx 44$. Since 22 and 44 are, in fact, the data obtained, 0.665 is indeed a good approximation for P(H) when the coin used in this experiment is tossed.

138. D: A fair coin has a symmetrical binomial distribution which peaks in its center. Since choice B shows a skewed distribution for the fair coin, it cannot be the correct answer. From the frequency histogram given for the misshapen coin, it is evident that the misshapen coin is more likely to land on heads. Therefore, it is more likely that ten coin flips would result in fewer tails than ten coin flips of a fair coin; consequently, the probability distribution for the misshapen coin would be higher than the fair coin's distribution towards the left of the graph since the misshapen coin is less likely to land on tails. Choice A shows a probability distribution which peaks at a value of 5 and which is symmetrical with respect to the peak, which verifies that it cannot be correct. (Furthermore, in choice A, the sum of the probabilities shown for each number of tails for the misshapen coin is not equal to 1.) The distribution for the misshapen coin in choice C is skewed in the wrong direction, favoring tails instead of heads, and must therefore also be incorrect. Choice D shows the correct binomial distribution for the fair coin and the appropriate shift for the misshapen coin.

Another way to approach this question is to use the answer from the previous problem to determine the probability of obtaining particular events, such as no tails and no heads, and then compare those probabilities to the graphs. For example, for the misshapen coin, P(0 tails)=P(10 heads) $\approx (0.67)^{10}$, or 0.018, and the P(10 tails) $\approx (0.33)^{10}$, which is 0.000015. For a fair coin, P(0 tails)=$(0.5)^{10}$=P(0 heads). To find values other than these, it is helpful to use the binomial distribution formula $({}_nC_r)p^r q^{n-r}$, where n is the number of trials, r is the number of successes, p is the probability of success, and q is the probability of failure. For this problem, obtaining tails is a success, and the probability of obtaining tails is $p = 0.33$ for the misshapen coin and $p = 0.5$ for the fair coin; so, $q = 0.67$ for the misshapen coin and $q = 0.5$ for the fair coin. To find the probability of, say, getting three tails for ten flips of the misshapen coin, find
$({}_nC_r)p^r q^{n-r} = ({}_{10}C_3)(0.33)^3(0.67)^7 = \frac{10!}{3!7!}(0.33)^3(0.67)^7 \approx 0.261$. The calculated probabilities match those shown in choice C.

139. C: When rolling two dice, there is only one way to roll a sum of two (rolling a 1 on each die) and twelve (rolling 6 on each die). In contrast, there are two ways to obtain a sum of three (rolling a 2 and 1 or a 1 and 2) and eleven (rolling a 5 and 6 or a 6 and 5), three ways to obtain a sum of four (1 and 3; 2 and 2; 3 and 1) or ten (4 and 6; 5 and 5; 6 and 4), and so on. Since the probability of obtaining each sum is inconsistent, choice C is not an appropriate simulation. Choice A is acceptable

since the probability of picking A, 1, 2, 3, 4, 5, 6, 7, 8, 9, or J from the modified deck cards of cards is equally likely, each with a probability of $\frac{4}{52-8} = \frac{4}{44} = \frac{1}{11}$. Choice B is also acceptable since the computer randomly generates one number from eleven possible numbers, so the probability of generating any of the numbers is $\frac{1}{11}$.

140. C: The number 00 represents the genotype aa. The numbers 11, 12, 21, and 22 represent the genotype bb.

```
28 93 97 37 92 00 27 21 87 13 62 63 10 31 55 09 47 07 54 88 38 88 10
98 34 01 45 14 34 46 38 61 93 22 37 39 57 03 93 50 53 16 28 65 81 60
21 12 13 10 19 91 04 18 49 01 99 30 11 16 00 48 04 63 59 24 02 42 23
06 32 52 19 18 94 94 46 63 87 41 79 39 85 20 43 20 15 03 39 33 77 45
66 77 70 92 25 27 68 71 89 35 98 55 85 47 60 97 12 92 53 44 45 41 51
22 09 23 81 33 04 35 43 48 32 80 36 95 64 56 34 74 55 37 64 84 51 50
25 99 51 94 19 46 10 44 17 25 75 52 47 35 70 65 08 50 98 09 02 24 30
59 00 03 21 40 30 86 16 53 91 28 17 97 58 75 76 73 83 54 40 54 13 38
36 67 74 80 63 12 41 27 96 61 66 05 60 69 96 15 56 82 57 31 83 26 24
78 42 76 49 56 06 57 78 67 02 96 40 82 29 14 07 29 62 90 31 08 26 71
61 18 22 84 23 33 49 29 90 07 08 05 14 59 72 86 44 69 68 99 06 11 95
43 72 58 28 93 97 37 92 00 27 21 87 13 62 61 15 31 55 09 47 07 54 88
38 88 10 98 34 01 45 14 34 46 38 61 93 22 37 39 57 03 93 50 53 16 28
65 81 60 21 12 13 10 19 91 04 18 49 01 99 30 11 16 00 48 04 63 59 24
02 42 23 06 32 52 19 18 94 94 46 63 87 41 79 39 85 20 43 20 15 03 39
33 77 45 66 77 70 92 25 27 68 71 89 35 98 55 85 47 60 97 12 92 53 44
45 41 51 22 09 23 81 33 04 35 43 48 32 80 36 95 64 56 34 74 55 37 64
84 51 50 25 99 51 94 19 46 10 44 17 25 75 52 47 35 70 65 08 50 98 09
02 24 30 59 00 03 21 40 30 86 16 53 91 28 17 97 58 75 76 73 83 54 40
54 13 38 36 67 74 80 63 12 41 27 96 61 66 05 60 69 96 15 56 82 57 31
83 26 24 78 42 76 49 56 06 57 78 67 02 96 40 82 29 14 07 29 62 90 31
08 26 71 61 18 22 84 23 33 49 29 90 07 08 05 14 59
```

There are six occurrences of 00, so the experimental probability of getting genotype aa is 6/500 = 0.012. There are 21 occurrences of 11, 12, 21, and 22, so the experimental probability of getting genotype bb is 21/500=0.042. The experimental probability of either getting genotype aa or bb is 0.012+0.042=0.054. Multiply this experimental probability by 100,000 to find the number of individuals expected to be homozygous for either allele in a population of 100,000. $0.054 \cdot 100{,}000 = 5{,}400$. Notice that this is higher than the expected number based on the theoretical probability. Since the allele frequencies are in a ratio of 1:2:7, the theoretical probability of getting either aa or bb is $\frac{1}{10} \cdot \frac{1}{10} + \frac{2}{10} \cdot \frac{2}{10} = \frac{5}{100} = 0.05$. Based on the theoretical probability, one would expect 5,000 members of a population of 100,000 to be homozygous for a or b.

141. D: A score of 85 is one standard deviation below the mean. Since approximately 68% of the data is within one standard deviation of the mean, about 32% (100%-68%) of the data is outside of one standard deviation within the mean. Normally distributed data is symmetric about the mean, which means that about 16% of the data lies below one standard deviation below the mean and about 16% of data lies above one standard deviation above the mean. Therefore, approximately 16% of individuals have IQs less than 85, while approximately 84% of the population has an IQ of at least 85. Since 84% of 300 is 252, about 252 people from the selected group have IQs of at least 85.

142. C: There are nine ways to assign the first digit since it can be any of the numbers 1-9. There are nine ways to assign the second digit since it can be any digit 0-9 EXCEPT for the digit assigned in place 1. There are eight ways to assign the third number since there are ten digits, two of which have already been assigned. There are seven ways to assign the fourth number, six ways to assign the fifth, five ways to assign the sixth, and four ways to assign the seventh. So, the number of combinations is $9 \cdot 9 \cdot 8 \cdot 7 \cdot 6 \cdot 5 \cdot 4 = 544{,}320$.

Another way to approach the problem is to notice that the arrangement of nine digits in the last six places is a sequence without reputation, or a permutation. (Note: this may be called a partial permutation since all of the elements of the set need not be used.) The number of possible sequences of a fixed length r of elements taken from a given set of size n is permutation ${}_nP_r = \frac{n!}{(n-r)!}$. So, the number of ways to arrange the last six digits is ${}_9P_6 = \frac{9!}{(9-6)!} = \frac{9!}{3!} = 60{,}480$. Multiply this number by nine since there are nine possibilities for the first digit of the phone number. $9 \cdot {}_9P_6 = 544{,}320$.

143. B: If each of the four groups in the class of twenty will contain three boys and two girls, there must be twelve boys and eight girls in the class. The number of ways the teacher can select three boys from a group of twelve boys is ${}_{12}C_3 = \frac{12!}{3!(12-3)!} = \frac{12!}{3!9!} = \frac{12 \cdot 11 \cdot 10 \cdot 9!}{3!9!} = \frac{12 \cdot 11 \cdot 10}{3 \cdot 2 \cdot 1} = 220$. The number of ways she can select two girls from a group of eight girls is ${}_8C_2 = \frac{8!}{2!(8-2)!} = \frac{8!}{2!6!} = \frac{8 \cdot 7 \cdot 6!}{2!6!} = \frac{8 \cdot 7}{2 \cdot 1} = 28$. Since each combination of boys can be paired with each combination of girls, the number of group combinations is $220 \cdot 28 = 6{,}160$.

144. B: One way to approach this problem is to first consider the number of arrangements of the five members of the family if Tasha (T) and Mac (M) must sit together. Treat them as a unit seated in a fixed location at the table; then arrange the other three family members (A, B, and C):

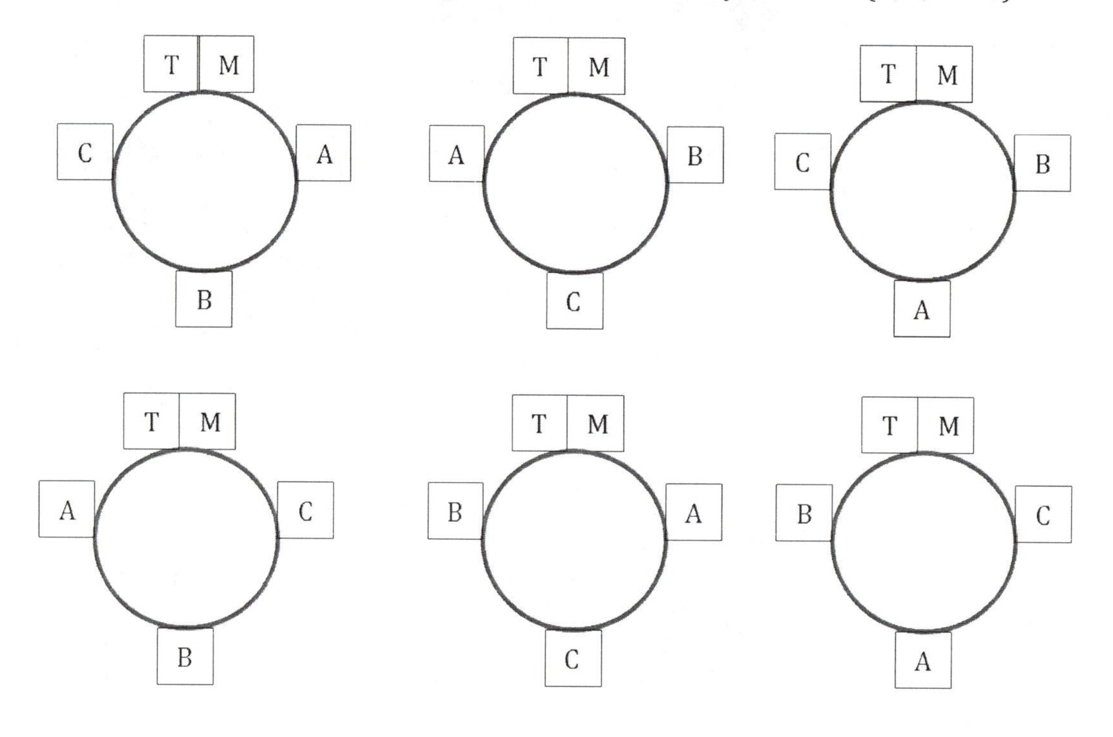

There are six ways to arrange four units around a circle as shown. (Any other arrangement would be a rotation in which the elements in the same order and would therefore not be a unique arrangement.) Note that there are $(n-1)!$ ways to arrange n units around a circle for $n > 1$.

Of course, Mac and Tasha are not actually a single unit. They would still be sitting beside each other if they were to trade seats, so there are twelve arrangements in which the two are seated next to one another. In all other arrangements of the five family members, they are separated. Therefore, to find the number of arrangements in which Tasha and Mac are not sitting together, subtract twelve from the possible arrangement of five units around a circle: $(5-1)! - 12 = 12$.

145. A: The recursive definition of the sequence gives the first term of the series, $a_1 = -1$. The definition also defines each term in the series as the sum of the previous term and 2. Therefore, the second term in the series is $-1 + 2 = 1$, the third term in the series is $1 + 2 = 3$, and so on.

n	a_n
1	-1
2	1
3	3

The relationship between n and a_n is linear, so the equation of the sequence can be found in the same way as the equation of a line. The value of a_n increases by two each time the value of n increases by 1.

n	$2n$	a_n
1	2	-1
2	4	1
3	6	3

Since the difference in $2n$ and a_n is 3, $a_n = 2n - 3$.

n	$2n-3$	a_n
1	2-3	-1
2	4-3	1
3	6-3	3

146. B: The series is an infinite geometric series, the sum of which can be found by using the formula $\sum_{n=0}^{\infty} ar^n = \frac{a}{1-r}, |r| < 1$, where a is the first term in the series and r is the ratio between successive terms. In the series 200+100+50+25+ ..., $a = 200$ and $r = \frac{1}{2}$. So, the sum of the series is $\frac{200}{1-\frac{1}{2}} = \frac{200}{\frac{1}{2}} = 400$.

147. A: The sum of two vectors is equal to the sum of their components. Using component-wise addition, $\boldsymbol{v} + \boldsymbol{w} = (4 + (-3), 3 + 4) = (1,7)$. To multiply a vector by a scalar, multiply each component by that scalar. Using component-wise scalar multiplication, $2(1,7) = (2 \cdot 1, 2 \cdot 7) = (2,14)$.

148. A: First, subtract the two column matrices in parentheses by subtracting corresponding terms.

$$[2 \quad 0 \quad -5]\left(\begin{bmatrix} 4-3 \\ 2-5 \\ -1-(-5) \end{bmatrix}\right) = [2 \quad 0 \quad -5]\begin{bmatrix} 1 \\ -3 \\ 4 \end{bmatrix}$$

Then, multiply the matrices. The product of a 1×3 matrix and a 3×1 matrix is a 1×1 matrix.

$$[2 \quad 0 \quad -5]\begin{bmatrix} 1 \\ -3 \\ 4 \end{bmatrix} = [(2)(1) + (0)(-3) + (-5)(4)] = [-18]$$

Note that matrix multiplication is NOT commutative. The product of the 3x1 matrix $\begin{bmatrix} 1 \\ -3 \\ 4 \end{bmatrix}$ and the 1x3 matrix $[2 \quad 0 \quad -5]$ is the 3x3 matrix $\begin{bmatrix} 2 & 0 & -5 \\ -6 & 0 & 15 \\ 8 & 0 & -20 \end{bmatrix}$.

149. B: The table below shows the intersections of each set with each of the other sets.

Set	{2,4,6,8,10,12,...}	{1,2,3,4,6,12}	{1,2,4,9}
{2,4,6,8,10,12,...}	**{2,4,6,8,10,12,...}**	{2,4,6,12}	{2,4}
{1,2,3,4,6,12}	{2,4,6,12}	**{1,2,3,4,6,12}**	{1,2,4}
{1,2,4,9}	{2,4}	{1,2,4}	**{1,2,4,9}**

Notice that {2,4} is a subset of {2,4,6,12} and {1,2,4}. So, the intersection of {1,2,4,9} and the even integers is a subset of the intersection of the even integers and the factors of twelve, and the intersection of the set of even integers and {1,2,4,9} is a subset of the intersection of {1,2,4,9} and the factors of twelve. So, while it is not possible to determine which set is A and which is B, set C must be the set of factors of twelve: {1,2,3,4,6,12}.

150. D: Use a Venn diagram to help organize the given information. Start by filling in the space where the three circles intersect: Jenny tutored three students in all three areas. Use that information to fill in the spaces where two circles intersect: for example, she tutored four students in chemistry and for the ACT, and three of those were students she tutored in all three areas, so one student was tutored in chemistry and for the ACT but not for math. Once the diagram is completed, add the number of students who were tutored in all areas to the number of students tutored in only two of the three areas to the number of students tutored in only one area. The total number of students tutored was 3+2+2+1+3+2+1=14.

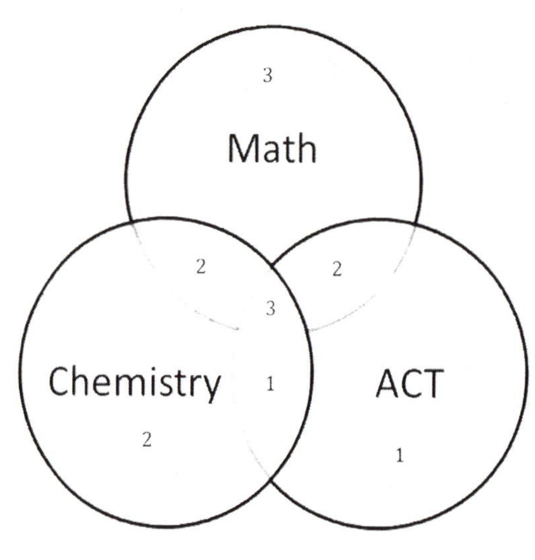

Science Practice Test

Practice Questions

1. Which of the following describes the process skill of concluding?
 a. Explaining or interpreting observations
 b. Making a determination based on the results of a controlled experiment
 c. Reading an instrument during an experiment
 d. Listing similarities and differences between two objects

2. A chemistry experiment is performed to determine the effect of a nonvolatile solute on the boiling point of water. Three trials are performed in which 10 mg, 20 mg and 30 mg of salt are added to 500 ml of distilled water. Each solution is heated on a hot plate, and the elevated boiling points are recorded. Which of the following correctly identifies the independent and dependent variables?
 a. The independent variable is the amount of salt, and the dependent variable is the temperature at which the water boils.
 b. The independent variable is the amount of water, and the dependent variable is the temperature at which the water boils.
 c. The independent variable is the temperature at which the water boils, and the dependent variable is the amount of salt.
 d. The independent variable is the amount of salt, and the dependent variable is the amount of water.

3. Which of the following is NOT true concerning forming and testing hypotheses?
 a. A controlled experiment should have only one independent variable.
 b. A controlled experiment may have several constants.
 c. A good hypothesis should take all of the available background material on the topic into consideration.
 d. A good hypothesis will not be disproved by testing.

4. Which of the following is the correct expression of 0.0034050 in scientific notation?
 a. 34.050×10^{-3}
 b. 3.4050×10^{-2}
 c. 3.4050×10^{-3}
 d. 3.4050×10^{3}

5. Which of the following numbers has 4 significant figures?
 a. 3020.5
 b. 0.003020
 c. 3.2005
 d. 0.0325

6. What is the correct expression of 91,000 × 87,000 using scientific notation and significant figures?
 a. 7.91×10^9
 b. 7.9×10^9
 c. 79.2×10^8
 d. 79×10^8

7. Students experimentally determine that the specific heat of copper is 0.410 $\frac{J}{g \cdot °C}$. If the known value of the specific heat of copper is 0.385 $\frac{J}{g \cdot °C}$, what is the percent error?
 a. 6.10%
 b. 16.4%
 c. 6.49%
 d. 15.4%

8. Two balances in a classroom laboratory are used to determine the mass of an object. The actual mass of the object is 15.374 grams. Which of the following statements is true concerning the accuracy and precision of these two balances?

Measurement	Triple Beam Balance	Digital Balance
1	15.38 grams	15.375 grams
2	15.39 grams	15.376 grams
3	15.37 grams	15.376 grams
4	15.38 grams	15.375 grams

 a. The triple beam balance is both more accurate and more precise.
 b. The triple beam balance is more accurate, but the digital balance is more precise.
 c. The digital balance is more accurate, but the triple beam balance is more precise.
 d. The digital balance is both more accurate and more precise.

9. Which of the following subskills best fits the process skill of observing?
 a. Using the five senses to collect evidence and write descriptions
 b. Grouping objects based on similarities, differences, and interrelationships
 c. Explaining or interpreting collected evidence
 d. Reporting to others what has been found by experimentation

10. Which of the following sets of quantities are equivalent?
 a. 2,310 mg and 2.310 g
 b. 2.310 g and 231.0 mg
 c. 2.310 kg and 231.0 g
 d. 2.310 kg and 231,000 mg

11. Which of the following best describes the relationship of this set of data?

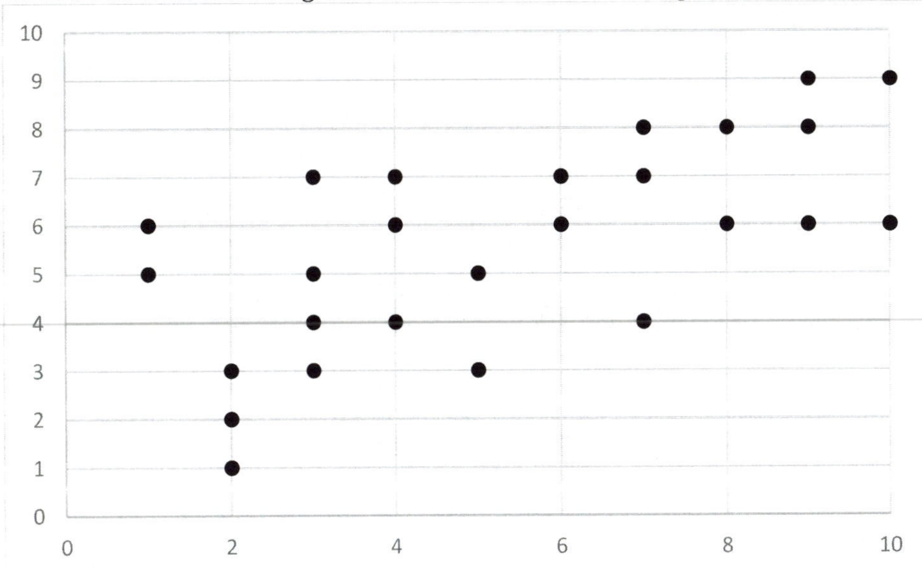

a. High positive correlation
b. Low positive correlation
c. Low negative correlation
d. No correlation

12. Which of the following is NOT true concerning correlation?
a. Correlation can show the relationship between variables.
b. Correlation can show cause and effect.
c. Correlation can show linear relationships.
d. Correlation can show nonlinear relationships.

13. Which of the following is NOT a recommended storage practice for laboratory chemicals?
a. Chemicals should be stored at the appropriate temperature and humidity.
b. Chemicals should be dated when received and when opened.
c. Chemicals may be routinely stored on bench tops.
d. Chemicals should be stored on shelves with raised outer edges.

14. Which of the following is the best prediction for solubility at 150 degrees Celsius?

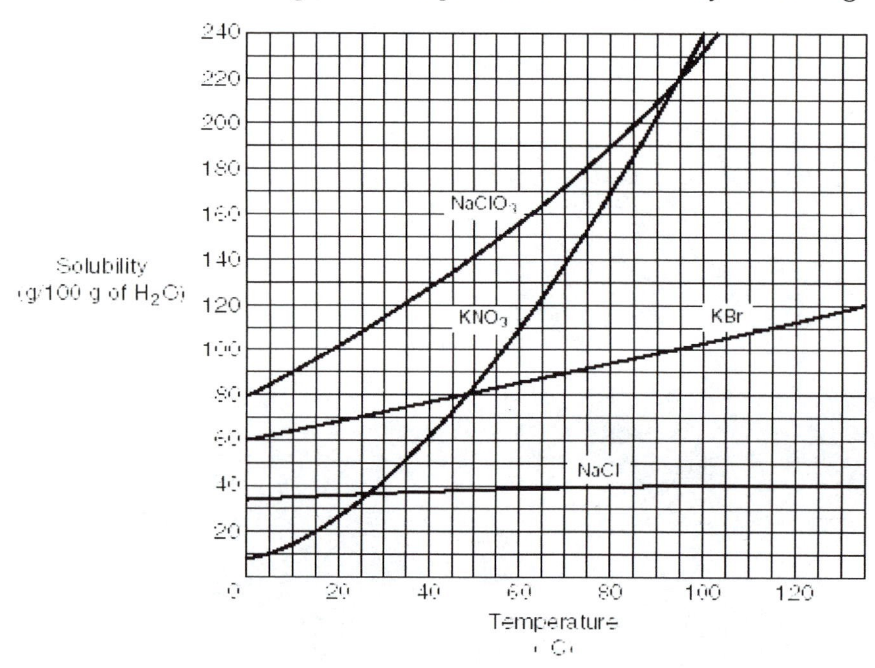

a. 260 g NaClO3 per 100 g H2O
b. 250 g KNO3 per 100 g H2O
c. 130 g KBr per 100 g H2O
d. 80 g NaCl per 100 g H2O

15. Which of the following conclusions can be drawn from the data presented in the graph below?

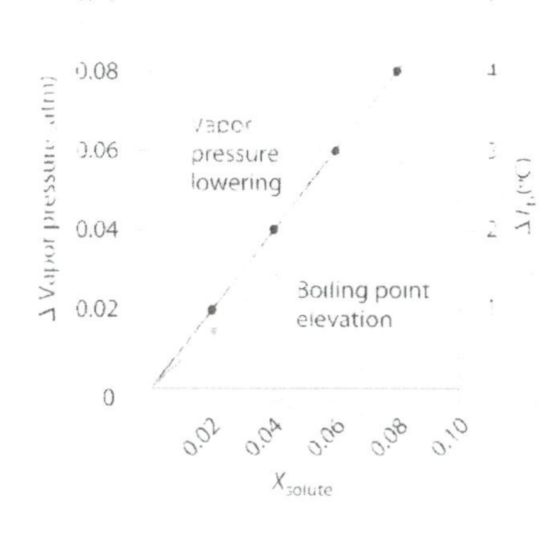

a. Increasing the solute increases the vapor pressure and decreases the boiling point of this solution.
b. Increasing the solute increases the vapor pressure and increases the boiling point of this solution.
c. Increasing the solute decreases the vapor pressure and decreases the boiling point of this solution.
d. Increasing the solute decreases the vapor pressure and increases the boiling point of this solution.

16. What are pure substances that consist of more than one type of atom?
   a. Elements
   b. Compounds
   c. Molecules
   d. Mixtures

17. Which of the following statements concerning the states of matter is NOT true?
   a. Plasmas are high temperature collections of ions and free electrons.
   b. Solids are the least compressible due to the more rigid positions of the particles.
   c. Gases have no definite volume and expand to fill their containers
   d. Liquids have no definite shape and no definite volume.

18. The symbol for a calcium ion is Ca^{2+}. Which of the following statements is true concerning this ion?
   a. This cation has fewer electrons than protons.
   b. This anion has fewer electrons than protons.
   c. This cation has more electrons than protons.
   d. This anion has more electrons than protons.

19. Which of the following subatomic particles has the smallest mass?
   a. Protons
   b. Electrons
   c. Quarks
   d. Neutrons

20. A uranium isotope is represented by the symbol $^{238}_{92}U$. How many neutrons does an atom of this isotope contain?
   a. 92
   b. 330
   c. 238
   d. 146

21. Which if the following represents an alpha particle?
   a. $_{-1}^{0}e$
   b. $_{1}^{2}H+$
   c. $_{2}^{4}He2+$
   d. $_{+1}^{0}e$

22. Which of the following is an example of a chemical change?
   a. Salt dissolving in water
   b. Water evaporating
   c. Silver tarnishing
   d. Dry ice sublimating

23. Which temperature scales have exactly 100 degrees between the freezing point and the boiling point of water?
  a. Celsius only
  b. Celsius and Kelvin
  c. Celsius and Fahrenheit
  d. Celsius, Fahrenheit, and Kelvin

24. Which is an example of convection as a method of heat transfer?
  a. A person warming his hands by placing them on an electric blanket
  b. A person warming his hands by placing them near the sides of a light bulb
  c. A person warming his hands by washing with hot water
  d. A person warming his hands by rubbing them together

25. The energy flow through an ecosystem is represented by an energy pyramid. In the energy pyramid for a terrestrial ecosystem, the producers utilize 6,000 kilocalories per square meter per year. What approximate amount of energy is transferred to the third trophic level of this ecosystem?
  a. 0.6 kilocalories per square meter per year
  b. 6 kilocalories per square meter per year
  c. 60 kilocalories per square meter per year
  d. 600 kilocalories per square meter per year

26. Which of the following general statements concerning ideal gases is true?
  a. Volume is inversely proportional to kinetic energy.
  b. Volume is inversely proportional to number of moles.
  c. Volume is inversely proportional to temperature.
  d. Volume is inversely proportional to pressure.

27. According to the kinetic theory of matter, which of the following statements is true?
  a. The average kinetic energy is inversely proportional to the square of the average velocity of the particles.
  b. The average kinetic energy is inversely proportional to the average velocity of the particles.
  c. The average kinetic energy is directly proportional to the square of the average velocity of the particles.
  d. The average kinetic energy is directly proportional to the average velocity of the particles.

28. In general, where in the periodic table of elements are the elements with the largest atomic radii located?
  a. Upper-right corner
  b. Upper-left corner
  c. Bottom-left corner
  d. Bottom-right corner

29. What is the name of the compound $CuCl_2$?
  a. Copper (I) chloride
  b. Copper (II) chloride
  c. Copper (I) chlorine
  d. Copper (II) chlorine

30. Which of the following molecules exhibits ionic bonding?
   a. NaCl
   b. CO2
   c. C6H12O6
   d. H2O

31. Given the chemical reaction $4Al(s) + 3O_2(g) \rightarrow 2Al_2O_3(s)$, how many moles of $O_2(g)$ are needed to produce 100.0 moles of $2Al_2O_3(s)$?
   a. 100.0
   b. 150.0
   c. 200.0
   d. 250.0

32. Which of the following is Avogadro's number?
   a. 2.063×10^{23}
   b. 6.023×10^{22}
   c. 6.022×10^{23}
   d. 2.063×10^{22}

33. What type of reaction is $Cu(s) + 2AgNO_3(aq) \rightarrow 2Ag(s) + Cu(NO_3)_2(aq)$?
   a. Single replacement
   b. Double replacement
   c. Synthesis
   d. Decomposition

34. Which of the following is NOT true regarding exothermic and endothermic processes or reactions?
   a. Exothermic reactions release heat energy.
   b. The melting of ice is an endothermic process.
   c. The burning of butane is an exothermic process.
   d. The change in enthalpy is positive for an exothermic reaction.

35. Which of the following substances has a pH closest to 1?
   a. Bleach
   b. Water
   c. Ammonia
   d. Vinegar

36. Which of the following describes the correct procedure to prepare 100.0 ml of 3.00 M HCl solution from an 18.0 M HCl stock solution?
   a. Dilute 16.7 ml of 18.0 M HCl to a total volume of 100.0 ml.
   b. Dilute 18.0 ml of 18.0 M HCl to a total volume of 100.0 ml.
   c. Dilute 54.0 ml of 18.0 M HCl to a total volume of 100.0 ml.
   d. Dilute 14.3 ml of 18.0 M HCl to a total volume of 100.0 ml.

37. Which of the following is NOT generally true regarding solubility?
    a. Increasing temperature increases the solubility of a solid in a liquid.
    b. Increasing temperature increases the solubility of a gas in a liquid.
    c. Increasing the pressure has little effect on the solubility of a solid in a liquid.
    d. Increasing partial pressure of a gas decreases the solubility of a gas in a liquid.

38. Which of the following would most likely dissolve in a nonpolar solvent?
    a. $AgNO_3$
    b. NH_3
    c. CCl_4
    d. KI

39. Which of the following characteristics is consistent with an acid?
    a. Turns litmus paper blue
    b. Accepts a proton
    c. Reacts with zinc to produce hydrogen gas
    d. Produces OH^- ions in aqueous solutions

40. Which of the following is a solute?
    a. Salt in a mixture of salt and pepper
    b. Air in mixture of ash and air
    c. Water in a mixture of salt and water
    d. Sugar in a mixture of sugar and water

41. Which of the following is a scalar quantity?
    a. Acceleration
    b. Velocity
    c. Speed
    d. Force

42. Which of Newton's laws explains why seatbelts are needed?
    a. Second Law of Motion
    b. Law of Universal Gravitation
    c. First Law of Motion
    d. Third Law of Motion

43. According to Newton's Law of Universal Gravitation, what happens to the force of attraction between two objects if the distance between them is doubled?
    a. The force is reduced to one half of the original amount.
    b. The force is reduced to one fourth of the original amount.
    c. The force is quadrupled.
    d. The force is doubled.

44. Which of the following is the best description of pressure?
    a. Mass per unit volume
    b. Force per unit area
    c. Force per unit volume
    d. Mass per unit area

45. What is the volume of a 378 gram block of quartz that has a density of 2.65 g/cm^3?
  a. 1012 cm3
  b. 143 cm3
  c. 375 cm3
  d. 721 cm3

46. Which of the following statements is NOT true about the period of a simple pendulum?
  a. As the mass of a pendulum increases, the period increases.
  b. For small amplitudes, the period of a pendulum is approximately independent of amplitude.
  c. A pendulum swings more slowly at higher elevation.
  d. To double the period of a pendulum, the length must be quadrupled.

47. A worker applies a force of 500.0 N to a pulley for a distance of 1.5 m to move a crate that weighs 1000.0 N a distance of 0.5 m. What is the ideal mechanical advantage of this pulley?
  a. 4
  b. 2
  c. 3
  d. 5

48. According to Coulomb's Law of Electric Force, which of the following statements is true?
  a. The force between two charged objects is directly related to the square of the distance between them.
  b. The force between two charged objects is inversely related to the square of the distance between them.
  c. The force between two charged objects is inversely related to the distance between them.
  d. The force between two charged objects is inversely related to the square root of the distance between them.

49. What is the current through a resistor of 20.0 ohms if the voltage is 6.0 volts?
  a. 0.30 amperes
  b. 120 amperes
  c. 3.3 amperes
  d. 0.20 amperes

50. An electromagnet has a lifting force of 5 N. If the current through the coil is doubled, what is the lifting force?
  a. 2 N
  b. 5 N
  c. 10 N
  d. 20 N

51. Which color of light has the highest frequency?
  a. Blue
  b. Red
  c. Green
  d. Violet

52. On what does the energy of a photon depend?

a. Speed
b. Mass
c. Frequency
d. Amplitude

53. Under which conditions will light undergo total internal reflection?

a. When the angle of incidence is equal to the critical angle
b. When the angle of incidence is greater than the critical angle
c. When the angle of incidence is less than the critical angle
d. When the angle of incidence is zero

54. Which of the following correctly describes the image of a double concave lens?

a. Reduced, upright, virtual image
b. Enlarged, upright, virtual image
c. Reduced, inverted, virtual image
d. Reduced, upright, real image

55. Which of the following can be described as the way the human ear perceives the amplitude of a sound wave?

a. Loudness
b. Pitch
c. Intensity
d. Frequency

56. Which substance is most likely to be a solid at STP?

a. Kr
b. Na
c. NH_3
d. Xe

57.Which of the following tend to increase the melting point of a solid?

I. Increasing molecular weight
II. Decreasing polarity
III. Increasing surface area

a. I and II
b. II
c. III
d. I and III

58. A gas at constant volume is cooled. Which statement about the gas must be true?

a. The kinetic energy of the gas molecules has decreased.
b. The gas has condensed to a liquid.
c. The weight of the gas has decreased.
d. The density of the gas has increased.

59. One mole of oxygen gas and two moles of hydrogen are combined in a sealed container at STP. Which of the following statements is true?

a. The mass of hydrogen gas is greater than the mass of oxygen.
b. The volume of hydrogen is greater than the volume of oxygen.
c. The hydrogen and oxygen will react to produce 2 mol of water.
d. The partial pressure of hydrogen is greater than the partial pressure of oxygen.

60. Graham's law is best used to determine what relationship between two different materials?

a. pressure and volume
b. volume and temperature
c. mass and diffusion rate
d. Diffusion rate and temperature

61. Which of the following statements is true about the physical properties of liquids and gases?

I. Liquids and gases are both compressible
II. Liquids flow, but gases do not
III. Liquids flow, and gases are incompressible
IV. Liquids flow and gases are compressible
V. Gases flow and liquids are incompressible

a. I and III
b. II and IV
c. III and V
d. IV and V

62. Which of the following statements **generally** describes the trend of electronegativity considering the Periodic Table of the Elements?

a. Electronegativity increases going from left to right and from top to bottom
b. Electronegativity increases going from right to left and from bottom to top
c. Electronegativity increases going from left to right and from bottom to top
d. Electronegativity increases going from right to left and from top to bottom

63. A solid is heated until it melts. Which of the following is true about the solid melting?

a. ΔH is positive, and ΔS is positive
b. ΔH is negative and ΔS is positive
c. ΔH is positive and ΔS is negative
d. ΔH is negative and ΔS is negative

64. A liquid is held at its freezing point and slowly allowed to solidify. Which of the following statements about this event are true?

a. During freezing, the temperature of the material decreases
b. While freezing, heat is given off by the material
c. During freezing, heat is absorbed by the material
d. During freezing, the temperature of the material increases

65. Which of the following radioactive emissions results in an increase in atomic number?

a. Alpha
b. Beta
c. Gamma
d. Neutron

66. A material has a half life of 2 years. If you started with 1 kg of the material, how much of it would still be the original material after 8 years?
    a. 1 kg
    b. 0.5 kg
    c. 0.06 kg
    d. 0.12 kg

67. The hydrogen bonds in a water molecule make water a good
    a. Solvent for lipids
    b. Participant in replacement reactions
    c. Surface for small particles and living organisms to move across
    d. Solvent for polysaccharides such as cellulose

68. The breakdown of a disaccharide releases energy which is stored as ATP. This is an example of a(n)
    a. Combination reaction
    b. Replacement reaction
    c. Endothermic reaction
    d. Exothermic reaction

69. Which of the following metabolic compounds is composed of only carbon, oxygen, and hydrogen?
    a. Phospholipids
    b. Glycogen
    c. Peptides
    d. RNA

70. When an animal takes in more energy that it uses over an extended time, the extra chemical energy is stored as:
    a. Fat
    b. Starch
    c. Protein
    d. Enzymes

71. Which of the following molecules is thought to have acted as the first enzyme in early life on earth?
    a. Protein
    b. RNA
    c. DNA
    d. Triglycerides

72. Which of the following organelles is/are formed when the plasma membrane surrounds a particle outside of the cell?
    a. Golgi bodies
    b. Rough endoplasmic reticulum
    c. Secretory vesicles
    d. Endocytic vesicles

73. Which of the following plant organelles contain(s) pigment that give leaves their color?
a. Centrioles
b. Cell walls
c. Chloroplasts
d. Central vacuole

74. Prokaryotic and eukaryotic cells are similar in having which of the following?
a. Membrane-bound organelles
b. Protein-studded DNA
c. Presence of a nucleus
d. Integral membrane proteins in the plasma membrane

75. Which of the following cell types has a peptidoglycan cell wall?
a. Algae
b. Bacteria
c. Fungi
d. Land plants

76. Enzymes catalyze biochemical reactions by
a. Lowering the potential energy of the products
b. Separating inhibitors from products
c. Forming a complex with the products
d. Lowering the activation energy of the reaction

77. Which of the following is not a characteristic of enzymes?
a. They change shape when they bind their substrates
b. They can catalyze reactions in both forward and reverse directions
c. Their activity is sensitive to changes in temperature
d. They are always active on more than one kind of substrate

78. In a strenuously exercising muscle, NADH begins to accumulate in high concentration. Which of the following metabolic process will be activated to reduce the concentration of NADH?
a. Glycolysis
b. The Krebs cycle
c. Lactic acid fermentation
d. Oxidative phosphorylation

79. Which of the following statements regarding chemiosmosis in mitochondria is not correct?
a. ATP synthase is powered by protons flowing through membrane channels
b. Energy from ATP is used to transport protons to the intermembrane space
c. Energy from the electron transport chain is used to transport protons to the intermembrane space
d. An electrical gradient and a pH gradient both exist across the inner membrane

80. In photosynthesis, high-energy electrons move through electron transport chains to produce ATP and NADPH. Which of the following provides the energy to create high energy electrons?
a. NADH
b. $NADP^+$
c. Water
d. Light

81. Which of the following kinds of plants is most likely to perform CAM photosynthesis?
a. Mosses
b. Grasses
c. Deciduous trees
d. Cacti

82. The combination of DNA with histones is called
a. A centromere
b. Chromatin
c. A chromatid
d. Nucleoli

83. In plants and animals, genetic variation is introduced during
a. Crossing over in mitosis
b. Chromosome segregation in mitosis
c. Cytokinesis of meiosis
d. Anaphase I of meiosis

84. DNA replication occurs during which of the following phases?
a. Prophase I
b. Prophase II
c. Interphase I
d. Interphase II

85. The synaptonemal complex is present in which of the following phases of the cell cycle?
a. Metaphase of mitosis
b. Metaphase of meiosis I
c. Telophase of meiosis I
d. Metaphase of meiosis II

86. A length of DNA coding for a particular protein is called a(n)
a. Allele
b. Genome
c. Gene
d. Transcript

87. In DNA replication, which of the following enzymes is required for separating the DNA molecule into two strands?
a. DNA polymerase
b. Single strand binding protein
c. DNA gyrase
d. Helicase

88. Which of the following chemical moieties forms the backbone of DNA?
a. Nitrogenous bases
b. Glycerol
c. Amino groups
d. Pentose and phosphate

89. Which of the following is required for the activity of DNA polymerase?
   a. Okazaki fragments
   b. RNA primer
   c. Single-strand binding protein
   d. Leading strand

90. Which of the following is the substrate for DNA ligase?
   a. Okazaki fragments
   b. RNA primer
   c. Single-strand binding protein
   d. Leading strand

91. Which of the following is true of the enzyme telomerase?
   a. It is active on the leading strand during DNA synthesis
   b. It requires a chromosomal DNA template
   c. It acts in the $3' \rightarrow 5'$ direction
   d. It adds a repetitive DNA sequence to the end of chromosomes

92. Which enzyme in DNA replication is a potential source of new mutations?
   a. DNA ligase
   b. Primase
   c. DNA gyrase
   d. DNA polymerase

93. Which of the following mutations is most likely to have a dramatic effect on the sequence of a protein?
   a. A point mutation
   b. A missense mutation
   c. A deletion
   d. A silent mutation

94. Which of the following best describes igneous rock?
   a. Includes intrusive and extrusive rock categories
   b. Includes foliated and non-foliated rock categories
   c. Includes chemical and mechanical rock categories
   d. Includes organic and inorganic rock categories

95. To which class of minerals do opal, corundum, magnetite, and quartz belong?
   a. Halides
   b. Silicates
   c. Native elements
   d. Oxides

96. Which of the following soil or rock types has a high porosity and a low permeability?
   a. Sand
   b. Granite
   c. Gravel
   d. Clay

97. In relation to the water cycle, which of the following statements concerning transpiration is NOT true?

a. As relative humidity increases, the rate of transpiration increases.
b. As winds increase, the rate of transpiration increases.
c. As temperatures increase, the rate of transpiration increases.
d. As soil moisture decreases, the rate of transpiration decreases.

98. Which of the following statements concerning earthquakes is NOT true?

a. The epicenter is located on the earth's surface directly above the focus.
b. Large earthquakes near or beneath a large body of water can generate deadly tsunamis.
c. The epicenter may be located by combining seismograms from two widely separate locations.
d. P waves, which travel faster than S waves, tend to have lower amplitude than S waves, causing little damage.

99. Which of the following statements regarding the principle of uniformitarianism is true?

a. Uniformitarianism is an argument for catastrophism.
b. Uniformitarianism is a key building block for Darwin's theory of evolution.
c. Uniformitarianism states that the past is the key to the present.
d. Uniformitarianism states that the fittest organisms will survive to reproduce.

100. According to the geologic time scale, which of the following statements is NOT true?

a. The rise of human civilization occurred between six thousand and twelve thousand years ago.
b. The Cambrian Explosion occurred after the Jurassic Period.
c. Amphibians appeared before reptiles, mammals, and birds.
d. Spontaneous generation of the first cells occurred approximately 4,000,000,000 years ago.

101. Which of the following is NOT a correct representation of the average salinity of seawater?

a. 35 parts per thousand
b. 3.5 parts per hundred
c. 3.5%
d. 35%

102. Which of the following is NOT a factor as to why lakes don't freeze solid in winter?

a. Water has its lowest volume at zero degrees Celsius.
b. As water freezes, the ice floats due to its lower density than the surrounding water.
c. Due to hydrogen bonding, water forms six-sided crystals that have a larger volume than six water molecules.
d. The water exposed to the cold air freezes first forming a good insulator between the air and the water beneath it.

103. Which of the following layers of the earth make up the lithosphere?

a. The crust only
b. The crust and the rigid upper portion of the upper mantle
c. The crust and the upper mantle
d. The crust, upper mantle, and lower mantle

104. Which of the following is a type of physical weathering?
a. Oxidation
b. Hydrolysis
c. Exfoliation
d. Carbonation

105. Which of the following states the correct atmospheric percentages of the major gases?
a. Nitrogen 78% and oxygen 21%
b. Oxygen 78% and carbon dioxide 21 %
c. Oxygen 78% and nitrogen 21%
d. Carbon dioxide 78% and oxygen 21%

106. Which of the following statements regarding the layers of the atmosphere is NOT true?
a. In the troposphere, temperature decreases as altitude increases.
b. In the mesosphere, temperature decreases as altitude increases.
c. In the stratosphere, temperature decreases as altitude increases.
d. In the thermosphere, temperature increases as altitude increases.

107. Which of the following correctly describes cloud formation?
a. Clouds form when evaporation and condensation are in dynamic equilibrium.
b. Clouds form when there are no condensation nuclei in the air.
c. Clouds form when the atmospheric temperature reaches the dew point.
d. Clouds form when the relative humidity is 0%.

108. Which of the following descriptions concerning air masses is true?
a. Maritime tropical air masses bring warm, dry weather.
b. Continental polar air masses bring warm, moist weather.
c. Continental tropical air masses bring cold, dry weather.
d. Maritime polar air masses bring cold, moist weather.

109. According to Kepler's Laws of Planetary Motion, which of the following statements is true?
a. The planets orbit the sun in circular paths.
b. While orbiting the sun, planets sweep out equal areas in equal amounts of time.
c. Planets located further from the sun have shorter periods than planets located nearer to the sun.
d. While orbiting the sun, the closer the planet is to the sun, the slower it travels.

110. Which of the following statements about the moon is NOT true?
a. Only one side of the moon is seen from earth.
b. The moon only rotates once in one orbit around the earth.
c. The moon is slowly moving closer to the earth.
d. The gravitational acceleration on the surface of the moon is approximately one sixth of the gravitational acceleration on the surface of the earth.

111. Between which two planets is the asteroid belt located?
a. Saturn and Uranus
b. Jupiter and Saturn
c. Earth and Mars
d. Mars and Jupiter

112. Which of the following apparent color of stars indicates the coolest temperature?

a. Orange red
b. Yellow orange
c. Yellow white
d. Blue white

113. Which of the following statements correctly describes a similarity or difference between rocks and minerals?

a. Minerals may contain traces of organic compounds, while rocks do not.
b. Rocks are classified by their formation and the minerals they contain, while minerals are classified by their chemical composition and physical properties.
c. Both rocks and minerals can be polymorphs.
d. Both rocks and minerals may contain mineraloids.

114. Which of the following is the best description of mineraloids?

a. Mineraloids are organic compounds found in rocks.
b. Mineraloids are inorganic solids containing two or more minerals with different crystalline structures.
c. Mineraloids are inorganic solids containing one or more minerals with the same crystalline structure.
d. Mineraloids are minerals that lack a crystalline structure.

115. All of the following are branches of petrology EXCEPT:

a. Metamorphic petrology.
b. Igneous petrology.
c. Mineralogical petrology.
d. Sedimentary petrology.

116. Which of the following is NOT one of the five major physical properties of minerals?

a. Chemical composition
b. Hardness
c. Luster
d. Streak

117. Which of these minerals would have the lowest score on the Mohs scale?

a. Gypsum
b. Fluorite
c. Talc
d. Diamond

118. A mineral's true color is observed by:

a. Conducting a streak test on white paper.
b. Conducting a streak test on unglazed porcelain tile.
c. Inspecting the mineral's outer surface.
d. Shining a light on the mineral to inspect its luster.

119. According to the Dana classification system, gold, silver, and copper belong to which class?
a. Organic
b. Elemental
c. Oxide
d. Sulfide

120. According to the Dana classification system, minerals that contain the anion SO_4^{2-} are part of which chemical class?
a. Sulfate
b. Sulfite
c. Halide
d. Phosphate

121. Which of the following is the most immediate effect of acid rain?
a. Loss of fish due to toxicity of water
b. Disease- and pest-ridden forest trees
c. Unwanted algae growth where a river enters the ocean
d. Deterioration of buildings and monuments

122. Which of the following options is a serious direct impact of climate change?
a. Soil erosion
b. Deforestation
c. Water pollution
d. Increase in average sea level

123. Which of the following is NOT an environmental impact of an irrigation scheme that draws water from a river?
a. Reduction in the downstream river discharge
b. Raising of the level of the water table
c. Decreased evaporation in the area
d. Increased drainage flow

124. Which of the following is a negative impact of reservoirs or dams?
a. Flood control
b. Decreased dissolved oxygen
c. Hydroelectricity
d. Irrigation

125. Which of the following is a negative effect of groundwater or aquifer depletion?
a. Possible saltwater contamination of the water supply
b. Decreased cost as water must be pumped further
c. Increased surface water supplies
d. Raising of the water table

126. Which of the following is NOT a result of ozone layer depletion?
a. Higher UV levels reaching the earth
b. More skin cancer, sunburn, and premature aging of skin
c. Damage to marine life such as plankton
d. Increased crop yields of wheat, corn, and soybeans

127. How does the loss of biodiversity impact the environment and society?
a. Increase of access to raw materials
b. Increase of access to clean water
c. Decrease of food supply
d. Decrease of vulnerability to natural disasters

128. Which of the following activities has impacted society with improved weather forecasting, development of a global positioning system, and the development of lightweight materials?
a. Conservation and recycling
b. Space exploration
c. Biotechnology
d. Land reclamation

129. Which of the following has the potential for negative impacts including soil contamination, surface water contamination, pollution, and leachate?
a. Landfills
b. Incinerators
c. Recycling centers
d. Irrigation systems

130. Which of the following is a source of renewable energy?
a. Nuclear power
b. Natural gas
c. Geothermal power
d. Crude oil

131. Which of the following is a source of nonrenewable energy?
a. Solar power
b. Wind power
c. Wood
d. Coal

132. Which type of plant does not produce fruits?
a. Monocots
b. Angiosperms
c. Gymnosperms
d. Nonvascular plants

133. Which of the following natural resource is NOT used in the manufacturing of glass?
a. Bauxite
b. Sand
c. Soda ash
d. Limestone

134. Which of the following is a benefit of wind energy?
a. Wind turbines are space efficient.
b. Wind is fluctuating as a source of energy.
c. Wind turbines are expensive to manufacture and install.
d. Wind turbines are a threat to wildlife.

135. Which of the following is a drawback of solar energy?
   a. Solar energy is environmentally friendly
   b. Solar energy is intermittent
   c. Solar energy is low maintenance
   d. Solar energy is silent

Answers and Explanations

1. B: Making a determination based on the results of a controlled experiment is a description of concluding. Inferring can be described as explaining or interpreting observations. Reading an instrument during an experiment is one type of quantitative observation. Comparing includes noting similarities and differences.

2. A: In a scientific experiment, the dependent variable is the condition that is being tested and measured. The independent variable is the condition that is being changed or controlled. In this example, the amount of salt is varied, and the boiling point of water is measured. Therefore, the independent variable is the amount of salt, and the dependent variable is the temperature at which the water boils.

3. D: A good hypothesis must be testable. This means it may be proved or disproved by testing using a controlled experiment. A controlled experiment may have several constants but only one independent variable.

4. C: The number 0.0034050 is written as 3.4050×10^{-3} in scientific notation. The correct form for scientific notation is $M \times 10^{n}$ in which M is a number between 1 and 10, and n is an integer. Numbers greater than or equal to 10 have a positive exponent, and numbers less than 1 have a negative exponent.

5. B: When working with numbers with decimals, the number of significant figures is determined by starting at the first nonzero digit on the left and counting to the last digit on the right. The number 0.003020 has 4 significant figures. The number 3020.5 has 5 significant figures. The number 3.2005 has 5 significant figures. The number 0.0325 has 3 significant figures.

6. B: Before taking significant figures into consideration, the product of 91,000 × 87,000 is 7,917,000,000. In scientific notation, the product is 7.917×10^{9}. Since each factor has two significant figures, the product should have two significant figures. The correct answer is 7.9×10^{9}.

7. C: Percent error is calculated by the following equation.

$$Percent\ error = \frac{Experimental\ value - Theoretical\ value}{Theoretical\ value} \times 100\%$$

$$Percent\ error = \frac{0.410 - 0.385}{0.385} \times 100\% = 6.49\%$$

The percent error for the students' specific heat of copper of 6.49%.

8. D: Accuracy is determined by finding the range of differences between the measured values and the actual value. The smaller the differences, the greater the accuracy. The range of differences for the triple beam balance is between 0.004 - 0.016. The range of differences for the digital balance is 0.001 - 0.002. Therefore, the digital balance is more accurate. Precision is determined by finding the difference between the highest and lowest readings for each balance. The smaller the difference, the greater the precision. This range for the triple beam balance is 0.02. This range for the digital balance is 0.001. Therefore, the digital balance is also more precise.

9. A: Observation includes collecting evidence, using the five senses, and writing descriptions. Classifying includes grouping items based on similarities, differences, and interrelationships.

Inferring includes explaining or interpreting collected evidence. Communication is reporting to others what has been found by experimentation.

10. A: Since 1 g is equal to 1,000 mg, 2,310 mg is equivalent to 2.310 g. Since 1 kg is equal to 1,000 g, 2.310 kg is equivalent to 2,310 g, and 2.310 kg is equivalent to 2,310,000 mg.

11. B: Since the points in this scatterplot "tend" to be rising, this is a positive correlation. However, since the points are not clustered to resemble a straight line, this is a low positive correlation.

12. B: Correlations may be positive or negative and linear or nonlinear. However, correlation does not determine cause and effect. Correlation does not necessarily mean causation.

13. C: Chemicals should not be stored routinely on bench tops. Each chemical should be stored in a location for that specific type of chemical. When in use chemicals maybe be temporarily kept on bench tops, but only in the quantities that are required for that particular situation. Chemicals should be returned to an appropriate location after use.

14. C: Predictions of the solubility of each chemical at 150 degrees Celsius can be made by extending the lines or curves. Since the data for KBr is relatively linear, it is reasonable to assume that the solubility may increase to about 130 g per 100 g H_2O. If the curves for $NaClO_3$ and KNO_3 continue along the same lines, then these predictions are too low. The prediction for NaCl is too high.

15. D: This graph shows the effect of increasing the amount of solute in a solution on both vapor pressure lowering and boiling point elevation. The change in vapor pressure is a decrease due to the label of *vapor pressure lowering*. As the amount of solute increases, the amount the vapor pressure is lowered continually increases. Increasing the solute decreases the vapor pressure. Increasing the solute also increases the amount the boiling point is elevated. Increasing the solute increases the boiling point of the solution.

16. B: Elements and compounds are both pure substances. Elements consist of only one type of atom. Compounds consist of more than one type of atom. Molecules may make up either elements or compounds. Mixtures are two or more substances that are physically combined but not chemically united.

17. D: Liquids have no definite shape, but they do have a definite volume. While the particles of liquids move more freely than those in solids, they do maintain a definite volume.

18. A: Cations are positively charged ions. Anions are negatively charged ions. Therefore, the ion Ca^{2+} is a cation. Cations are positively charged because they have lost one or more electrons. This cation has lost two electrons and has fewer electrons than protons.

19. B: Electrons, protons, and neutrons are subatomic particles. Electrons have the smallest mass. Protons and neutrons, which are nearly equal in mass, are several orders of magnitude more massive than electrons. Quarks are believed to be the components of protons and neutrons; while a quark has less mass than a complete proton or neutron, it still has more mass than an electron.

20. D: Since the atomic number of this isotope is 92, the atom contains 92 protons. Since the mass number is 238, the atom contains 238 protons and neutrons. Since the difference between 238 and 92 is 146, the atom contains 146 neutrons.

21. C: Alpha particles are identical to helium nuclei and may be represented as He^{2+}, ${}^{4}_{2}He$, or ${}^{4}_{2}He^{2+}$. They may also be represented by the Greek letter alpha as α, α^{2+} or ${}^{4}_{2}\alpha^{2+}$. Beta particles are high speed electrons or positrons and are designated by the Greek letter beta as β^- and β^+ or ${}^{0}_{-1}e$ and ${}^{0}_{+1}e$.

22. C: A chemical change involves a chemical reaction. New substances are produced. When silver tarnishes, a thin layer of corrosion is formed indicating a chemical change. A physical change does not produce new substances. Phase changes such as evaporation and sublimation are physical changes. Salt dissolving in water is also a physical change, because the ions just separate, and no new substances are formed.

23. B: On the Celsius scale, water freezes at 0 °C and boils at 100 °C. On the Kelvin scale, water freezes at 273.15 K and boils at 373.15 K. Both the Celsius and Kelvin scales have exactly 100 degrees between the freezing and boiling points of water. Since water freezes at 32 °F and boils at 212 °F on the Fahrenheit scale, the Fahrenheit scale has 180 degrees between the freezing and boiling points of water.

24. C: Methods of heat transfer include conduction, convection, and radiation. With convection, heat is transferred by moving currents in fluids such as air or water. When a person washes his hands with hot water, heat is transmitted to his hands by means of convection. With conduction, heat is transferred by direct contact such as when someone touches an electric blanket. In radiation, heat is transferred by electromagnetic waves such as when someone places his hands near the sides of a light bulb. When a person warms his hands by rubbing them together, heat is generated by friction.

25. C: Producers always form the base of an energy pyramid as the first trophic level. Each successive level receives about 10% of the energy from the previous level. In this energy pyramid, the second trophic level receives 10% of 6000 or 600 kilocalories per square meter per year. The third trophic level receives 10% of 600 or 60 kilocalories per square meter per year.

26. D: According to Boyle's Law, the volume of a gas is inversely proportional to pressure. As pressure increases, volume decreases. According to Avogadro's Law, the volume of a gas is proportional to the number of moles. As the number of moles increases, volume increases. According to Charles's Law, the volume of a gas is proportional to the temperature in Kelvins. As the temperature increases, volume increases. Since temperature is a measure of the kinetic energy of a gas, volume is proportional to the kinetic energy.

27. C: According to the kinetic theory of matter, the kinetic energy of a particle is found by $KE = \frac{1}{2}mv^2$ in which KE is the kinetic energy in Joules, m is the mass of the particle in kilograms, and v is the velocity of the particle in meters per second squared. This formula shows that the average kinetic energy is directly proportional to the square of the average velocity of the particles.

28. C: In general, atomic radius increases moving down a group due to the increasing number of electron shells. In general, atomic radius decreases moving from left to right across a period due to the increasing number of protons in the energy level. Therefore, atoms of elements in the bottom left corner of the periodic table tend to have the largest atomic radii.

29. B: The compound $CuCl_2$ is an ionic compound consisting of Cu^{2+} ions and Cl^- ions. Ionic compounds are named from the cation and anion names. The name of this compound is copper (II) chloride. The Roman number II inside the parentheses indicates which copper ion is present.

30. A: Sodium chloride exhibits ionic bonding due to the attraction between Na^+ ions and Cl^- ions. Typically, elements on the opposite sides of the periodic table (a metal and a nonmetal) form ionic bonds. Carbon dioxide, water, and glucose exhibit covalent bonding. Typically, elements on the same side of the periodic (two or more nonmetals) form covalent bonds.

31. B: The coefficients of the balanced chemical equation can be used to form a mole ratio to be used in dimensional analysis. Since 3 moles of $O_2(g)$ produce 2 moles of $2Al_2O_3(s)$, the needed mole ratio is $\left(\frac{3 \text{ moles } O_2}{2 \text{ moles } Al_2O_3}\right)$. Using dimensional analysis, $(100.0 \text{ moles } Al_2O_3)\left(\frac{3 \text{ moles } O_2}{2 \text{ moles } Al_2O_3}\right)$ yields 150.0 moles of $O_2(g)$.

32. C: Avogadro's number is the number of particles in one mole of a substance. Avogadro's number is 6.022×10^{23}. One mole of any substance contains 6.022×10^{23} particles of that substance.

33. A: This is a single replacement reaction in which copper replaces silver. The copper combines with the nitrate ions, and the silver precipitates out. Single replacement reactions have the general form of $A + BC \rightarrow AC + B$. Double replacement reactions have the general form of $AB + CD \rightarrow AD + CB$. Synthesis reactions have the general form of $A + B \rightarrow AB$. Decomposition reactions have the general form of $AB \rightarrow A + B$.

34. D: Exothermic reactions release heat energy while endothermic reactions absorb heat energy. Since the burning of butane releases heat energy, the reaction is exothermic. Since the melting of ice absorbs energy, the process is endothermic. Since an exothermic reaction releases heat energy, the change in enthalpy is negative.

35. D: Vinegar is a 5% solution of acetic acid. The pH scale ranges from 0 to 14. Substances with pH's near zero are strong acids, and substances with pH's near 14 are strong bases. Substances with pH's of 7 are neutral. Bleach is a strong base, and ammonia is a relatively weak base. Water is neutral. Since vinegar is the only acid listed, the pH of vinegar is the closest to a pH of 1.

36. A: The needed volume of the stock solution is found by $V_{Stock}M_{Stock} = V_{Dilute}M_{Dilute}$ in which V_{Stock} is the unknown variable, M_{Stock} is the molarity of the stock solution, V_{Dilute} is the volume of the diluted solution, and M_{Dilute} is the molarity of the diluted solution. Then, $V_{Stock} = \frac{V_{Dilute}M_{Dilute}}{M_{Stock}}$. For this problem, $V_{Stock} = \frac{(100.0 \text{ ml})(3.00 \text{ M})}{18.0 \text{ M}}$ is approximately 16.7 ml. To prepare 100.0 ml of 3.00 M HCl solution from an 18.0 M HCl stock solution, dilute 16.7 ml of 18.0 M HCl to 100.0 ml.

37. B: Solubility is the amount of solute present in saturated solution. For a gas solute in a liquid solvent, increasing the temperature increases the kinetic energy of the gas molecules, which decreases the solubility of the gas in the liquid. Increasing the pressure of the gas increases the number of particles escaping from the surface and decreases the solubility. For a liquid solute in a liquid solvent, increasing the temperature increases the kinetic energy, which increases the number of collisions and increases the solubility. Increasing the pressure of a solute in a liquid has little or no effect on solubility.

38. C: A general rule of thumb for solubility is "like dissolves like". Polar solutes tend to dissolve in polar solvents such as water. Nonpolar solutes tend to dissolve in nonpolar solvents. Since CCl_4 has a tetrahedral shape with the polar covalent bonds arranged symmetrically around the carbon atom, CCl_4 is a nonpolar molecule which should dissolve in a nonpolar solvent. Since $AgNO_3$, NH_3, and KI are polar molecules, they probably won't dissolve in a nonpolar solvent.

39. C: Acids react with metals like zinc to produce hydrogen gas. Acids turn litmus red, not blue. Acids donate protons, not accept them. Acids produce H^+ ions in aqueous solution, not OH^- ions.

40. D: In a homogeneous solution, the substance that is dissolved is the solute. A mixture of sugar and water is a homogenous solution in which the sugar is the solute, and the water is the solvent. A mixture of salt and water is a homogeneous solution in which the salt is the solute, and the water is the solvent. A mixture of ash in air is a description of smoke which is a colloid. A mixture of salt and pepper is a heterogeneous mixture.

41. C: Vectors are quantities with both magnitude and direction. Scalars are quantities with magnitude but not direction. Since a velocity, an acceleration, and a force have magnitude and direction, they are all vectors. Since speed only has magnitude, speed is a scalar.

42. C: Newton's first law of motion states that an object in motion tends to remain in motion at a constant velocity unless acted upon by an external force. This tendency to resist changes in motion is known as inertia. Newton's First Law of Motion is often referred to as the Law of Inertia.

43. B: According to the Law of Universal Gravitation, the force of attraction between two objects is inversely proportional to the square of the distance between the two objects. If the distance increases, the force decreases. If the distance is doubled, the force is reduced to one fourth of the original amount.

44. B: Pressure can be defined as force per unit area. This is evident from common pressure units such as lb/in^2 and N/m^2. Mass per unit volume is a description of density.

45. B: Density is mass per unit volume. Then volume can be calculated by dividing mass by density. For this block of quartz, $V = \frac{378\text{ g}}{2.65\text{ g/cm}^3}$, which equals 143 cm^3.

46. A: The period of a simple pendulum depends on the length and the rate of acceleration due to gravity. The period is independent of mass and amplitude (to a good approximation) for amplitudes less than about 15 degrees. The period of a pendulum is unaffected by increasing the mass.

47. C: The ideal mechanical advantage of a simple machine is determined by the ratio of input distance to output distance. Since the input distance is 1.5 m and the output distance is 0.5 m, the ideal mechanical advantage for this pulley is 3.

48. B: Coulomb's Law of Electric Force is represented by $F = k\frac{q_1 q_2}{d^2}$ in which F is the force of attraction, k is a constant related to the medium between the charges, q_1 and q_2 are the strengths of the charges, and d is the distance between the charges. Since the square of the distance is in the denominator, the force is inversely related to the square of the distance between the charges.

49. A: According to Ohm's Law, $V = IR$ in which V represents voltage in volts; I represents the current or amperage in amperes; and R represents resistance in ohms. Then current is found by $I = \frac{V}{R}$. For this situation, $I = \frac{6.0 \text{ Volts}}{20.0 \text{ Ohms}} = 0.30$ amperes.

50. D: The strength of an electromagnet is directly related to the square of the current flowing through the coil. If the current is doubled, the lifting force is quadrupled. Since the original lifting force is 5 N, when the current is doubled, the lifting force is 20 N.

51. D: The colors of the visible spectrum from the lowest to highest frequency are red, orange, yellow, green, blue, and violet. Therefore, violet has the highest frequency.

52. C: The energy of a photon is determined by $E = hf$ in which E represents the energy of a photon, h is Planck's constant, and f represents the frequency of the photon. Therefore, the energy of a photon depends on the frequency of the photon.

53. B: When the angle of incidence is zero, the angle of refraction is also zero. As the angle of incidence increases, the angle of refraction increases. When the angle of incidence reaches the critical angle, the angle of refraction is 90 degrees. When the angle of incidence is greater than the critical angle, the light undergoes total internal reflection. No light is refracted.

54. A: A double concave lens is a diverging lens in which the light rays are spread apart. Therefore, the image formed by a double concave lens is always reduced, upright and virtual regardless of the distance of the object from the lens.

55. A: The strength of a sound wave is the intensity, which is related to the amplitude. The effect of intensity on the way humans perceive sound is loudness. Pitch, which is the "highness" or "lowness" of a sound, is determined by the frequency of the sound.

56. B: Na (sodium) is a solid at standard temperature and pressure, which is $0^{\circ}C$ (273 K) and 100 kPa (0.986 atm), according to IUPAC. The stronger the intermolecular forces, the greater the likelihood of the material being a solid. Kr and Xe are noble gases and have negligible intermolecular attraction. NH_3 has some hydrogen bonding but is still a gas at STP. Sodium is an alkali metal whose atoms are bonded by metallic bonding and is therefore a solid at STP.

57. D: Generally, the larger and heavier the molecule, the higher the melting point. Decreasing polarity will lower intermolecular attractions and lower the melting point. Long, linear molecules have a larger surface area, and therefore more opportunity to interact with other molecules, which increases the melting point.

58. A: The kinetic energy of the gas molecules is directly proportional to the temperature. If the temperature decreases, so does the molecular motion. A decrease in temperature will not necessarily mean a gas condenses to a liquid. Neither the mass nor the density is impacted, as no material was added or removed, and the volume remained the same.

59. D: Since there are twice as many molecules of hydrogen present vs. oxygen, the partial pressure of hydrogen will be greater. The mass of hydrogen will not be greater than the mass of oxygen present even though there are more moles of hydrogen, due to oxygen having a higher molecular weight. Each gas will occupy the same volume. Hydrogen and oxygen gas can coexist in the

container without reacting to produce water. There is no indication given that a chemical reaction has occurred.

60. C: Graham's law of diffusion allows one to calculate the relative diffusion rate between two different gases based on their masses.

61. D: Both liquids and gases are fluids and therefore flow, but only gases are compressible. The molecules that make up a gas are very far apart, allowing the gas to be compressed into a smaller volume.

62. C: The most electronegative atoms are found near the top right of the periodic table. Fluorine has a high electronegativity, while Cesium, located near the bottom left of the table, has a low electronegativity.

63. A: Heat is absorbed by the solid during melting, therefore ΔH is positive. Going from a solid to a liquid greatly increases the freedom of the particles, therefore increasing the entropy, so ΔS is also positive.

64. B: Freezing is an exothermic event; therefore heat must be given off. The temperature of the material remains unchanged at the freezing point during the process.

65. B: Negative beta emission represents the spontaneous decay of a neutron into a proton with the release of an electron. Therefore the resulting nucleus will have one more proton than it did before the reaction, and protons represent the atomic number of an atom. Alpha decay results in the emission of a helium nucleus. The resulting nucleus of an alpha decay would lose two protons and two neutrons, causing a decrease in both the atomic number and the mass number. Gamma decay does not affect the numbers of protons or neutrons in the nucleus. It is an emission of a photon, or packet of energy.

66. C: Since each half life is 2 years, eight years would be 4 half lives. So the mass of material is halved 4 times. Therefore if we start with 1 kg, at two years we would have 0.5 kg, at four years we would have 0.25 kg, after 6 years we would have 0.12 kg, and after 8 years we would have 0.06 kg.

67. C: The hydrogen bonds between water molecules cause water molecules to attract each other (negative pole to positive pole. and "stick" together. This gives water a high surface tension, which allows small living organisms, such as water striders, to move across its surface. Since water is a polar molecule, it readily dissolves other polar and ionic molecules such as carbohydrates and amino acids. Polarity alone is not sufficient to make something soluble in water, however; for example, cellulose is polar but its molecular weight is so large that it is not soluble in water.

68. D: An exothermic reaction releases energy, whereas an endothermic reaction requires energy. The breakdown of a chemical compound is an example of a decomposition reaction ($AB \rightarrow A + B$.. A combination reaction ($A + B \rightarrow AB$. is the reverse of a decomposition reaction, and a replacement (displacement) reaction is one where compound breaks apart and forms a new compound plus a free reactant ($AB + C \rightarrow AC + B$ or $AB + CD \rightarrow AD + CB$.

69. B: Glycogen is a polysaccharide, a molecule composed of many bonded glucose molecules. Glucose is a carbohydrate, and all carbohydrates are composed of only carbon, oxygen, and hydrogen. Most other metabolic compounds contain other atoms, particularly nitrogen, phosphorous, and sulfur.

70. A: Long term energy storage in animals takes the form of fat. Animals also store energy as glycogen, and plants store energy as starch. , but these substances are for shorter-term use. Fats are a good storage form for chemical energy because fatty acids bond to glycerol in a condensation reaction to form fats (triglycerides). This reaction, which releases water, allows for the compacting of high-energy fatty acids in a concentrated form.

71. B: Some RNA molecules in extant organisms have enzymatic activity; for example the formation of peptide bonds on ribosomes is catalyzed by an RNA molecule. This and other information has led scientists to believe that the most likely molecules to first demonstrate enzymatic activity were RNA molecules.

72. D: Endocytosis is a process by which cells absorb larger molecules or even tiny organisms, such as bacteria, than would be able to pass through the plasma membrane. Endocytic vesicles containing molecules from the extracellular environment often undergo further processing once they enter the cell.

73. C: Chloroplasts contain the light-absorbing compound chlorophyll, which is essential in photosynthesis. This gives leaves their green color. Chloroplasts also contain yellow and red carotenoid pigments, which give leaves red and yellow colors in the fall as chloroplasts lose their chlorophyll.

74. D: Both prokaryotes and eukaryotes interact with the extracellular environment and use membrane-bound or membrane-associated proteins to achieve this. They both use diffusion and active transport to move materials in and out of their cells. Prokaryotes have very few proteins associated with their DNA, whereas eukaryotes' DNA is richly studded with proteins. Both types of living things can have flagella, although with different structural characteristics in the two groups. The most important differences between prokaryotes and eukaryotes are the lack of a nucleus and membrane-bound organelles in prokaryotes.

75. B: Bacteria and cyanobacteria have cell walls constructed from peptidoglycans – a polysaccharide and protein molecule. Other types of organisms with cell walls, for instance, plants and fungi, have cell walls composed of different polysaccharides. Plant cell walls are composed of cellulose, and fungal cell walls are composed of chitin.

76. D: Enzymes act as catalysts for biochemical reactions. A catalyst is not consumed in a reaction, but, rather, lowers the activation energy for that reaction. The potential energy of the substrate and the product remain the same, but the activation energy—the energy needed to make the reaction progress—can be lowered with the help of an enzyme.

77. D: Enzymes are substrate-specific. Most enzymes catalyze only one biochemical reaction. Their active sites are specific for a certain type of substrate and do not bind to other substrates and catalyze other reactions.

78. C: Lactic acid fermentation converts pyruvate into lactate using high-energy electrons from NADH. This process allows ATP production to continue in anaerobic conditions by providing NAD^+ so that ATP can be made in glycolysis.

79. B: Proteins in the inner membrane of the mitochondrion accept high-energy electrons from NAD and $FADH_2$, and in turn transport protons from the matrix to the intermembrane space. The

high proton concentration in the intermembrane space creates a gradient which is harnessed by ATP synthase to produce ATP.

80. D: Electrons trapped by the chlorophyll P680 molecule in photosystem II are energized by light. They are then transferred to electron acceptors in an electron transport chain.

81. D: CAM photosynthesis occurs in plants that grow where water loss must be minimized, such as cacti. These plants open their stomata and fix CO_2 at night. During the day, stomata are closed, reducing water loss. Thus, photosynthesis can proceed without water loss.

82. B: DNA wrapped around histone proteins is called chromatin. In a eukaryotic cell, DNA is always associated with protein; it is not "naked" as with prokaryotic cells.

83. D: In anaphase I, homologous chromosome pairs segregate randomly into daughter cells. This means that each daughter cell contains a unique combination of chromosomes that is different from the mother cell and different from its cognate daughter cell.

84. C: Although there are two cell divisions in meiosis, DNA replication occurs only once. It occurs in interphase I, before M phase begins.

85. B: The synaptonemal complex is the point of contact between homologous chromatids. It is formed when nonsister chromatids exchange genetic material through crossing over. Once prophase of meiosis I has completed, crossovers have resolved and the synaptonemal complex no longer exists. Rather, sister chromatids are held together at their centromeres prior to separation in anaphase II.

86. C: Genes code for proteins, and genes are discrete lengths of DNA on chromosomes. An allele is a variant of a gene (different DNA sequence.. In diploid organisms, there may be two versions of each gene.

87. D: The enzyme helicase unwinds DNA. It depends on several other proteins to make the unwinding run smoothly, however. Single-strand binding protein holds the single stranded DNA in place, and topoisomerase helps relieve tension at the replication fork.

88. D: DNA is composed of nucleotides joined together in long chains. Nucleotides are composed of a pentose sugar, a phosphate group, and a nitrogenous base. The bases form the "rungs" of the ladder at the core of the DNA helix and the pentose-phosphates are on its outside, or backbone.

89. B: DNA replication begins with a short segment of RNA (not DNA.. DNA polymerase cannot begin adding nucleotides without an existing piece of DNA (a primer).

90. A: DNA synthesis on the lagging strand forms short segments called Okazaki fragments. Because DNA polymerase can only add nucleotides in the $5' \rightarrow 3'$ direction, lagging strand synthesis is discontinuous. The final product is formed when DNA ligase joins Okazaki fragments together.

91. D: Each time a cell divides; a few base pairs of DNA at the end of each chromosome are lost. Telomerase is an enzyme that uses a built-in template to add a short sequence of DNA over and over at the end of chromosomes—a sort of protective "cap". This prevents the loss of genetic material with each round of DNA replication.

92. D: DNA polymerase does not match base pairs with 100% fidelity. Some level of mismatching is present for all DNA polymerases, and this is a source of mutation in nature. Cells have mechanisms of correcting base pair mismatches, but they do not fix all of them.

93. C: Insertions and deletions cause frameshift mutations. These mutations cause all subsequent nucleotides to be displaced by one position, and thereby cause all the amino acids to be different than they would have been if the mutation had not occurred.

94. A.: Igneous rock forms from solidified magma. If the magma solidifies while underground, it's called intrusive rock. If the magma reaches the surface as lava and then solidifies, it's called extrusive rock. Metamorphic rock includes foliated and non-foliated rock categories. Sedimentary rock includes chemical, mechanical, organic, and inorganic rock categories.

95. D: Opal, corundum, magnetite and quartz are oxides. Opal and quartz are silicon dioxides. Corundum is aluminum oxide, and magnetite is iron oxide. Halides contain a halogen. Silicates contain silicon and oxygen. Native elements such as copper and silver exist as uncombined elements.

96. D: Porosity is a measure of how much water the soil can retain. Permeability is a measure of how easily water can travel through that soil. Clay has a high porosity because it holds a lot of water. Clay has a low permeability. Since it is fine-grained, water flows very slowly through it. Sand and gravel have high porosities and high permeabilities. Granite has a low porosity and a low permeability.

97. A: As the relative humidity in the area surrounding a plant increases, the rate of transpiration decreases. It is more difficult for water to evaporate into the more saturated air. As the relative humidity decreases, the rate of transpiration increases.

98. C: In order to pinpoint the exact location of the epicenter, seismograms are needed from three widely separate locations. A circle is drawn around each location with a radius equal to the distance of the earthquake. Since two circles can cross in two locations, a third circle is needed to pinpoint which intersection is the location of the epicenter. The intersection of the three circles is the location of the epicenter.

99. B: Darwin studied Lyell's work *Principles of Geology* while sailing around South America and the Galapagos islands. He was able to apply this concept of *the present is the key to the past* to the evolutionary history of life on earth. Uniformitarianism is completely opposed to the idea of catastrophism. Natural selection states that the fittest organisms will survive to reproduce.

100. B: The Cambrian Explosion occurred during the Cambrian Period in the Paleozoic Era approximately 541,000,000 years ago. The Jurassic Period known for the first giant dinosaurs occurred during the Mesozoic Era approximately 201,000,000 years ago.

101. D: The average salinity of seawater is 3.5 %. This can also be written as 35 parts per thousand or 3.5 parts per hundred.

102. A: Water actually has its lowest volume at four degrees Celsius. Water stops contracting at four degrees Celsius. Water expands as it cools from four degrees Celsius to zero degrees Celsius.

103. B: The lithosphere is the solid outer section of the earth. This includes the crust and the upper portion of the upper mantle. The asthenosphere, which lies in the upper mantle, is below the lithosphere.

104. C: Exfoliation is a type of physical or mechanical weathering that occurs when rocks peel off in sheets or layers. No chemical change occurs. Oxidation, hydrolysis, and carbonation are all types of chemical weathering.

105. A: The two most abundant atmospheric gases are nitrogen (78%) and oxygen (21%). Argon (0.93%), and neon (0.0018%) are also present in much smaller amounts. Carbon dioxide is present in varying amounts typically ranging from 0.02 to 0.04%.

106. C: In the stratosphere, temperature increases as altitude increases. The stratosphere contains the ozone layer which absorbs ultraviolet radiation and then reemits this energy as heat.

107. C: Clouds form when water in the air condenses onto condensation nuclei in the air. Atmospheric water vapor will condense when the atmospheric temperature reaches the dew point.

108. D: Air masses are named for the areas over which they form. Since maritime polar air masses form over oceans in frigid regions, they bring cold, moist weather. Since maritime tropical air masses form over oceans in warmer regions, they bring warm, moist weather. Since continental polar air masses form over northern Canada or Alaska, they bring cold, dry weather. Since continental tropical air masses form over deserts, they bring warm, dry weather.

109. B: According to the 1st Law of Planetary Motion, planets move in elliptical orbits, not circular. According to the 2nd Law of Planetary Motion, a radius vector connecting a planet to the sun sweeps out equal areas in equal amounts of time. According to the 3rd Law of Planetary Motions, the square of the period of a planet is directly proportional to the cube of the mean distance.

110. C: The moon is slowly moving further away from the earth. The moon is moving a little less than 4 cm a year away from the earth. Since the moon only rotates once in every orbit around the earth, the same side is always seen from earth. The acceleration of gravity on the surface of the moon is approximately one sixth of the gravitational acceleration on the surface of the earth... although the moon has less than 1/80 the mass of the Earth, it also has a smaller radius, and the acceleration of gravity on the surface depends on both.

111. D: The main asteroid belt which contains millions of asteroids is between Mars and Jupiter.

112. A: Orange red stars have temperatures less than 3,700 K. Yellow orange stars range between 3,700 and 5,200 K. Yellow white stars range between 5,200 K and 6,000 K. Blue white stars range between 10,000 and 30,000 K.

113. B: It is true that rocks are classified by their formation and the minerals they contain, while minerals are classified by their chemical composition and physical properties. Answer A is incorrect because rocks may contain traces of organic compounds. Answers C and D are incorrect because only minerals can be polymorphs and only rocks contain mineraloids.

114. D: Mineraloids are best defined as minerals that lack a crystalline structure, and they are typically found in rocks. Inorganic solids containing two or more minerals with different crystalline structures are known as polymorphs.

115. C: Mineralogical petrology is not a branch of petrology. Petrologists study the various categories of rocks, including metamorphic, igneous, and sedimentary. Some petrologists, called experimental petrologists, also study changes in the geochemistry of materials that are exposed to extreme temperatures and pressures. Minerals are studied by mineralogists, not petrologists.

116. A: Chemical composition is not one of the physical properties used to classify minerals. The five major physical properties used to classify minerals are luster, hardness, cleavage, streak, and form. There is a separate classification system based on the chemical composition of minerals.

117. C: On Mohs scale of mineral hardness, talc has the lowest possible score (a one). Diamond is a ten, which is the highest possible score, and gypsum and fluorite have a score of two and four, respectively. Minerals can always scratch minerals that have a Mohs score lower than their own.

118. B: A mineral's true color is observed by conducting a streak test on unglazed porcelain tile. Paper is not appropriate for a streak test because it does not have the correct physical properties. External observation (inspecting the mineral's outer surface) is not sufficient to establish true color since streak tests sometimes reveal a color that is different from the substance's external hue. Finally, the luster test is not used to determine color.

119. B: According to the Dana classification system, gold, silver, and copper belong to the elemental class. Members of the oxide class include chromite and magnetite, and hydrocarbons and acetates are members of the organic class. Sulfide minerals include pyrite and galena.

120. A: According to the Dana system, minerals that contain the anion SO_4^{2-} are part of the sulfate class. Sulfate minerals are typically formed in environments where highly saline water evaporates. Gypsum is an example of a mineral that belongs to the sulfate class.

121. A: Fish may die suddenly after heavy rains due to the lower pH leading to high levels of substances such as aluminum in the water. Over time acid rain may slowly remove nutrients from the forest soil weakening defenses of trees making them more vulnerable to diseases and pests. Excess nitrogen may lead to overgrowth of algae in areas where rivers enter the ocean. Acid rain may slowly deteriorate buildings and monuments made from stone containing calcium carbonate.

122. D: Of these options, the only real direct impact of climate change is the rising sea level. This is due to the melting glaciers and ice sheets. Also, the oceans expand slightly as they get warmer.

123. C: An irrigation scheme that draws water from a river and redistributes the water in the local area leads to an increase in evaporation, not a decrease. This is largely due to the increase of the surface area of contact of the water and the atmosphere.

124. B: Water moves more slowly downstream of a dam. This results in less aeration and diffusion and lowers the dissolved oxygen content in the water.

125. A: Groundwater overuse and depletion has several negative effects including saltwater contamination of the water supply, increased cost as water must be pumped further, decreased surface water supplies, and lowering of the water table.

126. D: Ozone layer depletion results in higher UV levels reaching the earth. These higher levels of UV rays may result in more skin cancers, sunburn, and premature aging of skin, damage to marine life such as plankton, and decreased crop yields of wheat, corn, and soybeans.

127. C: The loss of biodiversity destabilizes ecosystems and impacts society by decreasing the food supply, decreasing the access to raw materials and clean water, and increasing the vulnerability to natural disasters.

128. B: Space exploration has provided many benefits for humanity. Aside from the inspiration for many to undertake further studies in science, many practical benefits have resulted such as improved weather forecasting, development of a global positioning system, and the development of lightweight materials.

129. A: While landfills are necessary, potential problems include soil contamination, surface water contamination, pollution, and leachate.

130. C: Sources of renewable energy include geothermal power, solar energy, and wind power. Sources of nonrenewable energy include nuclear power, natural gas, and fossil fuels like coal, natural gas, and crude oil.

131. D: Coal is a fossil fuel. Fossil fuels like coal, crude oil, and natural gas are nonrenewable.

132: D: Nonvascular plants do not produce fruits like angiosperms and gymnosperms do. They generally reproduce sexually, but produce spores instead of seeds.

133. A: Glass is manufactured from sand, soda ash, and limestone. Aluminum is manufactured from bauxite ore.

134. A: Pros of wind energy include space efficiency, no pollution, and low operational costs. Cons of wind energy include wind fluctuation, threats to wildlife, and the expense to manufacture and install.

135. B: Pros of solar energy include the facts that it is renewable, abundant, environmentally friendly, low maintenance, and silent. Cons of solar energy include that it is expensive and intermittent and requires space.

Secret Key #1 - Time is Your Greatest Enemy

Pace Yourself

Wear a watch. At the beginning of the test, check the time (or start a chronometer on your watch to count the minutes), and check the time after every few questions to make sure you are "on schedule."

If you are forced to speed up, do it efficiently. Usually one or more answer choices can be eliminated without too much difficulty. Above all, don't panic. Don't speed up and just begin guessing at random choices. By pacing yourself, and continually monitoring your progress against your watch, you will always know exactly how far ahead or behind you are with your available time. If you find that you are one minute behind on the test, don't skip one question without spending any time on it, just to catch back up. Take 15 fewer seconds on the next four questions, and after four questions you'll have caught back up. Once you catch back up, you can continue working each problem at your normal pace.

Furthermore, don't dwell on the problems that you were rushed on. If a problem was taking up too much time and you made a hurried guess, it must be difficult. The difficult questions are the ones you are most likely to miss anyway, so it isn't a big loss. It is better to end with more time than you need than to run out of time.

Lastly, sometimes it is beneficial to slow down if you are constantly getting ahead of time. You are always more likely to catch a careless mistake by working more slowly than quickly, and among very high-scoring test takers (those who are likely to have lots of time left over), careless errors affect the score more than mastery of material.

Secret Key #2 - Guessing is not Guesswork

You probably know that guessing is a good idea. Unlike other standardized tests, there is no penalty for getting a wrong answer. Even if you have no idea about a question, you still have a 20-25% chance of getting it right.

Most test takers do not understand the impact that proper guessing can have on their score. Unless you score extremely high, guessing will significantly contribute to your final score.

Monkeys Take the Test

What most test takers don't realize is that to insure that 20-25% chance, you have to guess randomly. If you put 20 monkeys in a room to take this test, assuming they answered once per question and behaved themselves, on average they would get 20-25% of the questions correct. Put 20 test takers in the room, and the average will be much lower among guessed questions. Why?

1. The test writers intentionally write deceptive answer choices that "look" right. A test taker has no idea about a question, so he picks the "best looking" answer, which is often wrong.

The monkey has no idea what looks good and what doesn't, so it will consistently be right about 20-25% of the time.
2. Test takers will eliminate answer choices from the guessing pool based on a hunch or intuition. Simple but correct answers often get excluded, leaving a 0% chance of being correct. The monkey has no clue, and often gets lucky with the best choice.

This is why the process of elimination endorsed by most test courses is flawed and detrimental to your performance. Test takers don't guess; they make an ignorant stab in the dark that is usually worse than random.

$5 Challenge

Let me introduce one of the most valuable ideas of this course—the $5 challenge:

You only mark your "best guess" if you are willing to bet $5 on it.
You only eliminate choices from guessing if you are willing to bet $5 on it.

Why $5? Five dollars is an amount of money that is small yet not insignificant, and can really add up fast (20 questions could cost you $100). Likewise, each answer choice on one question of the test will have a small impact on your overall score, but it can really add up to a lot of points in the end.

The process of elimination IS valuable. The following shows your chance of guessing it right:

If you eliminate wrong answer choices until only this many remain:	Chance of getting it correct:
1	100%
2	50%
3	33%

However, if you accidentally eliminate the right answer or go on a hunch for an incorrect answer, your chances drop dramatically—to 0%. By guessing among all the answer choices, you are GUARANTEED to have a shot at the right answer.

That's why the $5 test is so valuable. If you give up the advantage and safety of a pure guess, it had better be worth the risk.

What we still haven't covered is how to be sure that whatever guess you make is truly random. Here's the easiest way:

Always pick the first answer choice among those remaining.

Such a technique means that you have decided, **before you see a single test question**, exactly how you are going to guess, and since the order of choices tells you nothing about which one is correct, this guessing technique is perfectly random.

This section is not meant to scare you away from making educated guesses or eliminating choices;

you just need to define when a choice is worth eliminating. The $5 test, along with a pre-defined random guessing strategy, is the best way to make sure you reap all of the benefits of guessing.

Secret Key #3 - Practice Smarter, Not Harder

Many test takers delay the test preparation process because they dread the awful amounts of practice time they think necessary to succeed on the test. We have refined an effective method that will take you only a fraction of the time.

There are a number of "obstacles" in the path to success. Among these are answering questions, finishing in time, and mastering test-taking strategies. All must be executed on the day of the test at peak performance, or your score will suffer. The test is a mental marathon that has a large impact on your future.

Just like a marathon runner, it is important to work your way up to the full challenge. So first you just worry about questions, and then time, and finally strategy:

Success Strategy

1. Find a good source for practice tests.
2. If you are willing to make a larger time investment, consider using more than one study guide. Often the different approaches of multiple authors will help you "get" difficult concepts.
3. Take a practice test with no time constraints, with all study helps, "open book." Take your time with questions and focus on applying strategies.
4. Take a practice test with time constraints, with all guides, "open book."
5. Take a final practice test without open material and with time limits.

If you have time to take more practice tests, just repeat step 5. By gradually exposing yourself to the full rigors of the test environment, you will condition your mind to the stress of test day and maximize your success.

Secret Key #4 - Prepare, Don't Procrastinate

Let me state an obvious fact: if you take the test three times, you will probably get three different scores. This is due to the way you feel on test day, the level of preparedness you have, and the version of the test you see. Despite the test writers' claims to the contrary, some versions of the test WILL be easier for you than others.

Since your future depends so much on your score, you should maximize your chances of success. In order to maximize the likelihood of success, you've got to prepare in advance. This means taking practice tests and spending time learning the information and test taking strategies you will need to succeed.

Never go take the actual test as a "practice" test, expecting that you can just take it again if you need to. Take all the practice tests you can on your own, but when you go to take the official test, be prepared, be focused, and do your best the first time!

Secret Key #5 - Test Yourself

Everyone knows that time is money. There is no need to spend too much of your time or too little of your time preparing for the test. You should only spend as much of your precious time preparing as is necessary for you to get the score you need.

Once you have taken a practice test under real conditions of time constraints, then you will know if you are ready for the test or not.

If you have scored extremely high the first time that you take the practice test, then there is not much point in spending countless hours studying. You are already there.

Benchmark your abilities by retaking practice tests and seeing how much you have improved. Once you consistently score high enough to guarantee success, then you are ready.

If you have scored well below where you need, then knuckle down and begin studying in earnest. Check your improvement regularly through the use of practice tests under real conditions. Above all, don't worry, panic, or give up. The key is perseverance!

Then, when you go to take the test, remain confident and remember how well you did on the practice tests. If you can score high enough on a practice test, then you can do the same on the real thing.

General Strategies

The most important thing you can do is to ignore your fears and jump into the test immediately. Do not be overwhelmed by any strange-sounding terms. You have to jump into the test like jumping into a pool—all at once is the easiest way.

Make Predictions
As you read and understand the question, try to guess what the answer will be. Remember that several of the answer choices are wrong, and once you begin reading them, your mind will immediately become cluttered with answer choices designed to throw you off. Your mind is typically the most focused immediately after you have read the question and digested its contents. If you can, try to predict what the correct answer will be. You may be surprised at what you can predict.

Quickly scan the choices and see if your prediction is in the listed answer choices. If it is, then you can be quite confident that you have the right answer. It still won't hurt to check the other answer choices, but most of the time, you've got it!

Answer the Question
It may seem obvious to only pick answer choices that answer the question, but the test writers can create some excellent answer choices that are wrong. Don't pick an answer just because it sounds right, or you believe it to be true. It MUST answer the question. Once you've made your selection, always go back and check it against the question and make sure that you didn't misread the question and that the answer choice does answer the question posed.

Benchmark
After you read the first answer choice, decide if you think it sounds correct or not. If it doesn't, move on to the next answer choice. If it does, mentally mark that answer choice. This doesn't mean that you've definitely selected it as your answer choice, it just means that it's the best you've seen thus far. Go ahead and read the next choice. If the next choice is worse than the one you've already selected, keep going to the next answer choice. If the next choice is better than the choice you've already selected, mentally mark the new answer choice as your best guess.

The first answer choice that you select becomes your standard. Every other answer choice must be benchmarked against that standard. That choice is correct until proven otherwise by another answer choice beating it out. Once you've decided that no other answer choice seems as good, do one final check to ensure that your answer choice answers the question posed.

Valid Information
Don't discount any of the information provided in the question. Every piece of information may be necessary to determine the correct answer. None of the information in the question is there to throw you off (while the answer choices will certainly have information to throw you off). If two seemingly unrelated topics are discussed, don't ignore either. You can be confident there is a relationship, or it wouldn't be included in the question, and you are probably going to have to determine what is that relationship to find the answer.

Avoid "Fact Traps"
Don't get distracted by a choice that is factually true. Your search is for the answer that answers the question. Stay focused and don't fall for an answer that is true but irrelevant. Always go back to the question and make sure you're choosing an answer that actually answers the question and is not just a true statement. An answer can be factually correct, but it MUST answer the question asked. Additionally, two answers can both be seemingly correct, so be sure to read all of the answer choices, and make sure that you get the one that BEST answers the question.

Milk the Question
Some of the questions may throw you completely off. They might deal with a subject you have not been exposed to, or one that you haven't reviewed in years. While your lack of knowledge about the subject will be a hindrance, the question itself can give you many clues that will help you find the correct answer. Read the question carefully and look for clues. Watch particularly for adjectives and nouns describing difficult terms or words that you don't recognize. Regardless of whether you completely understand a word or not, replacing it with a synonym, either provided or one you more familiar with, may help you to understand what the questions are asking. Rather than wracking your mind about specific detailed information concerning a difficult term or word, try to use mental substitutes that are easier to understand.

The Trap of Familiarity
Don't just choose a word because you recognize it. On difficult questions, you may not recognize a number of words in the answer choices. The test writers don't put "make-believe" words on the

test, so don't think that just because you only recognize all the words in one answer choice that that answer choice must be correct. If you only recognize words in one answer choice, then focus on that one. Is it correct? Try your best to determine if it is correct. If it is, that's great. If not, eliminate it. Each word and answer choice you eliminate increases your chances of getting the question correct, even if you then have to guess among the unfamiliar choices.

Eliminate Answers

Eliminate choices as soon as you realize they are wrong. But be careful! Make sure you consider all of the possible answer choices. Just because one appears right, doesn't mean that the next one won't be even better! The test writers will usually put more than one good answer choice for every question, so read all of them. Don't worry if you are stuck between two that seem right. By getting down to just two remaining possible choices, your odds are now 50/50. Rather than wasting too much time, play the odds. You are guessing, but guessing wisely because you've been able to knock out some of the answer choices that you know are wrong. If you are eliminating choices and realize that the last answer choice you are left with is also obviously wrong, don't panic. Start over and consider each choice again. There may easily be something that you missed the first time and will realize on the second pass.

Tough Questions

If you are stumped on a problem or it appears too hard or too difficult, don't waste time. Move on! Remember though, if you can quickly check for obviously incorrect answer choices, your chances of guessing correctly are greatly improved. Before you completely give up, at least try to knock out a couple of possible answers. Eliminate what you can and then guess at the remaining answer choices before moving on.

Brainstorm

If you get stuck on a difficult question, spend a few seconds quickly brainstorming. Run through the complete list of possible answer choices. Look at each choice and ask yourself, "Could this answer the question satisfactorily?" Go through each answer choice and consider it independently of the others. By systematically going through all possibilities, you may find something that you would otherwise overlook. Remember though that when you get stuck, it's important to try to keep moving.

Read Carefully

Understand the problem. Read the question and answer choices carefully. Don't miss the question because you misread the terms. You have plenty of time to read each question thoroughly and make sure you understand what is being asked. Yet a happy medium must be attained, so don't waste too much time. You must read carefully, but efficiently.

Face Value

When in doubt, use common sense. Always accept the situation in the problem at face value. Don't read too much into it. These problems will not require you to make huge leaps of logic. The test writers aren't trying to throw you off with a cheap trick. If you have to go beyond creativity and make a leap of logic in order to have an answer choice answer the question, then you should look at the other answer choices. Don't overcomplicate the problem by creating theoretical relationships or explanations that will warp time or space. These are normal problems rooted in reality. It's just that the applicable relationship or explanation may not be readily apparent and you have to figure things out. Use your common sense to interpret anything that isn't clear.

Prefixes

If you're having trouble with a word in the question or answer choices, try dissecting it. Take advantage of every clue that the word might include. Prefixes and suffixes can be a huge help. Usually they allow you to determine a basic meaning. Pre- means before, post- means after, pro - is positive, de- is negative. From these prefixes and suffixes, you can get an idea of the general meaning of the word and try to put it into context. Beware though of any traps. Just because con- is the opposite of pro-, doesn't necessarily mean congress is the opposite of progress!

Hedge Phrases
Watch out for critical hedge phrases, led off with words such as "likely," "may," "can," "sometimes," "often," "almost," "mostly," "usually," "generally," "rarely," and "sometimes." Question writers insert these hedge phrases to cover every possibility. Often an answer choice will be wrong simply because it leaves no room for exception. Unless the situation calls for them, avoid answer choices that have definitive words like "exactly," and "always."

Switchback Words
Stay alert for "switchbacks." These are the words and phrases frequently used to alert you to shifts in thought. The most common switchback word is "but." Others include "although," "however," "nevertheless," "on the other hand," "even though," "while," "in spite of," "despite," and "regardless of."

New Information
Correct answer choices will rarely have completely new information included. Answer choices typically are straightforward reflections of the material asked about and will directly relate to the question. If a new piece of information is included in an answer choice that doesn't even seem to relate to the topic being asked about, then that answer choice is likely incorrect. All of the information needed to answer the question is usually provided for you in the question. You should not have to make guesses that are unsupported or choose answer choices that require unknown information that cannot be reasoned from what is given.

Time Management
On technical questions, don't get lost on the technical terms. Don't spend too much time on any one question. If you don't know what a term means, then odds are you aren't going to get much further since you don't have a dictionary. You should be able to immediately recognize whether or not you know a term. If you don't, work with the other clues that you have—the other answer choices and terms provided—but don't waste too much time trying to figure out a difficult term that you don't know.

Contextual Clues
Look for contextual clues. An answer can be right but not the correct answer. The contextual clues will help you find the answer that is most right and is correct. Understand the context in which a phrase or statement is made. This will help you make important distinctions.

Don't Panic
Panicking will not answer any questions for you; therefore, it isn't helpful. When you first see the question, if your mind goes blank, take a deep breath. Force yourself to mechanically go through the steps of solving the problem using the strategies you've learned.

Pace Yourself
Don't get clock fever. It's easy to be overwhelmed when you're looking at a page full of questions, your mind is full of random thoughts and feeling confused, and the clock is ticking down faster than you would like. Calm down and maintain the pace that you have set for yourself. As long as you are on track by monitoring your pace, you are guaranteed to have enough time for yourself. When you

get to the last few minutes of the test, it may seem like you won't have enough time left, but if you only have as many questions as you should have left at that point, then you're right on track!

Answer Selection
The best way to pick an answer choice is to eliminate all of those that are wrong, until only one is left and confirm that is the correct answer. Sometimes though, an answer choice may immediately look right. Be careful! Take a second to make sure that the other choices are not equally obvious. Don't make a hasty mistake. There are only two times that you should stop before checking other answers. First is when you are positive that the answer choice you have selected is correct. Second is when time is almost out and you have to make a quick guess!

Check Your Work
Since you will probably not know every term listed and the answer to every question, it is important that you get credit for the ones that you do know. Don't miss any questions through careless mistakes. If at all possible, try to take a second to look back over your answer selection and make sure you've selected the correct answer choice and haven't made a costly careless mistake (such as marking an answer choice that you didn't mean to mark). The time it takes for this quick double check should more than pay for itself in caught mistakes.

Beware of Directly Quoted Answers
Sometimes an answer choice will repeat word for word a portion of the question or reference section. However, beware of such exact duplication. It may be a trap! More than likely, the correct choice will paraphrase or summarize a point, rather than being exactly the same wording.

Slang
Scientific sounding answers are better than slang ones. An answer choice that begins "To compare the outcomes..." is much more likely to be correct than one that begins "Because some people insisted..."

Extreme Statements
Avoid wild answers that throw out highly controversial ideas that are proclaimed as established fact. An answer choice that states the "process should used in certain situations, if..." is much more likely to be correct than one that states the "process should be discontinued completely." The first is a calm rational statement and doesn't even make a definitive, uncompromising stance, using a hedge word "if" to provide wiggle room, whereas the second choice is a radical idea and far more extreme.

Answer Choice Families
When you have two or more answer choices that are direct opposites or parallels, one of them is usually the correct answer. For instance, if one answer choice states "x increases" and another answer choice states "x decreases" or "y increases," then those two or three answer choices are very similar in construction and fall into the same family of answer choices. A family of answer choices consists of two or three answer choices, very similar in construction, but often with directly opposite meanings. Usually the correct answer choice will be in that family of answer choices. The "odd man out" or answer choice that doesn't seem to fit the parallel construction of the other answer choices is more likely to be incorrect.

Special Report: How to Overcome Test Anxiety

The very nature of tests caters to some level of anxiety, nervousness, or tension, just as we feel for any important event that occurs in our lives. A little bit of anxiety or nervousness can be a good thing. It helps us with motivation, and makes achievement just that much sweeter. However, too much anxiety can be a problem, especially if it hinders our ability to function and perform.

"Test anxiety," is the term that refers to the emotional reactions that some test-takers experience when faced with a test or exam. Having a fear of testing and exams is based upon a rational fear, since the test-taker's performance can shape the course of an academic career. Nevertheless, experiencing excessive fear of examinations will only interfere with the test-taker's ability to perform and chance to be successful.

There are a large variety of causes that can contribute to the development and sensation of test anxiety. These include, but are not limited to, lack of preparation and worrying about issues surrounding the test.

Lack of Preparation

Lack of preparation can be identified by the following behaviors or situations:

- Not scheduling enough time to study, and therefore cramming the night before the test or exam
- Managing time poorly, to create the sensation that there is not enough time to do everything
- Failing to organize the text information in advance, so that the study material consists of the entire text and not simply the pertinent information
- Poor overall studying habits

Worrying, on the other hand, can be related to both the test taker, or many other factors around him/her that will be affected by the results of the test. These include worrying about:

- Previous performances on similar exams, or exams in general
- How friends and other students are achieving
- The negative consequences that will result from a poor grade or failure

There are three primary elements to test anxiety. Physical components, which involve the same typical bodily reactions as those to acute anxiety (to be discussed below). Emotional factors have to do with fear or panic. Mental or cognitive issues concerning attention spans and memory abilities.

Physical Signals

There are many different symptoms of test anxiety, and these are not limited to mental and emotional strain. Frequently there are a range of physical signals that will let a test taker know that he/she is suffering from test anxiety. These bodily changes can include the following:

- Perspiring
- Sweaty palms
- Wet, trembling hands
- Nausea
- Dry mouth
- A knot in the stomach
- Headache
- Faintness
- Muscle tension
- Aching shoulders, back and neck
- Rapid heart beat
- Feeling too hot/cold

To recognize the sensation of test anxiety, a test-taker should monitor him/herself for the following sensations:

- The physical distress symptoms as listed above
- Emotional sensitivity, expressing emotional feelings such as the need to cry or laugh too much, or a sensation of anger or helplessness
- A decreased ability to think, causing the test-taker to blank out or have racing thoughts that are hard to organize or control

Though most students will feel some level of anxiety when faced with a test or exam, the majority can cope with that anxiety and maintain it at a manageable level. However, those who cannot are faced with a very real and very serious condition, which can and should be controlled for the immeasurable benefit of this sufferer.

Naturally, these sensations lead to negative results for the testing experience. The most common effects of test anxiety have to do with nervousness and mental blocking.

Nervousness

Nervousness can appear in several different levels:

- The test-taker's difficulty, or even inability to read and understand the questions on the test
- The difficulty or inability to organize thoughts to a coherent form
- The difficulty or inability to recall key words and concepts relating to the testing questions (especially essays)
- The receipt of poor grades on a test, though the test material was well known by the test taker

Conversely, a person may also experience mental blocking, which involves:

- Blanking out on test questions
- Only remembering the correct answers to the questions when the test has already finished

Fortunately for test anxiety sufferers, beating these feelings, to a large degree, has to do with proper preparation. When a test taker has a feeling of preparedness, then anxiety will be dramatically lessened.

The first step to resolving anxiety issues is to distinguish which of the two types of anxiety are being suffered. If the anxiety is a direct result of a lack of preparation, this should be considered a normal reaction, and the anxiety level (as opposed to the test results) shouldn't be anything to worry about. However, if, when adequately prepared, the test-taker still panics, blanks out, or seems to overreact, this is not a fully rational reaction. While this can be considered normal too, there are many ways to combat and overcome these effects.

Remember that anxiety cannot be entirely eliminated, however, there are ways to minimize it, to make the anxiety easier to manage. Preparation is one of the best ways to minimize test anxiety. Therefore the following techniques are wise in order to best fight off any anxiety that may want to build.

To begin with, try to avoid cramming before a test, whenever it is possible. By trying to memorize an entire term's worth of information in one day, you'll be shocking your system, and not giving yourself a very good chance to absorb the information. This is an easy path to anxiety, so for those who suffer from test anxiety, cramming should not even be considered an option.

Instead of cramming, work throughout the semester to combine all of the material which is presented throughout the semester, and work on it gradually as the course goes by, making sure to master the main concepts first, leaving minor details for a week or so before the test.

To study for the upcoming exam, be sure to pose questions that may be on the examination, to gauge the ability to answer them by integrating the ideas from your texts, notes and lectures, as well as any supplementary readings.

If it is truly impossible to cover all of the information that was covered in that particular term, concentrate on the most important portions, that can be covered very well. Learn these concepts as best as possible, so that when the test comes, a goal can be made to use these concepts as presentations of your knowledge.

In addition to study habits, changes in attitude are critical to beating a struggle with test anxiety. In fact, an improvement of the perspective over the entire test-taking experience can actually help a test taker to enjoy studying and therefore improve the overall experience. Be certain not to overemphasize the significance of the grade - know that the result of the test is neither a reflection of self worth, nor is it a measure of intelligence; one grade will not predict a person's future success.

To improve an overall testing outlook, the following steps should be tried:

- Keeping in mind that the most reasonable expectation for taking a test is to expect to try to demonstrate as much of what you know as you possibly can.
- Reminding ourselves that a test is only one test; this is not the only one, and there will be others.
- The thought of thinking of oneself in an irrational, all-or-nothing term should be avoided at all costs.

- A reward should be designated for after the test, so there's something to look forward to. Whether it be going to a movie, going out to eat, or simply visiting friends, schedule it in advance, and do it no matter what result is expected on the exam.

Test-takers should also keep in mind that the basics are some of the most important things, even beyond anti-anxiety techniques and studying. Never neglect the basic social, emotional and biological needs, in order to try to absorb information. In order to best achieve, these three factors must be held as just as important as the studying itself.

Study Steps

Remember the following important steps for studying:

- Maintain healthy nutrition and exercise habits. Continue both your recreational activities and social pass times. These both contribute to your physical and emotional well being.
- Be certain to get a good amount of sleep, especially the night before the test, because when you're overtired you are not able to perform to the best of your best ability.
- Keep the studying pace to a moderate level by taking breaks when they are needed, and varying the work whenever possible, to keep the mind fresh instead of getting bored.
- When enough studying has been done that all the material that can be learned has been learned, and the test taker is prepared for the test, stop studying and do something relaxing such as listening to music, watching a movie, or taking a warm bubble bath.

There are also many other techniques to minimize the uneasiness or apprehension that is experienced along with test anxiety before, during, or even after the examination. In fact, there are a great deal of things that can be done to stop anxiety from interfering with lifestyle and performance. Again, remember that anxiety will not be eliminated entirely, and it shouldn't be. Otherwise that "up" feeling for exams would not exist, and most of us depend on that sensation to perform better than usual. However, this anxiety has to be at a level that is manageable.

Of course, as we have just discussed, being prepared for the exam is half the battle right away. Attending all classes, finding out what knowledge will be expected on the exam, and knowing the exam schedules are easy steps to lowering anxiety. Keeping up with work will remove the need to cram, and efficient study habits will eliminate wasted time. Studying should be done in an ideal location for concentration, so that it is simple to become interested in the material and give it complete attention. A method such as SQ3R (Survey, Question, Read, Recite, Review) is a wonderful key to follow to make sure that the study habits are as effective as possible, especially in the case of learning from a textbook. Flashcards are great techniques for memorization. Learning to take good notes will mean that notes will be full of useful information, so that less sifting will need to be done to seek out what is pertinent for studying. Reviewing notes after class and then again on occasion will keep the information fresh in the mind. From notes that have been taken summary sheets and outlines can be made for simpler reviewing.

A study group can also be a very motivational and helpful place to study, as there will be a sharing of ideas, all of the minds can work together, to make sure that everyone understands, and the studying will be made more interesting because it will be a social occasion.

Basically, though, as long as the test-taker remains organized and self confident, with efficient study habits, less time will need to be spent studying, and higher grades will be achieved.

To become self confident, there are many useful steps. The first of these is "self talk." It has been shown through extensive research, that self-talk for students who suffer from test anxiety, should be well monitored, in order to make sure that it contributes to self confidence as opposed to sinking the student. Frequently the self talk of test-anxious students is negative or self-defeating, thinking that everyone else is smarter and faster, that they always mess up, and that if they don't do well, they'll fail the entire course. It is important to decreasing anxiety that awareness is made of self talk. Try writing any negative self thoughts and then disputing them with a positive statement instead. Begin self-encouragement as though it was a friend speaking. Repeat positive statements to help reprogram the mind to believing in successes instead of failures.

Helpful Techniques

Other extremely helpful techniques include:

- Self-visualization of doing well and reaching goals
- While aiming for an "A" level of understanding, don't try to "overprotect" by setting your expectations lower. This will only convince the mind to stop studying in order to meet the lower expectations.
- Don't make comparisons with the results or habits of other students. These are individual factors, and different things work for different people, causing different results.
- Strive to become an expert in learning what works well, and what can be done in order to improve. Consider collecting this data in a journal.
- Create rewards for after studying instead of doing things before studying that will only turn into avoidance behaviors.
- Make a practice of relaxing - by using methods such as progressive relaxation, self-hypnosis, guided imagery, etc - in order to make relaxation an automatic sensation.
- Work on creating a state of relaxed concentration so that concentrating will take on the focus of the mind, so that none will be wasted on worrying.
- Take good care of the physical self by eating well and getting enough sleep.
- Plan in time for exercise and stick to this plan.

Beyond these techniques, there are other methods to be used before, during and after the test that will help the test-taker perform well in addition to overcoming anxiety.

Before the exam comes the academic preparation. This involves establishing a study schedule and beginning at least one week before the actual date of the test. By doing this, the anxiety of not having enough time to study for the test will be automatically eliminated. Moreover, this will make the studying a much more effective experience, ensuring that the learning will be an easier process. This relieves much undue pressure on the test-taker.

Summary sheets, note cards, and flash cards with the main concepts and examples of these main concepts should be prepared in advance of the actual studying time. A topic should never be eliminated from this process. By omitting a topic because it isn't expected to be on the test is only setting up the test-taker for anxiety should it actually appear on the exam. Utilize the course syllabus for laying out the topics that should be studied. Carefully go over the notes that were made in class, paying special attention to any of the issues that the professor took special care to emphasize while lecturing in class. In the textbooks, use the chapter review, or if possible, the chapter tests, to begin your review.

It may even be possible to ask the instructor what information will be covered on the exam, or what the format of the exam will be (for example, multiple choice, essay, free form, true-false). Additionally, see if it is possible to find out how many questions will be on the test. If a review sheet or sample test has been offered by the professor, make good use of it, above anything else, for the preparation for the test. Another great resource for getting to know the examination is reviewing tests from previous semesters. Use these tests to review, and aim to achieve a 100% score on each of the possible topics. With a few exceptions, the goal that you set for yourself is the highest one that you will reach.

Take all of the questions that were assigned as homework, and rework them to any other possible course material. The more problems reworked, the more skill and confidence will form as a result. When forming the solution to a problem, write out each of the steps. Don't simply do head work. By doing as many steps on paper as possible, much clarification and therefore confidence will be formed. Do this with as many homework problems as possible, before checking the answers. By checking the answer after each problem, a reinforcement will exist, that will not be on the exam. Study situations should be as exam-like as possible, to prime the test-taker's system for the experience. By waiting to check the answers at the end, a psychological advantage will be formed, to decrease the stress factor.

Another fantastic reason for not cramming is the avoidance of confusion in concepts, especially when it comes to mathematics. 8-10 hours of study will become one hundred percent more effective if it is spread out over a week or at least several days, instead of doing it all in one sitting. Recognize that the human brain requires time in order to assimilate new material, so frequent breaks and a span of study time over several days will be much more beneficial.

Additionally, don't study right up until the point of the exam. Studying should stop a minimum of one hour before the exam begins. This allows the brain to rest and put things in their proper order. This will also provide the time to become as relaxed as possible when going into the examination room. The test-taker will also have time to eat well and eat sensibly. Know that the brain needs food as much as the rest of the body. With enough food and enough sleep, as well as a relaxed attitude, the body and the mind are primed for success.

Avoid any anxious classmates who are talking about the exam. These students only spread anxiety, and are not worth sharing the anxious sentimentalities.

Before the test also involves creating a positive attitude, so mental preparation should also be a point of concentration. There are many keys to creating a positive attitude. Should fears become rushing in, make a visualization of taking the exam, doing well, and seeing an A written on the paper. Write out a list of affirmations that will bring a feeling of confidence, such as "I am doing well in my English class," "I studied well and know my material," "I enjoy this class." Even if the affirmations aren't believed at first, it sends a positive message to the subconscious which will result in an alteration of the overall belief system, which is the system that creates reality.

If a sensation of panic begins, work with the fear and imagine the very worst! Work through the entire scenario of not passing the test, failing the entire course, and dropping out of school, followed by not getting a job, and pushing a shopping cart through the dark alley where you'll live. This will place things into perspective! Then, practice deep breathing and create a visualization of the opposite situation - achieving an "A" on the exam, passing the entire course, receiving the degree at a graduation ceremony.

On the day of the test, there are many things to be done to ensure the best results, as well as the most calm outlook. The following stages are suggested in order to maximize test-taking potential:

- Begin the examination day with a moderate breakfast, and avoid any coffee or beverages with caffeine if the test taker is prone to jitters. Even people who are used to managing caffeine can feel jittery or light-headed when it is taken on a test day.
- Attempt to do something that is relaxing before the examination begins. As last minute cramming clouds the mastering of overall concepts, it is better to use this time to create a calming outlook.
- Be certain to arrive at the test location well in advance, in order to provide time to select a location that is away from doors, windows and other distractions, as well as giving enough time to relax before the test begins.
- Keep away from anxiety generating classmates who will upset the sensation of stability and relaxation that is being attempted before the exam.
- Should the waiting period before the exam begins cause anxiety, create a self-distraction by reading a light magazine or something else that is relaxing and simple.

During the exam itself, read the entire exam from beginning to end, and find out how much time should be allotted to each individual problem. Once writing the exam, should more time be taken for a problem, it should be abandoned, in order to begin another problem. If there is time at the end, the unfinished problem can always be returned to and completed.

Read the instructions very carefully - twice - so that unpleasant surprises won't follow during or after the exam has ended.

When writing the exam, pretend that the situation is actually simply the completion of homework within a library, or at home. This will assist in forming a relaxed atmosphere, and will allow the brain extra focus for the complex thinking function.

Begin the exam with all of the questions with which the most confidence is felt. This will build the confidence level regarding the entire exam and will begin a quality momentum. This will also create encouragement for trying the problems where uncertainty resides.

Going with the "gut instinct" is always the way to go when solving a problem. Second guessing should be avoided at all costs. Have confidence in the ability to do well.
For essay questions, create an outline in advance that will keep the mind organized and make certain that all of the points are remembered. For multiple choice, read every answer, even if the correct one has been spotted - a better one may exist.

Continue at a pace that is reasonable and not rushed, in order to be able to work carefully. Provide enough time to go over the answers at the end, to check for small errors that can be corrected.

Should a feeling of panic begin, breathe deeply, and think of the feeling of the body releasing sand through its pores. Visualize a calm, peaceful place, and include all of the sights, sounds and sensations of this image. Continue the deep breathing, and take a few minutes to continue this with closed eyes. When all is well again, return to the test.

If a "blanking" occurs for a certain question, skip it and move on to the next question. There will be time to return to the other question later. Get everything done that can be done, first, to guarantee all the grades that can be compiled, and to build all of the confidence possible. Then return to the weaker questions to build the marks from there.

Remember, one's own reality can be created, so as long as the belief is there, success will follow. And remember: anxiety can happen later, right now, there's an exam to be written!

After the examination is complete, whether there is a feeling for a good grade or a bad grade, don't dwell on the exam, and be certain to follow through on the reward that was promised...and enjoy it! Don't dwell on any mistakes that have been made, as there is nothing that can be done at this point anyway.

Additionally, don't begin to study for the next test right away. Do something relaxing for a while, and let the mind relax and prepare itself to begin absorbing information again.

From the results of the exam - both the grade and the entire experience, be certain to learn from what has gone on. Perfect studying habits and work some more on confidence in order to make the next examination experience even better than the last one.

Learn to avoid places where openings occurred for laziness, procrastination and day dreaming.

Use the time between this exam and the next one to better learn to relax, even learning to relax on cue, so that any anxiety can be controlled during the next exam. Learn how to relax the body. Slouch in your chair if that helps. Tighten and then relax all of the different muscle groups, one group at a time, beginning with the feet and then working all the way up to the neck and face. This will ultimately relax the muscles more than they were to begin with. Learn how to breathe deeply and comfortably, and focus on this breathing going in and out as a relaxing thought. With every exhale, repeat the word "relax."

As common as test anxiety is, it is very possible to overcome it. Make yourself one of the test-takers who overcome this frustrating hindrance.

Additional Bonus Material

Due to our efforts to try to keep this book to a manageable length, we've created a link that will give you access to all of your additional bonus material.

Please visit http://www.mometrix.com/bonus948/mtelmsmathsci to access the information.